W9-BKS-955

THE FUTURE OF CONSERVATISM

50¢

Author of

REVOLT ON THE CAMPUS

THE LIBERAL ESTABLISHMENT

THE POLITICS OF SURRENDER

THE FUTURE OF CONSERVATISM

From Taft to Reagan and Beyond

BY *M. Stanton Evans*

Holt, Rinehart and Winston

New York Chicago San Francisco

For Susie

Published simultaneously in Canada by Holt, Rinehart
and Winston of Canada, Limited.

Library of Congress Catalog Card Number: 68-12044

FIRST EDITION

Designer: Vincent Torre
8683955
Printed in the United States of America

Contents

ACKNOWLEDGMENTS

Countless people have contributed over a span of years to the ideas and points of information around which this book is organized. Among those to whom particular thanks is owed are Senators Peter Dominick, Paul Fannin, George Murphy, Strom Thurmond, and John Tower, all of whom granted me highly instructive interviews; Representatives John Ashbrook and Richard Roudebush; F. Clifton White, Lyn Nofziger, Wiliam A. Rusher, Kieran O'Doherty, and Ferdinand L. Mayer.

For help in providing specific items of political fact and assistance in preparation of the manuscript, I would like to thank Brady Black, George Gallup Jr., Charles McManus, Thomas Winter, Allan Ryskind, Dawne Cina, David Franke, Ross Hermann, W.J. Griffith III, Carol Bauman, Sharon Page, Antoni Gollan, Allan Brownfeld, Frederic Andre, and Barbara Brown. And, for their exemplary job with the index, Mr. and Mrs. Lawrence Arany.

Finally, a special word of thanks to Tom Wallace, Neil McCaffrey, and Miss Jo Mohr, and to my wife Sue Ellen— who suffered through many a lonely evening while this book was in preparation. Needless to remark, responsibility for all sentiments and conclusions expressed in this essay is entirely mine.

THE FUTURE OF CONSERVATISM

1:: Introduction: THE GROWING EDGE

For the past half-century or so, Western politicians have been regularly warned—and warning each other—that they must put themselves in league with the future. This is a famous but, on reflection, essentially pointless bit of practical wisdom, rather like telling investors to buy low and sell high. Most people would do it if they could; the question is, how? The future is hard to foresee and difficult to get in league with.

There are plenty of people around, of course, who think they can sense the rising impulse of the age. We are somewhat relentlessly lectured about population explosions and technology mutations, not to mention such random affrightments as urban sprawl, school crises, bus fumes, black power, white backlash, and the poignant gentleness of unwashed hippies. Each of these is said to imply some major upheaval in the American soul, rich with consequence for tomorrow's politics.

Whether any of this prophecy will prove itself out, or how, is a matter of debate; some of it has already disappointed expectation. The population explosion, for one, seems to have lost the galvanic energy imputed to it six or seven years ago, although population figures remain a topic of non-sensational interest. The urban revolution has turned out to be something quite different from what we were led to believe. It seems likely that other supposedly futuristic items will suffer similar deflation in their turn.

Yet history teaches us that various kinds of revolution do occur, and that there is survival value in the ability to see them coming. If the spinning jenny is going to catch on or the stock market to collapse, people who know about it in advance will generally be better off than those who don't. The same thing holds for politics. As long as men are interested in winning elections and wielding power, the effort to outguess the political hereafter will probably continue.

While there is no guaranteed method for casting the national horoscope, there are some obvious guidelines available to us. We know, for example, that major transpositions, in industrial development or financial dealings or government, seldom strike from the blue. They tend to occur when the existing state of opinion or institutional arrangements is ready for them. The '29 collapse was a stunning surprise to a lot of people who weren't paying very much attention, but to a few economists who had followed and warned against the overexpansion of credit it was not especially astonishing.

It follows that we can get an approximate reading on some aspects of the future by seeking out long-term developments beneath the flow of circumstance. The point of interest is not change *per se*, but change which is of germinal importance—which proves its transforming power by continued increase from year to year, around which other kinds of associated change will tend to cluster; change, in sum, which bears the hallmark of impending permanence. To tell much of anything about the coming political era, we must cut through the web of incident and find the growing edge.

The argument of this book is that American life today is marked by a number of such changes—each closely related to or interacting with the others, each pointing to a common result. We have been witnessing, I think, the emergence of a new sort of power grouping which, over time and through an intelligent strategy, can become the leading element of our politics. The preliminary shifts of mood and shadings of opinion have for the most part been accomplished. It remains for decisive events and appropriate leadership to effect the transformation.

This new tendency is hard to talk about in conventional terms, since it conforms only imperfectly to accepted rules of political calculation. It embraces economic groups, intellectual subcommunities and scattered individuals who differ widely in occupation, ethnic background, educational level, and other qualities, but who have forged a kind of implicit agreement on the central questions of government—an agreement which departs abruptly from the prevailing outlook of the recent past.

Our incipient coalition is also hard to discuss because its members often do not consider themselves to be members of it or even tacitly allied with one another. Like Sumner's forgotten man, to whom they bear other resemblances, they do not form an identifiable claque with recognized interests. The unifying themes have begun to surface nonetheless: The primacy of the individual, consequent need for constitutional restraints on power, resulting antagonism to the Federal establishment in Washington. Whatever their disagreements on other questions, the coalitionists tend to agree on these essential items.

In keeping with common usage (which I believe compatible with philosophical usage), I take the word "conservative" to describe this new constituency. I am aware that many of the participants are not conservatives in the Edmund Burke-John Adams sense of the word and that others are openly hostile to given aspects of the present-day conservative position. In general discourse, however, "conservative" has become a passable designation for those who resist the extension of Federal authority. By the same token, I use the word "liberal" to mean the point of view which favors centralization of power in Washington.

If the nation is in fact gearing up for a revival of limited-government conservatism, then this is obviously a development of some importance; but it does not, of itself, tell us anything about the political future. The task of gaining political representation, as we shall see, is complex. To decide whether our asserted revolution will be effective, we must also examine the instruments available for its political expression. The most obvious of these, for a number of reasons, is the Republican Party; but whether the conservative coalescence will gain lodging there is a question open to dispute.

The magnetic pull between the Republican party and a resurgent conservatism is plain enough on the record. Despite confusions in the presidential arena, the legislative wing of the GOP has fought long and hard to prevent the absorption of our national energies into a single power-center. It has protested the expansion of the welfare state with its accompanying burden of taxes and controls. It has tried to contain the growth of the executive bureaucracy. All of these happen to be major stress points of the new conservative coalition.

The coincidence of interests suggests the GOP has an excellent chance to become the beneficiary of a major shift in national outlook: That the party can do in the 1970's what the Democrats did in the 1930's—align itself with a rising force which could dominate our politics, not merely for one or two elections, but over a span of decades. A few discerning liberals, in fact, have come to precisely this conclusion—expressing concern that the Democrats, wedded to their own opposing formula, can do little or nothing to prevent it. The only people who might forestall the Republican success, it seems, are the Republicans themselves; unfortunately, some of their number seem determined to do exactly that.

In effect, the garrison is being told to surrender just as the cavalry is riding over the hill. Precisely as the limited-government impulse has pressed toward the political surface, certain Republican strategists are advising the party to abandon its limited-government position. The GOP, they assert, must concede that the battle against welfarism has been lost, grant the final triumph of the big-government approach, and fashion its policies in the image of the opposition. As signs of a conservative counterrevolution push up around them, Republicans are told to turn their back on conservatism.

Were the contours of the Republican party the only issue at stake in all of this, we would be dealing with an admittedly meager apocalypse. In the long view of history, the ideological stance of any given political group is not a topic of overmastering concern. It happens, however, that other interests are also in the balance—most notably, the shape and quality of American life in the decades just ahead. For the issues the Republican party is called upon to decide are nothing less than the root issues of civil authority itself—the essential questions of freedom and concentrated power. And, in the long view of history, these are very significant indeed.

The battle within the GOP is important because it reflects the battle taking place in the United States as a whole. To a large extent, in fact, it *is* that battle, since the Republican party is at present the only major forum where the limited-government view can obtain a national hearing or lay a believable claim to national power. The campaign to excise conservative opinion from the GOP is thus a campaign to dislodge the limited-government view from its last significant foothold in the political structure of the nation. Should the suggested change of Republican front occur, surface unanimity in behalf of the liberal position would be made complete—an event of profound political implication.

Such a development would not bring the conservative impulse in American politics to a halt; but it would almost certainly result in fragmentation of the dawning conservative coalition and the confusion of its members. It would deny the partisans of limited government access to any important means of political expression and require them to invent or adapt other institutions to their uses. This would in the short run be immensely damaging to the Republican party and the conservative movement alike. What it would do to long-term prospects for limiting governmental power is a subject for melancholy speculation.

Possible Republican motives for embracing such confusions are obscure. One may simply be the fact that years of battle fatigue have dulled the instincts and befogged the analytical powers. The long string of Democratic triumphs has, understandably, left psychic lacerations from which the GOP has yet to recover. Having been disappointed so frequently in the past, some Republican leaders are perhaps afraid to hope for authentic victory; having been out of power so long, they may simply be incapable of recognizing major opportunities or of acting on them if recognized.

A further source of difficulty is the fact that antagonists in the internal GOP debate quite frequently talk about such different things. Conservatives tend to stress the moralistic side of the matter, liberals to depict themselves as pragmatists, concerned only with winning elections. The steady propagation of these self-images has spread the notion that liberal Republicans *can* win while conservatives cannot. This has become a kind of planted axiom of the Republican dialogue, exerting a silent pressure on the thought waves of both conservatives and liberals.

The present book tries to close up this ellipsis in the discussion—to consider the merits of conservatism, not as an exercise in secular theology, but as a recipe for successful politics. Beyond the sermonizing implicit in the assertion of its major premises, the pages which follow contain no moral preachment in behalf of the conservative position. Rather than arguing that conservatism should be a major force in our politics (I assume it should), I have tried to focus on the question of whether it can be such a force in fact.

To approach this discussion, we must traverse still another zone of darkened counsel—the question of the media. Among the factors working for the confusion of Republican strategies, the influence of TV, radio, magazines, and newspapers is in many ways the most important. We live in the age of the image, of fleeting sense impressions which mould our minds in ways we do not fully understand. The impact of these things on our view of ourselves and the world around us is, I believe, enormous.

There is, for example, the homogenizing power of the media, particularly television and the national magazines. The ability to transmit precisely the same thought patterns and images to the whole of the nation, every night of the week and every week of the year, is awesome to contemplate. The effect of this power in terms of politics has yet to be satisfactorily explored. Greater still, perhaps, is the "certifying" function of the media—their ability to define reality for us by what they say and what they fail to say.*

* Marshall McLuhan refers to the curious fact that one of the first things people read about in a newspaper is an event they themselves have witnessed. He thinks this occurs because people enjoy the act of reliving a pleasant experience. Perhaps. But this omits the fact that the same thing occurs even with respect to experiences which are not very pleasant, like natural disasters or fires or automobile accidents. The real reason for this phenomenon, I think, is that by reading about the event in which we participated or which we witnessed, we assure ourselves of its importance and, in a sense, of its reality; we "certify" it by seeing it in print or on film,

The existence of such considerable powers to affect the course of political opinion is obviously a matter of significance; but it becomes the more so when we reflect that the national media, on any close reading of their performance, have a bias toward illusion. Professor Daniel Boorstin has noted the rise of what he calls the "pseudo-event," an artificial happening contrived for the purpose of getting itself reported. An obvious case in point is the modern-day street demonstration, which exists for the media—most notably television, with its emphasis on visual appeal and movement rather than content—and which would not occur, in anything like its present form, without the media. Equally suggestive is today's increasing emphasis on political candidates who are physically attractive—a natural political tendency which seems, with the Orthicon tube, to have reached its final perfection.

Keeping pace with the march of the pseudo-event, we also have the pseudo-opinion. We are told that the late President Kennedy employed a so-called "people machine" to discover exactly what people wanted to hear and therefore what ought to be said. And more than one politician, Kennedy included, has approached the same objective through antiphonal sentence structures whose either-or assertions take both sides of an issue by surrounding it, thus allowing people of opposing views to believe they have heard something in agreement with their opinions.

The potential for illusion in all of this is very great. It is altogether likely that, somewhere along the way, we are going to wind up with a pseudo-personality confecting a pseudo-statement in response to a pseudo-event, all earnestly reported to the nation as the "news" of the day. An ambiguously worded White House press release concerning

---

in exactly the same form in which thousands of other people see it. Media reality thus becomes superior to that which is experienced directly. This effect has been most clearly described, not by Boorstin or McLuhan, but by novelist Walker Percy.

somebody's latest march on Washington, of which there have been a large number, obviously fulfils the requirements of this ultimate unreality. There is evidence that a fair proportion of what gets conveyed to the American public about the world of politics consists of items of this sort.

The national media have not, it should be noted, simply manufactured these things out of the whole cloth; like the other implements of man, they project the frailties as well as the virtues of their creators. Yet they have given those frailties a scope and influence which had not, until a few years ago, been considered possible; and they have in consequence come to occupy a unique position of psychological leverage. They trade, to measurable degree, in make-believe; yet because of their power to objectify and authenticate experience, they are the arbiters of reality.

Republicans who have been wandering for years across this crepuscular moonscape may be forgiven if they have some trouble separating fact from fiction. The instruments of knowledge are prior to knowledge itself, and if those instruments are clouded, misinformation is an expectable result. It becomes apparent that there can be no talk of Republican or conservative prospects in America until this curious effect is understood; before we can set foot on open political terrain, we must make our way through a cave of shadows.

2:: THE TWO AMERICAS

There are, politically speaking, two entirely separate and distinct Americas.

There is, first of all, the America we read about in the glossy magazines, glimpse in some portions of the daily press, hear discussed on the national TV programs. In this favored land, political issues are cut and dried—in favor of the liberal position. Major societal questions have long since been determined, and everyone is agreed on the proper goals of political action. These consist of increased governmental services from the Federal authorities in our quest for social justice, and a program of cautious accommodation of the Soviet Union and other Communist powers in our quest for global peace.

In this version of America, most of the nation's problems have been solved or are on their way to getting there; we have achieved an economic sophistication that knows how to keep depressions away; we are making sure everybody gets what he needs from government; we are successfully building bridges to the Communist nations. Under the leadership of the Democratic party from the time of Franklin Roosevelt onward, we have come a long way and are getting most things pretty well taken care of.

There are, of course, some remaining pockets of discontent—but we are working on these, too. Obviously, we must provide still more in the way of governmental services. We must enlarge the poverty program, pass more and stiffer civil-rights bills, enact bigger and better urban renewal and public-housing programs. This will take care of the remaining problems and close the circle of our felicity.

In this scheme of things, the Republican party has a fixed and modest role to play. It is essentially an adjunct to the liberal program, affirming the necessity of all the government largess at home and bridge-building overseas. In the past, the Republicans tried to combat such programs. But those days, except for a few obstructionists, are gone forever.

The Republican party now has a "mainstream" of bright new leaders, liberals like John Lindsay and Nelson Rockefeller, who are tired of losing elections, and realize that if they offer more imaginative solutions to problems than do the Democrats, the GOP can once more attain majority status. Until this happens, the party can serve as a goad to progress by urging constructive proposals on the Democrats—who, after being in power so long, may be a little too complacent.

That's the way it is in the first America.

The second America is different. This is a nation one can discover by putting down his magazine, turning off his TV set, and walking out the front door. It is the America you encounter by talking to your neighbors, by tracing the accumulation of political detail in various local communities, by noting the daily shape of American social life and American ideas.

This is the America which consists of actual living, breathing people. Within its boundaries, things look a good deal different from the way they look on television or in the latest issue of your favorite magazine. For one thing, the concerns are different: People don't always—or even usually—talk about the same things that are talked of in the media; or if they do, they talk about them in a different way.

The political climate is different, too—particularly among Republicans. Unless you live in New York, it is hard to find the Republicans who look to John Lindsay or Nelson Rockefeller as their leader. It is equally hard to find Republicans who adopt attitudes on the issues comparable to those expounded by such spokesmen.

You find in this America that rank-and-file Republicans are not, by and large, liberals; they tend to be pretty conservative about things, and more often than not explicitly so. They don't want more welfarism and more spending in Washington, but less; they don't want their party to be an adjunct to the liberal program, but to oppose the liberal program.

That's the way it is in the second America.

The curious contrast between these two nations—the America characteristically presented in the media, and the America one can observe with a little independent effort—is the theme of this book. That the contrast exists, as a matter of empirical determination, is the burden of my argument. Why it exists—a fascinating subject in its own right—cannot be explored in a volume of this sort, although some of the reasons will be touched on at a later stage of the discussion.

The "two Americas" argument is, of course, an enormous simplification—a metaphor rather than a diagram. The conceptual America of the media and the corporeal America of everyday experience are bound together by webs of thought and circumstance. The contours of the media world bear a rough general relationship to the lineaments of the actual one, and sometimes the resemblance is more faithful than at others.

To suggest that the predominant media version of America is off the mark is not to imply that it is irrelevant, or without influence. It is very influential indeed. The role of the media conforms to Heisenberg's uncertainty principle. The act of observing intrudes upon the normal course of things and influences it into other channels. The media are not merely sensors recording impulses. They are a causative factor; they make things happen, or keep them from happening, or cause them to happen in different ways. By what they report and how they report it, they can and do achieve a powerful effect on our politics and other aspects of our lives.

The people who write for newspapers and magazines and put TV shows together are, of course, individuals, with individual virtues and failings; my shorthand use of the term "media" is not, therefore, meant to encompass all such people, or even the same people all of the time. Nor is it meant to suggest concerted malice or dishonesty. It is intended instead to refer to a predominant tendency, demonstrated in many individual cases over a considerable period of time, to impose certain favored theorems of the imaginary America on the refractory data of the real one. That this tendency exists, particularly with respect to the Republican party, can easily be documented.

Let us take a specific example: media treatment of two prominent Republicans, Mayor John Lindsay of New York, liberal, and Governor Ronald Reagan of California, conservative. The different ways in which these two officials have been publicized in the nation's leading magazines will mark the boundary between the two Americas, I think, with some precision.

John Lindsay is, by any conceivable standard, an extremely liberal Republican. As a congressman, he compiled an exceptionally high rating for votes in opposition to his party, frequently siding with the Democratic administration on crucial roll calls, and helping achieve passage of New Frontier and Great Society legislation. His 1964 voting record was adjudged by the liberal group, Americans for Democratic Action (ADA), to be 87 per cent correct—that is, liberal. He was recorded as in favor of abolishing the House Committee on Un-American Activities. When he ran for mayor, he sought and received the endorsement of ADA and New York's Liberal party, put a liberal Democrat on his ticket, and in general tried to outflank his Democratic opposition on the left. He is, on anybody's assessment, a liberal's liberal.

When Lindsay announced his mayoral candidacy early in 1965, the response of the media was, to say the least, enthusiastic. *Life*, for example, ran a cover story on Lindsay which bore no less than four different headlines, as follows: "John Lindsay: A GOP Star Rises in the East"; "Young GOP Star Rises in the East"; "Lindsay Runs for Mayor: The GOP Is Smiling Again . . ."; and "Why the GOP Is Smiling Again: Lindsay Is Running." You begin to get the idea.

The suggestion that Lindsay might be a bit of all right is further spelled out in the text, which announces: "With youthful verve and the long-legged grace of a heron, John Vliet Lindsay, 6 feet 3 inches tall, strode into the race for mayor of New York and Republicans all over the country broke into ear-to-ear smiles."

This send-off seemed almost reticent in comparison to the simultaneous cover story which appeared in *Newsweek*. In an article headlined, "GOP Hope: Lindsay of N.Y.," *Newsweek* informed us that Lindsay's campaign headquarters was "the embryonic nerve center of the most exciting and important political operation in America today. Indeed, the scene might even be the first chapter of the making of the president, 1972." The reason for all the excitement was the fact that "lithe, vibrant Rep. John Vliet Lindsay—the hottest young Republican hope in the nation—" was getting ready to run for mayor. The appeal of the candidate was suggested by the observation that "when Lindsay lopes through the lobby of the Roosevelt or handshakes his way through a crowd, women's eyes glaze and men's faces glow...."

Newsweek further observed that "Lindsay's unexpected entry into the race electrified Washington pols on both sides of the political aisle . . . the excitement in the Capital last week was all Lindsay. He was, to hear the talk, the greatest thing to happen to the GOP since Eisenhower, and, besides, he was better looking. 'It doesn't make any difference whether he wins or whether he loses by a little or a lot,' burbled one top GOP leader. 'What matters is that he's running.'" Anonymous observers encountered by *Newsweek* invariably burbled about Lindsay, it seemed, since another unnamed figure is quoted as telling the lithe, vibrant candidate: "I'm a fraternity brother of Bob Wagner's but I'll do anything I can to help you win. This city needs you."

The net impact of these lyric passages is so obvious as to require no comment. The effect is heightened, however, if we turn for the moment to the subject of Reagan. The California governor is, of course, identified with the opposite wing of the Republican party, having launched his political career in 1964 with a ringing speech in support of Barry Goldwater. He represents the conservative element quite as clearly as Lindsay does the liberal. It is therefore interesting to compare *Newsweek*'s treatment of Reagan, when he was seeking the gubernatorial nomination, with the coverage it gave to Lindsay.

In Reagan's case, the headline on the article does not read: "GOP Hope." Instead it says: "Reagan in the Wilderness." The article tells us, among other things, that Reagan is "trimming his views," and that this exercise has "taken a physical toll." It has, indeed, "transformed Reagan into California's coiled spring candidate, the one noticeably tense politician in the gubernatorial sweepstakes. . . ." Reagan's liberal GOP opponent, George Christopher, while not particularly adroit, "has the one quality Reagan notably lacks . . . executive experience" and "is slowly, steadily picking up strength." Although "disarmingly effective" on TV, Reagan is beset by "inner strain," which shows up "in the thin, creased neck and in the lined and lately haggard face under incongruously youthful chestnut hair." No lithe, vibrant fireball, this. A Reagan altercation with Christopher is described as "just the kind of emotional performance that a movie actor and political novice, seeking to dissociate himself from the rabid right wing, could least afford."

Unlike the anonymous observers who dote on Lindsay, *Newsweek*'s unnamed authorities are uniformly hostile to Reagan. One nameless Reagan staffer is quoted as saying, after the Reagan-Christopher tiff referred to above: "One more like that, and it's curtains." At a meeting in Pasadena, a "haughty lady" tells "a friend" concerning Christopher: "At least he's a cut above that actor person." These anonymous quotes are brought forward in substantiation of "the enthusiasm gap over Reagan."

It takes no cryptographer to observe the bias threaded into the disparate treatment of these two Republican hopefuls. The deck, quite clearly, is being stacked in favor of Lindsay's race for the New York mayoralty, against Reagan's bid in California: And, it seems, rather awkwardly stacked at that. One could only have surmised from these stories that John Lindsay, "the hottest young Republican hope in the nation," was destined to take the GOP by storm, and that Ronald Reagan, an emotional basket case with a thin, creased neck, was a man going nowhere in particular. Subsequent election results and events within the Republican party have yielded, however, an entirely different picture

Lindsay was elected Mayor of New York, but squeaked in with less than a majority of the votes cast and has since failed to make any noticeable appearance in the various Republican surveys of presidential preference. Reagan, on the other hand, won a smashing two-to-one victory over Christopher (who had been "slowly, steadily picking up strength") and went on to defeat Democratic Governor Edmund G. ("Pat") Brown by a million-vote plurality in the fall (demonstrating the growing "enthusiasm gap over Reagan.") After that, he emerged in the winter 1967-1968 as a strong contender in the presidential surveys—where small trace of Lindsay, two years after his election, was to be found. Events have, in sum, contradicted the essential message of the media in both of these instances.

Mistakes happen, of course, and if these were isolated matters they might simply be chalked up to the inevitable hazards of journalistic soothsaying. But they are not, in point of fact, isolated. They represent the kind of thing which occurs with predictable regularity in a large segment of the national media—not all the time, to be sure, but often enough to keep the real America and the imaginary one widely separated.

Other such examples could be cited at length, but one more, I think, will serve to illustrate the point. The episode in question concerned Governor Nelson Rockefeller of New York, who represents roughly the same fraction of Republican opinion as does Lindsay, and who has been at least an equal beneficiary of media solicitude. In the fall of 1963, when Rockefeller and Arizona's Senator Barry Goldwater were contending for Republican leadership, the New York governor made a flying trip to the state of Illinois in an effort to drum up Midwestern support. The experience could not have been, on the whole, reassuring.

For one thing, when Rockefeller arrived at the Rockford, Ill., airport, he found that none of the state's Republican dignitaries was on hand to greet him. The absentees included Secretary of State Charles Carpentier, Cook County Republican Chairman Hayes Robertson, and industrialist Charles Percy—all of whom were then running for governor. Also absent were Senator Everett Dirksen and the local Republican congressman, John Anderson. All of these Republican leaders, it seemed, had other things to do.

There was one political aspirant who did, however, show up to welcome Rockefeller to the state. This was Lar (America First) Daly, an individual well known to students of Midwestern politics for two striking characteristics: He invariably dresses in an Uncle Sam suit, and he constantly enters primary elections, Republican and Democratic alike, in the states of Indiana and Illinois. Lar Daly was on hand at the Rockford airport, and greeted the New York governor with characteristic fervor. "I'm Lar Daly," he told Rockefeller, "and I'm one candidate for governor who's not afraid to be here."

The significance of this episode in political terms was quite apparent. As Robert Novak puts it, Daly "was indeed the *only* avowed candidate who cared so little about his chances in the April 1964 primary to rub elbows with Rockefeller in September, 1963. Goldwaterism had become the established religion in rural Illinois and any contact—even the most casual contact—with the Rockefeller heresy was dangerous business."

That Novak's assessment was correct was made clear a few days later when Goldwater traveled to Chicago to make a speech. The various gubernatorial candidates who hadn't been able to make time for the Rockefeller visit—including Percy—showed up *en masse* to be seen with Goldwater. Novak comments that at this time "Goldwater was the leader of the Republican Party, in fact if not in name. Illinois in early September was no exception. Everywhere that autumn, it was the open-armed welcome for Goldwater and the cold shoulder for Rockefeller."

So much for Nelson Rockefeller's trip to Illinois. Now let

us turn to the New York *Times* coverage of this event, demonstrating that Rockefeller was out in the cold and that Goldwater was "the leader of the Republican Party in fact if not in name." This was the *Times'* story:

GOLDWATER AREA
LIKES ROCKEFELLER

Reception Warm in Illinois
Bastion of Conservatism

By Austin C. Wehrwein

ROCKFORD, ILL., Sept. 8—Republican Party leaders view Governor Rockefeller's surprisingly successful visit to this Goldwater bastion yesterday as evidence that the Governor could command conservative support in a race for the presidency.

The governor departed glowing all over.

He was received eagerly here and at a corn-on-the-cob picnic at nearby Oregon despite the effort of local supporters of Barry Goldwater. . . . The visit was also a triumph for Mrs. Rockefeller. . . .

And so forth. No mention of the absent dignitaries. No mention of Lar Daly.

Again, the gap between reality and press portrayal is too obvious to require comment. In the real Illinois, where Republican leaders took thought for their political future, Rockefeller was a flop; in the imaginary Illinois of the *Times*, he was a smash hit. It was from triumphs of precisely this sort that the erroneous impression was circulated that Rockefeller was a popular favorite in the Republican party.

My purpose in bringing up these things—which are merely random samples from a fat and constantly expanding folder—is not to argue that the magazines or newspapers in question are "unfair." In a diagnostic survey, the issue of "fairness" is neither here nor there; the point is that such startling discrepancies between Republican fact and Republican image constitute an important datum of our political experience, and unless we take account of them and correct for them we cannot hope to understand the shape of popular opinion, the prospects of the Republican party, the future of conservatism, or anything else.

Overloading the "news" in this fashion introduces a skew factor into our politics, profoundly hostile to rational discourse. Multiply the Lindsay and Rockefeller examples many times over, repeat them at consistent intervals over a period of years, and the potential disparity between fact and image becomes immense. An accumulation of such things must produce a blurring of vision and a distraction of critical energies. The real world, its outlines vaguely discernible, is mantled in obscurity; its inhabitants become correspondingly disoriented, keying their actions to an eccentric conception of the political landscape.

Above all, the continuing disparity has profound effects on the Republican party, particularly on the average citizens who comprise the rank and file. The dissociation of sensibility experienced by such citizens would make a worthy subject for a doctoral thesis by some young researcher. For the average Republican is daily confronted by a situation in which his own sympathies and observations tell him one thing, while the authenticators to whom he looks for validation tell him something altogether different. The result is a kind of political schizophrenia, a disorganization of the reasoning process in political matters which affects every Republican within reach of a TV set or a magazine stand.

It is doubtful that publicity in behalf of John Lindsay can make Republicans in Kankakee or Zanesville adopt him as their own particular favorite; but it may very well convince them that, even if they don't like him, somebody else does. And if that somebody else is supposed to symbolize the prevailing drift of Republican sentiment, then their prospects for having their own views represented in the party are seemingly diminished. They may become resigned to the fact that they will have to accept a candidate whom they do not particularly want, but who is cherished by all those *other* Republicans who are smiling from ear to ear, coast to coast. In which case the nomination of a Lindsay or someone like him inches a little closer to reality.

The Rockefeller example demonstrates this effect with statistical clarity. Throughout the early 1960's, Rockefeller enjoyed a number of triumphs like his visit to Illinois—triumphs, that is, in the Potemkin Village GOP that shines out so brightly from the media. It was repeatedly stated by the media commentators, particularly the political columnists, that Rockefeller was a shoo-in for the 1964 nomination. Walter Lippmann, for one, opined that Rockefeller could have the prize simply for the asking, while James Reston put it, more colorfully, that Rockefeller had "as much chance of losing the nomination as he has of going broke." The front-runningness of Rockefeller was accepted as a kind of absolute, like the value of Pi or the formula for making Coca-Cola.

The effect of all this assured commentary was, in part, to *make* Rockefeller the favorite, even though the rank and file of the Republican party didn't want him to be. He became the front runner by media say-so. Political surveys by *U.S. News and World Report*, *Newsweek*, and *Congressional Quarterly*, conducted among Republican state leaders, county chairmen, and former delegates, all reflected a curious discrepancy in the shape of Republican opinion. In each case a majority of the party officials thought Rockefeller was going to be the Republican candidate in 1964. But also in each case, a majority let it be known that they didn't *want* Rockefeller to be the nominee; they wanted Goldwater. The typical respondent, that is, did not favor Rockefeller as the candidate but thought his fellow respondents did.*

* This same disparity showed up consistently with respect to Goldwater's popularity among Republican officials. Surveys throughout 1963

Principal victims of this divergence between fact and image are the conservative Republicans who tend to show up badly, or not at all, in the media presentation. But, oddly enough, the liberal GOPers who are the immediate beneficiaries also pay a kind of psychological tariff. It is apparent, for example, that such items as the *Times* report of Rockefeller's Illinois triumph can have misleading effects for liberals as well as conservatives. Rockefeller partisans in the state of New York would all too probably peruse this glowing dispatch and conclude that Rockefeller had scored an important victory when he had in fact suffered a political disaster. The misinformation could induce the kind of self-defeating euphoria which seeks to premise impossible strategies on invisible resources.

In this connection, it is interesting to note Theodore White's observation that, in early 1963, "the unknowing young Rockefeller men" contentedly believed the Republican nomination was "Rockefeller's for the taking." Similar attitudes were widespread in the liberal Republican community—if not about Rockefeller personally, then about the general ability of the liberals to win the convention in their own good time. Given the true state of Republican sentiment, and given the results at San Francisco, this was very unknowing indeed. It was, however, precisely the kind of thing Rockefeller's *naïfs* were reading and hearing all the time, as well as what they wanted to believe, so it was natural they should have accepted it.

Nor, it should be added, have Rockefeller's several embarrassments or the 1964 convention done much to change things. In the 1965 play given Lindsay and in subsequent

---

disclosed there were more Republican officials who wanted Goldwater to be the nominee than there were officials who thought he actually would be the nominee. This was evident both before and after the Kennedy assassination; prior to Dallas, some 1,194 party leaders out of 1,361 polled thought Goldwater would be the strongest candidate, but only 901 thought he was the most likely candidate. After Dallas, when Goldwater's stock fell precipitously, the gap remained roughly the same.

treatment of other themes—principally the outcome of the 1966 elections—the two-Americas policy persists. The notion of an essentially liberal Republican party, reflecting the essential liberalism of the nation, is with us still, its powers of mischief unabated.

fered by a liberal Republican organization called the Ripon Society, which argues the unwisdom of Republican attack on Democratic programs. "There is *no* future," Ripon says in its own italics, "in calling for wholesale repeal of major items of Great Society legislation. Certainly there is room for responsible Republican criticism of the administrative failures. But progressive Republicans must themselves join in the search for sensible and efficient answers. The American people sense that the war on poverty, crime, disease, illness, and illiteracy is moving in the right direction."

Another source, the research journal *Congressional Quarterly*, tells us essentially the same thing. Since World War II, a CQ essay says, a "consensus" has arisen in American politics, and both parties must adhere to it if they want to survive as relevant political entities. The ingredients of the postwar consensus are "an acceptance of government's role in the social welfare field and close industry-government ties at home, coupled with a desire to avoid nuclear confrontation with the Soviet Union abroad."

The incarnations of this argument are various, sometimes fixing on particular reasons for the inevitable drift to liberalism, sometimes stating the matter as a sweeping generalization. Among the specific items sometimes offered in evidence are the following:

—The conservative position has derived its strength from the overrepresented rural areas of the South and Midwest. Now, with the increased urbanization of America and recent Supreme Court decisions giving greater representation to the cities, the conservative era has passed. Political power is devolving on the big-city states, where welfare-minded interest groups are clustered. To survive in an era when the conservative rural population is declining and the liberal urban population is increasing, the Republican party must make drastic changes in its rhetoric and ideology.

—Conservatism has no appeal to younger Americans, who have shown a historic tendency to side with the Democrats.

The median age of the voting population is rapidly declining and by 1970 some 50 per cent of the American people will be under twenty-five. To appeal to these younger voters, the Republican party must get rid of its stodgy conservatism and start addressing itself to the subjects in which these non-conservative young people are interested.

—Conservatism has no answer to the characteristic problems of our era, and by its insistence on states' rights and local autonomies ignores the increased complexity of modern life. The rise of megalopolis, urban blight, housing problems, traffic congestion, and assorted kinds of pollution require both increased Federal "aid" and augmented regulation. Centralization of power is a necessary feature of a complicated age, and the Republican party must recognize this fact.

—The conservative position is negative, always denying rather than affirming. This creates a distasteful image for the Republican party. The American people want politicians to take a positive approach to problems, and the Republican party must come up with constructive alternatives to Democratic proposals rather than simply opposing them. It must be problem-solving and pragmatic, rather than inflexible and simplistic.

These and countless other such arguments have occupied center stage in the Republican drama ever since 1964. It is in consequence widely believed that the American people will brook no interference with their demand for liberal nirvana, and that, to avoid being inexorably crushed, the Republican party must come to terms.

But—is it so? Is it really true that the American consensus is liberal, and that to achieve political success the Republican party must also be liberal? The present writer believes it is not—and in particular believes that sweeping statements about a liberal "consensus," or what the "American people sense" in the way of liberal affirmation, are quite clearly in error. Contrary to the prevailing analysis, I believe recent political history demonstrates the existence of a "conservative majority" in America—or, rather, a cluster of different conservative majorities, some latent and some explicit, which have tended to become crystallized in the years since 1960.

If this view is correct, the implications for the Republican party are of course the reverse of what has been suggested by Senator Javits and others like him. It is in the Republican interest not to abandon its traditional stance, but to become even more explicitly conservative than has hitherto been the case. Indeed, I go beyond even these outrageous sentiments by venturing to believe conservative victory in the nation, taking the evidence all in all, is more probable than otherwise.

I do not suggest that there is anything inevitable about the ultimate triumph of the conservative impulse, because there is virtually no human tendency which is not subject to some kind of change, and because it is altogether possible that confusion at the leadership level will prevent the Republican party, the natural vehicle for conservative expression, from capitalizing on the opportunities which lie before it. I do suggest, however, that the effort of this impulse to achieve political expression in one form or another is about as certain as such things can be, and that all the signs indicate it is growing stronger with each passing year.

Before launching this inquiry, it is necessary to explain my reason for referring to conservative "majorities," rather than to a single "majority." I do so because, in terms relevant to politics, there is in fact no such thing as an American "majority," or "consensus," at all. Such terms are analytical conventions, not political fact, and if their chiefly heuristic value is forgotten, the result can be a hindrance to analysis rather than a help. To understand this point is, indeed, the beginning of political wisdom.

The most striking feature of the American governmental system is, precisely, its exceeding complexity. Unless one grasps this fact, has at least a rough working idea of the intricate machinery of the system and the many levers which make the machinery go, he will understand very little about the shape of American politics. Our system knows nothing of abstract propositions. It moves, by design and by circumstance, through the slow accretion of detail, and it comprises not one majority but many.

Brief inquiry into the nature of these majorities will suggest some of the questions with which serious students of our politics should be concerned. For purposes of convenience, the subject is here divided into six principal categories. The number could as easily be compressed to four or five, or extended to ten or twelve. The net meaning, in terms of complexities and overlays of power, would be essentially the same.

The first majority in American politics is the one with which we are all familiar, and to which the commentators quoted above apparently refer when they talk about what "the American people sense" or what "the American consensus" wants, namely: A *plebiscitary majority* in which the voting population makes its will known on selected subjects—most usually, candidates for the office of President. This is the majority assumed by the Gallup Poll statistics: If the country were to choose up sides between two well-known candidates, one liberal and one conservative, which one would you favor? The side which gets 50.1 per cent or more of the votes has the majority.

This is the kind of thing most people think of when questions of political sentiment are debated. Yet, ironically enough, it does not, in a practical sense, exist. It is in fact a sort of mythical phenomenon which is never fully achieved, and Dr. Gallup's statistics are merely an instrument for seeking an approximation of it. The closest approach to it in real life is the quadrennial popular vote for the presidency—which, however, is usually much less tidy and conclusive than Dr. Gallup's percentages.

A spin-off from the Gallup Poll majority is the *ideological majority*: the state of popular opinion, not in terms of a given candidate but in terms of issues and general principle. As a number of opinion surveys have shown, this ideological majority, although susceptible to the same cautionary rules as the Gallup Poll majority, often turns out to be quite different from the presidential choices suggested by Gallup. From Gallup's own surveys and similar ones conducted by Louis Harris, it appears that the general mood of the country and its feelings on certain specific points are often distinct from its asserted presidential preferences.

This larger ideological majority includes a specific kind of majority supremely important in terms of our present subject—the ideological consensus within the Republican party itself. What Republicans in the aggregate think about issues, and how they want these issues handled in public discourse, is a topic of considerable dispute. This subdivision of the national consensus in turn has several subdivisions of its own, so that the shape of the Republican "majority" may appear in different guises according to whether we are considering candidates, or leadership, or issues.

Hovering somewhere behind the ideological majority, related to it by multiple ties of cause and effect, is the *intellectual majority*. By which I mean the point of view on seminal issues of government and politics which is dominant or becoming so among political theorists and others professionally engaged in the dissemination of ideas. Of particular relevance is the consensus of those who are breaking new ground and advancing new ideas, molding the political attitudes of the future rather than simply reflecting those which are currently in vogue. Needless to remark, determination of such things is a highly subjective matter—yet there is evidence, as we shall note, that just such a consensus is now emerging. Developments at this level will obviously have a shaping influence, over the long pull, on the ideological predispositions of the nation at large.

Yet a fourth kind of majority—and here we move away from mythical percentages and subjective speculation to the more hard-nosed business of working political authority—might be described as the *congressional majority*. This is, precisely as the name implies, the point of view on matters of practical legislation which is capable of commanding more than half the votes cast in divisions of the House or Senate.

That point of view is itself, moreover, merely a surface manifestation of a deeper system of majorities—the complex of opinions which prevails in the different states and hundreds of congressional districts which must combine to elect the requisite number of legislators. This system of majorities, which controls much of American politics, can and often does differ from the Gallup Poll majority or the ideological majority, although it is also susceptible to being influenced by both. A recent case in point was the effort to secure repeal of Section 14(b) of the Taft-Hartley Act, permitting states to adopt right-to-work laws. Opinion surveys showed a majority of public sentiment against repeal; yet because of the particular leverage of the labor unions and the White House, the proposal passed the House and came close to passing in the Senate. Finally, of course, the pressures of public opinion did win out.*

Our fifth majority is the *Electoral College majority*. This is, for immediate purposes, the most important of all. It is the majority which decides who shall be President of the United States. And since the election of a President is what people usually mean when they bring up the subject of majorities, it is the species most crucial to our discussion. The Electoral College majority is yet again distinctive from all of the other majorities. It can in theory be opposed to either

* To underline the complexity of a subject ordinarily discussed in simplistic terms, we should probably at this point make mention of another sort of legislative consensus—the constitutional majority. Under the American system, this is the most potent authority of all, and un-

a Gallup Poll, or plebiscitary, majority and it very often turns up in conflict—as the late Professor Willmoore Kendall and others have pointed out—with the prevalent view in Congress.

The main point about the Electoral College majority, however, is not so much that it may be opposed to other majorities as that it is *different from* them: it must be solicited by techniques and byways discrete from those considered useful in accumulating other majorities. This point is not always clearly understood. In particular, there is a tendency to confuse the Electoral College requirement for winning the presidency with the rough popularity figures of the Gallup Poll surveys, which are for many practical purposes misleading. Measures of mass popular sentiment do not tell us who will win the presidency. When expressed as national averages, they specifically do not tell us where the popular sentiment is located, and what its impact will be on the Electoral College. A candidate who gets four million votes in New York state might as well get none if his opponent gets four million plus; he will in either case lose all of New York's 43 electoral votes. The same candidate, with only a fraction of that many votes, might on the other hand pick up the 33 electoral votes of the Rocky Mountain states.

Our last majority I shall term the *majority of the future* —that is, the constellation of political attitudes which will become dominant in the years ahead, and out of which all the other majorities, from Gallup Poll to Electoral College, will eventually be derived. In assessing the future of our politics, we cannot rest content with a static analysis of

doubtedly the least understood—the 3/4ths vote of the state legislatures by which the American Constitution can be amended. This is the majority capable of making the most definitive statements about the shape of government in our country, the ultimate expression of American political sovereignty. Yet it may very well be opposed to any or all of the other majorities—*e.g.*, as in the case of the demand for a constitutional convention, opposed to the existing majority attitude in Congress.

public opinion or intellectual tendencies; we must try to discern what the likely shape of these will be five, ten, and fifteen years from now. We must examine, that is, the political possibilities of the rising generation. If the outlook is favorable for conservatives (or liberals), then contrary developments here and now are mitigated; if the outlook is unfavorable, then hopeful data which might now be assembled will avail us little.

In this category—as with the intellectual majority to which it is intimately connected—we are admittedly reduced to speculation. Who can really say how American young people will react to political issues in the years ahead? There are some attitude surveys available, but in political terms these suggest nothing so much as a striking volatility and therefore provide no solid foundation for analysis. Although the guidelines are not so precise as we could wish, this is obviously a topic of key importance and one which requires at least an attempted answer. From the decisions of these young people, sooner or later, everything else will flow.

If we run through these categories one by one, it becomes apparent that the question, "Is there a conservative—or liberal—majority?" will require several different answers—and that any or all of these may differ, in one fashion or another, from the popular generalizations. The discussion which follows tries to sort the data of our politics into the relevant bins, to seek out the particular facts which repose beneath the film of words. By viewing the system in the concrete rather than the abstract, by observing its various permutations through the selective filter of each particular majority, we can, I think, discover many things the conventional analysis systematically fails to notice. What we can discover, indeed, is nothing less than a revolution in American politics.

4:: WHERE THE VOTES ARE

"Our problem," Josh Billings wrote, "is not ignorance; it is just that we know so many things that aren't true."

The accuracy of that observation is nowhere more apparent than in discussing future tendencies of the American electorate. Consider, for example, the argument that our politics in general and the Republican party in particular are being pushed inexorably toward liberalism by the sheer force of population trends—a theory which has found acceptance in some Republican circles.

A Senate Republican Policy Committee staff study offers a fairly typical statement of this view. This report maintains that an urban-youthful "new power group" in American politics "will vote in terms of a reaction to problems, not an allegiance to philosophies. . . . Whichever party offers the most rational solutions may well win the respect and long-term allegiance of this New Electorate."

Underlining the implication that conservative principle

must be abandoned for governmental problem-solving, the report adds: "The denser the population, the more government tends to multiply and extend itself, if only because a dense population depends increasingly upon common services." The new electorate, disregarding questions of philosophy, will demand government-supplied solutions to things, and the Republican party must pitch in and supply them.

How valid is this liberal argument-from-population?

Examination of the data indicates it is completely mistaken—that there is in fact nothing in the population figures suggesting a necessary trend toward liberalism, and a good deal of evidence suggesting the opposite. Much of this latter evidence is, however, usually omitted from liberal pronouncements on the subject of the "new electorate."

The census figures show that, far from producing a population mix attuned to liberal sentiment, the urbanization wave is more nearly doing the reverse. The conventional view of the matter derives from a hazy popular image of urban life which consists solely of ghettos, concrete canyons, crowded masses shoehorned into the downtown areas of our major cities. People in such circumstances have generally responded to the political left, and if there are going to be more and more such people, it stands to reason there is also going to be more leftism.

But, taken in context, this doleful vision is a trick of the imagination. There are of course plenty of people who live in such circumstances. But relatively speaking, as a result of present population trends, the downtown areas thus populated are going to be having less and less political influence, not more and more.

This seeming paradox is explained by the fact that the technical meaning of the word "urban" is quite different from the popular image—so that urbanization can and does include many different kinds of population change. Strictly speaking, an urban area is any community of more than 2,500 people—a definition which obviously embraces thousands of hamlets, small towns and middle-sized cities with political convictions the reverse of those which prevail in Manhattan. Most important, the urban definition includes the rapidly expanding suburban communities which surround the big cities. It is in these suburbs, in fact, that the major urban population increase of the past three decades has occurred.

Between 1930 and 1960, the rural population of America underwent a precipitious decline, falling from 50 per cent to 37 per cent of the total. This is the statistic from which most of the commentary about our urban society proceeds—but a good deal of that commentary misses the point. The big cities, in the aggregate, did *not* pick up any of this percentage redistribution. The central city share of the total U.S. population actually dropped during this same thirty-year span—from 33 to 32 per cent. All of the proportionate gains were in the suburbs, where the figure rose from 18 to 31 per cent. It is in suburbia that the population bomb has done most of its exploding.

The absolute numbers involved in suburban growth are staggering. Robert Wood noted in 1958 that no less than 47 million Americans then lived in the suburbs, and that over 12 million people had migrated to suburbia in the preceding decade. Between 1950 and 1960, the population increase in the supposedly puissant central cities amounted to 5.6 million people. But suburban growth amounted to more than three times that figure—17.9 million.

This trend has continued just as markedly since 1960. The GOP Policy Committee itself notes the continued flow of the American people to the suburbs—without, however, drawing any political conclusions from it. "Today," the report observes, "over 58 million Americans live in the suburbs, a gain of almost 50 per cent in the last census decade." This vast increase compares with an 11 per cent gain in the central cities.

Urban authority Victor Gruen pinpoints an even more radical disparity between downtown and suburban population trends in the case of New York City, the archetypical American metropolis. Total population in downtown New York, Gruen observed in 1961, has actually decreased, so that "during the last 10 years, Manhattan has lost about 200,000 inhabitants in spite of the fact that there was an immigration of large numbers of economically underprivileged inhabitants. The meaning behind these figures is that about half a million or more persons of middle-class status . . . have settled in the suburbs."

It is estimated that population movements of this sort during the decade 1950–1960 caused the central cities of the East Coast, from Boston to Baltimore, to sustain a net loss of half-a-million people. In the same span, the suburbs of this area experienced a net gain of about five million inhabitants. Nationwide, the figures for the period show that, of the 16 major cities, 11 suffered population loss; and among the five cities which did not lose population, the only three experiencing substantial gains—Los Angeles, Houston, and Dallas—are newer Western cities which differ notably from the compacted urban centers of the East.

The political implications of all this may be determined by comparing the distribution of metropolitan-area votes in recent election years. In 1962, the total vote for Congress cast in metropolitan districts came to 7.25 million, split down the middle between central city and suburban areas. In 1966, the total vote changed very little—up slightly to 7.27 million. But the distribution of it changed dramatically. The suburban vote was *up* 12 per cent over 1962, while the central city vote was *down* by 11.5 per cent. On net balance, the suburban vote, which had constituted 50 per cent of the metropolitan total in 1962, had risen to 56 per cent.

Equally to the point, the Republican share of the suburban vote increased—from 56.5 per cent to 60 per cent. The net result of these developments was that, even though the 1966 Republican vote was down in the assertedly crucial city precincts, the party racked up a historic landslide.

It is apparent that talk of urban explosion is highly misleading. What is referred to in most such cases is chiefly a *sub*urban explosion—with implications quite different from those the population-crisis rhetoric leads us to expect. Suburban voting habits in most sections of the country are not liberal but conservative. The suburbanite is, typically, a property-owner and taxpayer, sensitive to the cost of government. He is more concerned about schools, roads, and law enforcement than he is about welfare programs, Medicare, and the war on poverty. In so far as he evinces much interest in the latter, it tends to be hostile—since they cost him money.

In general, suburbanites are distinguished by high educational levels, high incomes, good housing, and good jobs. The increase of people in such circumstances clearly reflects the growth of the middle class, and is in fact simply another way of looking at the same phenomenon. Raymond Moley noted in 1964 that "whereas a little over a decade ago the bulk of our voting population and the center of political power were families with incomes ranging between $2,000 and $5,000 . . . the middle income group in 1960 centered between $4,000 and $10,000, constituting 50 per cent of the nation's families. . . . Increased average income and an impressive upward shift of families along the income scale have been consistent since the second world war."

A generation ago, only five per cent of America's families had annual incomes of $5,000 or more; by 1967, more than 50 per cent had incomes of that level. Between 1959 and 1967, the number of families below the $5,000 mark decreased by four million; in the same span, families with incomes of $10,000 or better more than doubled—from 17 per cent of the total to 35 per cent. Moreover, the number of people in middle-class and upper-middle-class brackets is destined to increase still further in the years to come. *Fortune* estimates that by 1975 the proportion of families with annual incomes of more than $10,000 will be above 50 per cent.

The result of these tendencies is to produce an increasing number of people accessible to the conservative appeal, for one reason if not for others: They have crossed over or are in the process of crossing over an imaginary line where one begins to view the Federal Government not as benefactor but as menace. They become cognizant, not of what government can "give" them, but of what it can take away. They become increasingly sensitive on the subject of taxes and inflation, and concerned to have these things brought in check; their proprietary interest in their local schools and other civic functions makes them hostile, or potentially so when the occasion arises, to the idea of these things being taken over by distant authorities in Washington. This is particularly true in the case of the schools.

That the growth of middle-class suburbia in most parts of the country also means the growth of conservative sentiment seems rather apparent from recent election results. Suburban voting patterns in most sections of the country have tended to contradict the mid-50's suggestion of Samuel Lubell and Bennett Berger, that voters who had been Democrats when they lived in the city would stay that way in the suburbs.

Some of the reasons for this development were indicated by a 1967 poll of union member attitudes conducted for the national AFL-CIO by Joseph Kraft, Inc. This survey reflected two rather startling facts. One was that almost 50 per cent of the union members now live in the suburbs; the other was that, in certain categories, these union members are changing their political outlook, not because they had become conservative ideologues, but because they have new and different interests. Concerning these results AFL-CIO official Alexander Barkan says: " . . . in terms of issues, [the poll] found that suburban living naturally has directed members' attention to suburban problems, often in higher priority than national issues. Members in the suburbs share their neighbors' concern about local tax assessments, zoning, sewage and garbage disposal, street repairs, transportation and school-bond issues. It is not that they change from liberal Jekylls to conservative Hydes the moment they cross the city line into the suburbs; it is that in many cases their roster of interests is shuffled and becomes more locally-oriented."

Suburban voters in the South, Midwest, and West have moved heavily toward conservatism and the Republican party. The development of a suburban way of life in the South has been accompanied by a rapidly ascending Republican vote (from 18 per cent in the 1932 presidential election, to 37 per cent in 1952, to 49 per cent in 1964). It is precisely the suburban areas of the South—around Houston, Dallas, Atlanta, Louisville, Charlotte, Arlington, Columbia, Chattanooga, Memphis, Miami, St. Petersburg—that have produced the new breed of Southern Republican congressmen, usually much more conservative than the Democrats they replace. The same holds true of the younger conservative GOPers from the Midwest and West. The Los Angeles-Orange County complex in Southern California, suburbia incarnate, is perhaps the most conservative area in the nation.

What has caused this development is a matter of some debate, with certain theorists giving greater weight to the obvious economic factors, others to deeper psychological influences. For purposes of the present discussion, however, speculation on the underlying reasons for suburban conservatism is unnecessary. The relevant point is not a matter of analytical subtlety but of raw political fact: that the suburbs are growing so rapidly as to become the dominant force in American political life; and that these same suburbs are increasingly conservative in their political inclinations.

It appears, then, that the liberal argument from urbanization is not very persuasive. And it becomes less so when one examines the other pre-eminent fact of population movement in America today—a fact which a number of theoreticians, claiming to discuss the question of population in depth, entirely omit. This is America's great westward migration—which even more decisively than the growth of the suburbs points the way toward conservative, not liberal, politics.

With few exceptions, liberals in general and Republican liberals in particular are oriented to the East. They think New York state is the key to winning elections, the giant political powerhouse which can carry everything before it. Just as New York is the implicit standard of urban living, so is it the implicit model for big-city voting patterns. A good deal of talk about what Republicans "must" do to win in the big-city states is predicated on what is necessary to sway the leftward-leaning electorate of New York and its East Coast satellites.

But the shift of population away from the East has rendered this thinking obsolete. New York, Pennsylvania, and New Jersey are decreasingly able to dominate Republican conventions and national elections. The American people, following the impulse that has ruled them since they touched down at Jamestown and Plymouth Rock, are heading West. The population parade is rapidly leaving New York and other Eastern states behind.

What has been happening over the long pull may be simply demonstrated by tracing the movement of the geographical center of population across a map of the United States. In 1790 this hypothetical balance point was a spot some twenty-three miles east of Baltimore, Maryland. By 1860, it was twenty miles south by east of Chillicothe,

Ohio. In 1900, it was six miles northeast of Columbus, Indiana. In 1960, it was only fifty miles east of St. Louis, and still heading west.

That westward-tending mythical dot symbolizes a momentous change in political power relationships. It means that the northeastern quadrant of the United States, where liberalism is most firmly entrenched, is growing at a pace considerably slower than the other sectors of the country —and drastically below the growth rate of the West. The East, between 1950 and 1960, grew in population by 13.2 per cent; the Midwest and the South, by 16.1 per cent and 16.5 per cent, respectively, the burgeoning West, by a whopping 38.9 per cent.

If these trends continue in the decades ahead, the once-mighty East could well become the least populous section of the country. Consider these figures: Between 1940 and 1960, the population of the eastern quadrant increased from 36 million to 45 million. In the same period, the Midwest increased from 40 million to 52 million; the South, from 42 million to 55 million; and the West—doubling in size—from 14 million to 28 million. The day when demographic realities will demand a Western-oriented rather than Eastern-oriented politics is not far distant.

Equally interesting is the fact that our mythical dot, while tending mostly in a westerly direction, is also drifting south. The Southern United States is, indeed, the great unsung population giant of American demography. It is the largest single section of the country, the home, according to the 1960 census, of some 55 million people. Its growth rate is surpassed only by the phenomenal expansion of the West, and it contains two of the nation's political behemoths, Texas and Florida. All in all, political calculators would be well advised to take this sector of the nation into account. As B. J. Wattenberg and Richard Scammon observe:

"Southerners comprise almost a third of our population

and are in the second-fastest growing area in the nation . . . the South comprises a sizeable proportion of the population, and when we cease thinking of it as a minority culture, and when critics stop thinking of ways to bring it into 'the mainstream,' we will be striking a blow for accuracy. One third of a nation, after all, is nearly a mainstream in itself."

What kind of Republican politics do they favor in the South and West? Not, by and large, the Rockefeller-Javits-Lindsay line suggested in the Senate GOP report. On the contrary, California celebrated its arrival as the largest state in the union by taking a decided turn to the political right, and electing conservative standard-bearer Ronald Reagan as its governor. In the same election, our sixth largest state, Texas, re-elected conservative GOP Senator John Tower. And Florida, the eighth largest state, elected conservative Republican Claude Kirk, the state's first GOP governor since Reconstruction.

Taken as a whole, the 1966 elections were in fact an almost perfect illustration of the rising political importance of the West and South. The GOP's net gains in the U.S. House of Representatives over its performance in the preceding by-elections were almost entirely owing to the South (a subject to be explored at greater length in Chapter 11), and its dramatic resurgence in the governors' races was almost entirely due to the South and West combined. The GOP elected ten new governors in 1966, of whom seven were in the South and West (California, Arizona, Nevada, New Mexico, Alaska, Arkansas, and Florida). Two new Republican governors were elected in the Midwest (Nebraska and Minnesota), and one in the East; but since these two sections also lost two GOP incumbents (Kansas and Maine), their contribution to the party's net gubernatorial gain amounted to one new chief executive.

Particularly indicative of the new Western influence in

the GOP is the fact that as of 1967 11 of the nation's 26 Republican governors held office in this region. Only two Western states—Utah and Hawaii—had Democratic chief executives after the 1966 balloting. Also suggestive is the fact that, of the 11 Republican governors in the West, 7 are generally considered to be conservatives (Hickel of Alaska, Williams of Arizona, Reagan of California, Samuelson of Idaho, Babcock of Montana, Laxalt of Nevada, Hathaway of Wyoming). Of which, also, more anon.

These findings suggest that the influence of the South and West in Republican political circles is on the increase, and that this influence militates in favor of conservatism. It becomes clear, in fact, that the emergence of conservative strength is not merely a futuristic possibility. As things now stand, the predominantly conservative areas of the nation taken together have massive superiority over the liberal areas if and when they co-ordinate their interests and political aspirations. So steady has been the movement of American population West and South that an analysis of the existing big-city states, as of the 1960 census, shows the balance swinging perceptibly toward the conservative areas of the country.

It is usually assumed that the big-city states must be liberal in politics. This may have been true once, but it is obviously true no longer. If we examine a list of the ten largest states in the Union, we discover there are as many of these with generally conservative political inclinations as there are with liberal leanings. Handing down broad political characterizations of entire states is, of course, a presumptuous and risky business. Since the issue has been more or less thrust upon us by the prevailing analysis, however, some effort in this direction is necessary.

Employing some rather rough-hewn but widely accepted standards of analysis, we discover that the ten largest states of the union split down the middle in matters of conservative-liberal predilection.* The generally liberal states are New York, Pennsylvania, Michigan, New Jersey, and Massachusetts. The generally conservative states, by the same criteria, are California, Illinois, Ohio, Texas, and Florida. The fact that these ten states split evenly is in itself instructive, but for several reasons underplays the growing strength of the conservative element. Population relationships among them are not static. They are constantly changing—in favor of the conservatives. With California leading the way, the Western and Southern states have moved ahead of the Eastern ones in aggregate population.

In 1950, the five generally liberal states had a comfortable population bulge over their more conservative counterparts—41,226,000 to 37,727,000. By 1960 the relationship was reversed. The generally liberal states had increased their aggregate population to 47,140,000, but the generally conservative ones had shot forward to an aggregate population of 50,036,000—a total increase of more than 12 million.

Even the foregoing tends to stack the analysis in favor of the liberal position, since liberal strength is considerably greater in these states than it is further down the line. A

* In general, I rely upon an analytical approach suggested in 1962 by *The Annals* of the American Academy of Political and Social Science, judging a state's tendencies by the preponderant voting records of its congressmen. Since our dual purpose is to discern political tendencies at large *and* tendencies within the Republican party, however, I have refined the procedure a few steps further—considering the general complexion of the GOP in a given state, plus the relative ability of the party to gain major electoral victories in congressional and statewide races.

Even with these provisos, of course, the results are mixed. Thus New Jersey cast half its convention votes in 1964 for Goldwater, but is clearly liberal, and liberal Republican, in its over-all political tendencies; Illinois has elected Charles Percy, a prominent Republican liberal, to the Senate, but other indices, including the voting records of its GOP congressmen, its performance in national conventions, and the general inclinations of its Republican leadership combine to place it in the conservative column.

roll call of the next ten states in terms of population size leads us directly into the Midwest and South, where conservative political muscle is far more prominent. These states, with an aggregate 1960 population of 38,905,000, are, in order: Indiana, North Carolina, Missouri, Virginia, Wisconsin, Georgia, Tennessee, Minnesota, Alabama, and Louisiana.

All of these except Minnesota have a recent history of conservatism within the Republican party, and that state elected a conservative Republican, Harold LeVander, as its governor in 1966. Six of the ten (Indiana, Virginia, Wisconsin, Georgia, Alabama, and Louisiana) may reasonably be expected to give their electoral votes to an attractive conservative Republican candidate in future elections. And, depending on local circumstances, Tennessee and North Carolina might well do likewise.

The rising political importance of the West is a major theme of the new Republican figures who have come out of the Rocky Mountain region. Senator Paul Fannin of Arizona describes the transformation which has come over his state, once a stronghold of the opposition. "Arizona had been a rural state and a Democratic one," Fannin says. "There is still a 61 per cent Democratic majority in registration. But there has been a change—tremendous growth through immigration, bringing in people from all over the United States, members of the scientific community, businessmen, retirement communities. These developments have helped increase Republican registration. . . . Arizona people are concerned about big government, high taxes, and inflation. There is great mobility in the West. The people have a strong sense of independence and individual responsibility. Many of them have saved their money so they can stand on their own two feet, and they don't like to see their savings eaten up by inflation."

Senator Peter Dominick of Colorado, one of the GOP's bright new faces, believes people in the Eastern states are in many cases largely unaware of what is happening in the burgeoning West. And, as a native of Connecticut, Dominick doesn't speak from a spirit of sectional animosity. "People in the East used to think anybody West of the Alleghenies had feathers in his hair," Domnick says. "We are trying to get the true story of Western development across—through 'Colorado ambassadors' who talk with representatives of Eastern industry. We are attracting an increasing number of bright young business people, and Colorado is one of the fastest growing states in the union.* There has been a tremendous shift of population to the West—and of political power. The problem is to get people on the Eastern seaboard to understand what is happening. I think they're learning."

On the increasing Republicanism of the area, Dominick says: "The Republican successes are owing to the fact that people in the West are moving into an area where their own individual ability has a chance to be recognized; there's room to move around, unlimited opportunity. The Western atmosphere is one of individual freedom, not of cutting down on choice through government regulation."

The Westward-conservative thrust of American political power has also been confirmed, ironically enough, by a man who has become a casualty of it. Former Idaho Governor Robert Smylie, a moderate Republican, wound up casting an unwilling delegate vote for Barry Goldwater at the 1964 Republican National Convention, and subsequently found himself being ousted from office by a conservative Republican opponent. Smylie reflected on the new Western conservatism, and Eastern failure to reckon with it, in an interview with Theodore White.

"This continent tilts," Smylie said. "But Easterners don't

* Between 1950 and 1960, Colorado had the eighth highest rate of growth in the nation—32 per cent. The seven states above it on the list are, significantly, all either Western or Southern states—with a single exception. These include: Florida (79 per cent); Nevada (78 per cent); Alaska (76 per cent); Arizona (74 per cent); California (49 per cent); Delaware (40 per cent); New Mexico (40 per cent).

recognize it. You have an 'overflight' complex. You think the first stop after Idlewild is Los Angeles. You don't recognize the condition of explosive growth and development—and Kennedy did more to emphasize that fact that you don't care than anybody. What did he care about the little mountain states of the West?

"Our state of Idaho has only one trade mission abroad —in Tokyo. It's Idaho wheat that makes the Japanese kids grow so fast—and we sell it, we don't give it away. We can get a pretty good-sized loan in San Francisco these days; we don't have to go to New York. If I buy stock, I'm more apt to do it through Schwabacher and Co. in San Francisco than with Merrill Lynch."

The westward and southerly migration of people and voting power, the growth of the middle-class suburbs—these are the great central facts of American politics today. Taken together, they suggest new and dazzling opportunities for Republican conservatives.

5:: How POPULAR IS "CONSERVATIVE"?

Talk with certain Republican politicians these days and you get the distinct impression that "conservative" is a swear word. Liberal Republicans have never been very partial to it, of course. But even some GOP officeholders who are themselves essentially conservative have seemed reluctant to use the term.

"I prefer to say I'm in favor of good Republican principles." That, or something like it, is a frequent answer to questions of ideological style. The idea seems to be that, since 1964, conservatism is a political albatross, mere mention of which will alienate voters. Better to be a plain garden variety "Republican."

Analysis of public opinion surveys suggests that, should this attitude persist and spread, it could be fatal to Republican aspirations. For the ironic fact is that there are far more people in the United States who call themselves conservative than there are Republicans. It is "Republican," not "conservative," which is the unpopular designation.

On the same evidence, the overt liberalism of the self-styled moderate Republicans is even more mistaken. The opinion polls indicate that an effort to endorse or emulate Democratic proposals for accommodation abroad or welfarism at home will screen out key issues that could engender Republican success and foreclose the GOP's major opportunities.

The present writer grants—indeed, insists on—the fallibility of such polls. The variation in the figures, the acknowledged margin of error, the mistakes of 1948 and 1964, are warning enough. But as general guides to public attitudes, the polls are obviously useful; and since they have seldom been accused of bias toward conservatism, pro-conservative poll findings have an added kind of utility.

So, against that backdrop, how popular is the term "conservative"? The truth is that it has far more acceptance—by as much as a two-to-one margin, depending on which figures you use—than does the term "Republican." Current surveys show barely one quarter of the American people now consider themselves Republicans. A far higher percentage, up to one half the electorate, think of themselves as conservatives.

Polls taken by Dr. George Gallup clearly reflect this disparity. In a 1964 survey Gallup found 53 per cent of the respondents considered themselves to be Democrats, while only 25 per cent said they were Republicans. This contrasted sharply with a survey the previous year which found the conservative position commanding the allegiance of nearly half the electorate. In the 1963 canvass, voters were asked: "Suppose there were only two major parties in the United States, one for liberals, and one for conservatives, which one would you be most likely to prefer?" The answers: liberal, 51 per cent; conservative, 49 per cent.

Noting that liberal-conservative polls of one sort or another had been taken periodically since 1936, Gallup commented that "in nearly every one of these surveys the vote across the nation has been found to be almost equally divided." During this same period, of course, the Republican party, assiduously projecting as nonconservative an image as possible at the presidential level, saw its public support shrink to roughly one quarter of the electorate.

Interestingly enough, this conservative strength does not seem to have been diminished by the 1964 election. In a September 1966 interview—two full years after the Goldwater campaign—Gallup remarked that conservative sentiment in America seemed to be on the increase, and added: "*The country is split almost evenly between 'conservatives' and 'liberals.' Strangely enough, the word 'conservative' doesn't carry the onus that the word 'Republican' does.*"

Gallup's findings are confirmed, with different figures but similar conclusions, by other national surveys. A 1964 canvass conducted by the Opinion Research Corp. showed 48 per cent of those responding considered themselves to be Democrats, while only 26 per cent said they were Republicans. But when the question was posed in terms of conservative-liberal designations, the conservatives came out well in front—41 per cent choosing this label as opposed to 31 per cent who called themselves "liberals," with 28 per cent saying they were "in between."

Parallel data emerge from the surveys of Louis Harris, whose figures also show the conservative position considerably stronger than the liberal one. In a 1964 Harris poll, 39 per cent of the respondents viewed themselves as conservatives, only 23 per cent as liberals, with 38 per cent saying they were "middle of the road." In 1967, a similar Harris survey disclosed that 35 per cent of the respondents said they were conservatives as opposed to 17 per cent who chose the designation liberal, with 48 per cent saying they were "middle of the road."

Thus, if we take the lowest of these estimates—Harris' 35 per cent of mid-1967—it becomes apparent that there are considerably more conservatives in the United States than there are Republicans. And if we take the highest—Gallup's over-all 50-50 split—it appears that the conservatives outnumber the Republicans by almost two-to-one.

If conservatives are just as numerous as liberals, why do the liberals keep electing Presidents? The chief answer seems to be that American elections are not ideological plebiscites but highly complicated affairs in which popular sentiment is refracted through subcommunities and diffused by conflicting pressures. Also a factor is the difficulty of establishing political cause and effect (if you are angry about inflation or recession, who do you blame?) and the demonstrated tendency of politicians to conduct their campaigns in terms irrelevant to ideology.

Equally important is the fact that conservatives over the years have been outclassed by the liberals in presenting their case to the public. The surveys suggest the American people have mixed political attitudes. They tend to take a conservative position on broad questions of government policy (more spending or less, more Federal intervention or less), but on particular issues (Federal aid to schools, Medicare) their views are heavily influenced by the emotive terms in which the matter is presented.

Also suggesting a failure in articulation is the fact that even when the public does take the conservative view on particular issues—and this has happened repeatedly—the electorate has not been convinced that these are more important than the contrary issues being pressed by the liberal Democrats. It is interesting to note, for example, that a 1964 survey taken by Harris found conservatism on a number of key subjects to be not merely strong but overwhelming. Harris concluded that the voters agreed with Goldwater on prayer in the schools (88 per cent), government security regulations (94 per cent), the demoralizing effect of government welfare programs (60 per cent) and the general increase of government power (60 per cent).

The fact that these same voters were getting ready to cast their ballots against the candidate who represented their views on these questions, and in favor of the candidate who opposed them, illustrates the difficulty of putting a strictly ideological interpretation on any given set of election results. That difficulty is further underlined by the observation of election statistician and former Census Bureau Chief Richard Scammon, that many voters felt Johnson was the conservative candidate and Goldwater the "radical" one. Harris found almost half of the voters polled by his organization chose the designation "radical" rather than "conservative" to describe Goldwater's position.

Indicative of rising rather than declining conservative strength is the fact that the trend in recent years has been toward more public concern on issues conservatives consider important, instead of less. This seems an obvious corollary to the demographic changes we have noted, although an improvement in conservative rhetoric and a variety of troubles afflicting liberal programs may also have played a role. In any case, it is a development suggesting that opportunities for the politically effective deployment of conservative principle are becoming increasingly numerous.

The Gallup organization, for example, has conducted polls testing the relative concern of the public respecting "the biggest threat to the country in the future"—posing the alternatives of "big business," "big labor," and "big government." A survey on this question in 1960 showed 15 per cent of the people thought big business was the principal threat. Forty-one per cent gave the accolade to big labor, and only 14 per cent said their chief concern was the danger of big government.

In 1965, Gallup found the situation radically altered. In the later survey, 16 per cent said big business was the major threat, 28 per cent said big labor, and 37 per cent—more than twice the '60 figure—said big government. On that evidence, concern over big government is not only substantial but rapidly increasing.

Nor has the rate of increase shown signs of leveling off. In 1967, the percentage of Gallup respondents who pinpointed government as "the biggest threat" took still another upward leap. No less than 49 per cent saw government as the principal danger, while 21 per cent said big labor and 16 per cent said big business. This represented a 12 per cent increase in concern over government in the preceding two years, and three times the level which had prevailed only seven years before.

Two other Gallup surveys published in January, 1967, pointed to similar conclusions. Asked whether tax money could be spent more wisely by state or Federal government, the respondents, by a wide margin, gave the nod to the states—49 per cent to 18 per cent. An even larger plurality—70 per cent to 18 per cent—favored bloc-grant return of revenues to the states and local communities without Federal strings attached.

The same sort of anxiety about government is reflected in a 1966 Opinion Research survey on the subject of inflation. This poll found 84 per cent of the American people concerned about inflation, 67 per cent saying they had been hurt by it, and the same percentage saying that Federal programs should be curtailed to halt the upward price spiral. Asked to choose between spending cuts and increased income taxes as a method for stopping inflation, 71 per cent favored decreased spending. Only 7 per cent thought the answer was to raise taxes.

These are obviously attitudes favorable to the conservative emphasis on economy, low taxes, and balanced budgets. Other data in the poll underline, however, the need for further educational effort. Twenty-eight per cent of the respondents blamed government for inflation, but 13 per cent thought the responsible parties were "the people themselves"; 10 per cent said labor unions, 6 per cent said big business, and 41 per cent said they didn't know who was responsible.

Interestingly enough, antagonism to taxes and inflation has been showing up in that segment of the public which is supposed to provide the welfare economy with its strongest support—the labor unions. The 1967 poll conducted for the national AFL-CIO, testing the attitudes of union members on various subjects, found American workers to be far more conservative in their political views than is usually assumed. The poll showed that union members are deeply concerned about such issues as taxes, the spiraling cost of living, and crime in the streets.

When the members were asked to state "the big problems on your mind," the highest percentages focused on the twin issues of taxes and the cost of living. Some 53 per cent of the respondents listed economic issues as a topic of major concern, and picked these items in one-two order. Among younger members, the high cost of living came first—20 per cent mentioning this. Among older members, taxes were considered to be the more important problem. Twenty-eight per cent of the members between 30 and 49 years of age listed this as the single issue which concerned them most, and 21 per cent of those 50 and over did the same.

On foreign affairs, the second major item of broad concern (principally Vietnam), union members of all ages took an essentially conservative position. The vast majority distributed their answers among backing for President Johnson's policy of combating Vietnamese Communist aggression, calls for escalation of the war, expressions of patriotic sentiment and the like. Only a small minority—between 6 and 8 per cent—took the dove line on the Vietnamese conflict.

The third area of major anxiety, "civil rights and law

2. If Republicans fail to attack such things as trade with the enemy and Federal welfarism, they will be abandoning issues on which the concern of the American people is deep and has in recent years become increasingly acute.

Beyond these more obvious implications, the data suggest a deeper meaning as well. The demographic revolution and the poll results, taken together, indicate that the Democratic welfare formula of the past thirty years is extremely vulnerable. In the twin issues of taxes and inflation, it has not one Achilles heel but two. Public anxiety on these subjects shows that the asserted consensus in behalf of welfarism is on the verge of collapse.

The opinion surveys clearly indicate that the American people have almost no conceptual attachment to the centralized welfare-state idea as such. As an abstract proposition, welfarism is unpopular—surprisingly so considering the ideological campaign conducted in its behalf for thirty years and more. Democratic victories have been built, not on a consensus of belief in favor of welfarism, but on a coalition of interest blocs whose particular benefits from the welfare apparatus secure their allegiance to the general system.

This fact was as plain in the 1930's as in the 1960's. It is assumed by many commentators that Roosevelt was swept into power by widespread popular demand for inauguration of the welfare state. In point of fact, Roosevelt and the Democratic platform of 1932 strenuously attacked Hoover and the Republicans for irresponsible waste of the taxpayer's money, demanding balanced budgets and a 25-per-cent reduction in the cost of government.* It should be apparent that the nation to which such sentiments were addressed was not being asked to provide the new regime with a mandate for indiscrimi-

* The Democratic platform stated, for example:

"We advocate an immediate and drastic reduction of governmental expenditures by abolishing useless commissions and offices, consolidating

nate welfarism. It was only when the Democrats' coalition of interest groups had been formed and cemented by Federal checks that the new welfarist majority began to be assembled.

Now this alliance is obviously beginning to come apart. The growth of the suburban home-owning group, the rapid increase in the percentage of people who view government as the "biggest threat to the country in the future," the deep-going alteration in the views of suburban labor-union members, all point in the same direction: The costs of the welfare state, in terms of tax levies and rising prices through currency inflation, are beginning to outstrip the benefits as decisive political factors.

The costs of welfarism and the resulting tax burden have pressed the nation consistently toward a point of political transition—the point at which people who look upon themselves as taxpayers become more numerous and politically aroused than the people who look upon themselves chiefly as the beneficiaries of government largess. Thanks to Democratic adroitness and Republican lassitude, this day of reckoning has long been postponed. How much longer it can be forestalled is an interesting question. In the age of the $186 billion Federal budget, taxes to pay for benefits to all and sundry are high and rising. These levies, once thought to be a matter of "soaking the

---

departments and bureaus and eliminating extravagance, to accomplish a saving of not less than 25 per cent in the cost of the Federal government. . . .

"Maintenance of the national credit by a Federal budget annually balanced on the basis of accurate executive estimates within the revenues . . . a sound currency to be preserved at all hazards. . . .

"We condemn . . . the open and covert resistance of administrative officials to every effort made by congressional committees to control the extravagant expenditures of government. . . ."

Roosevelt himself spoke along the same lines, saying that "we must abolish useless offices. We must eliminate . . . functions . . . that are not definitely essential to the continuance of government." And: "Any government, like any family, can for a year spend a little more than it earns. But you and I know that a continuation of that habit means the poorhouse."

rich," are now felt at every level of the economy. This is true of property taxes, state taxes, Federal taxes, and special Federal levies like the Social Security tax.

Feeling the pinch on the tax issue, the Democrats have tried the age-old expedient of inflation. Spending more and taxing less helps fend off the final accounting because a rising price table is less direct in consequence and harder to pinpoint as to source. But, as the 1966 elections suggested, the expedient is wearing thin. The polls show the cost of living is politically as damaging an issue as is taxation. Realization of this fact was an obvious component in President Johnson's 1967 decision to seek a tax hike rather than face the consequences of an estimated $29 billion Federal deficit.

The political importance of the cost-of-living issue is suggested by a late 1967 Gallup survey in which three out of five respondents said their most urgent problem was "to make ends meet." Cited as a characteristic complaint was the statement of one respondent: "You think you're making money and getting ahead, but after you've paid the bills you are back in the hole." This issue far outranked Vietnam, which only one American in 20 saw as the major difficulty facing him or his family.

The Democrats are confronted by an obvious dilemma. Committed to an enormous welfare program that must be paid for either through taxes or inflation, they oscillate between the two according to which seems for the moment to be politically less dangerous. As public concern on both counts rises, their situation becomes increasingly untenable.

Samuel Lubell noted the opening out of this process in the early 1950's. He quotes as a typical example of rising discontent a housewife from a Democratic family who told him "we're being taxed to death," denounced the Brannan Plan, and opposed "giving all that stuff away abroad." The key to her anxiety, he says, was "anger over inflation" and "a resentment against all forms of government spending." He adds the significant comment: "Listening to her, I wondered how many times in the past she had heard the same criticism of 'New Deal Socialism' without paying any attention to it. As long as the New Deal was painless, the Republican attacks failed to register. Once the bite of taxes was felt, the welfare state took on a new aspect." Lubell concludes that "inflation has clearly become the breaking point of the Roosevelt coalition."*

The same effect is visible in the Opinion Research poll data and the AFL-CIO survey. Vast numbers of the American people are moving into the category where they are more sensitive to the things government is taking away from them than they are to the things government is giving them. The resulting problems for Democrats, and opportunities for Republicans, are apparent.

Broadly viewed, it may be stated that the Democratic coalition will collapse at last (1) when the relevant majorities have passed the dividing line between their old self-conception as beneficiaries of government and their new self-conception as victims of it, and (2) when the Republican party acts effectively to elicit this majority sentiment at the polls. The suburban revolution and the explicit concern of the American people over big government, taxes, and inflation indicate this point is being

* Fourteen years later, Lubell found the same attitude persisted, as further observation of welfarism in action had made the American people increasingly suspicious of government. "Expanded government spending," he discovered in a June 1966 survey, "seems to be strengthening, not weakening, public support for the private enterprise system. . . . An overwhelming majority thought that a government-run operation is 'bound to be less efficient than private business.' Their reasoning was that 'since private industry has to be competitive and show a profit, it must cut costs.' But 'the government can stay in business without a profit' so 'it never thinks about saving money.'" Lubell emphasized that responses to his questions were "intensely practical" rather than ideological; "nearly always," he said, "they divided on the basis of their own interests." His respondents, that is, had come increasingly to view expanded government as harmful to them rather than helpful.

reached if it has not been reached already. It remains for the Republican party to do something about it. If the GOP takes its stand in behalf of the groaning taxpayer and the home-owning suburbanite, it could dramatically improve its political position. If it settles for increased welfarism and still more taxation, the result could be disastrous.

This is not mere conjecture. History shows the GOP fumbling a similar opportunity once before. In 1952 the Republicans received an enormous vote from suburbanites and middle-class Americans generally who had had enough of New Deal and Fair Deal welfarism and wanted relief from taxes and inflation. Lubell's irate lady quoted above was one of these, and he pinpoints such sentiments as a principal reason for Eisenhower's victory. Chicago Democratic boss Jake Arvey put it succinctly: "The suburbs beat us."

The expectations of these middle-class voters were, however, rudely disappointed. The net result of the Eisenhower years was not to make things better for this echelon of society but to make things worse, shifting the tax burden even more heavily onto the middle class. In 1950, middle-class Americans paid 33 per cent of the total tax burden. By 1958, they found themselves paying 47 per cent of it—and the aggregate burden was, of course, considerably larger. Result: The Republican party was swept under in the 1958 elections, sustaining a defeat second only to the disaster of 1936 in modern Republican history.

In 1966, the suburbanites and other Americans concerned about rising taxes and inflation clearly indicated they were willing once again to trust the Republican party to hold the line on taxes and stop the trend toward welfare government. If the GOP is wise it will not disappoint them again.

6:: The Republican Mainstream

Strong in the nation generally, conservative sentiment is even stronger in the Republican party. For those accustomed to viewing the GOP as the more conservative of the two national parties, this may seem to be a prosaic if not pointless observation. But it is in fact a matter of controversy, hotly contested by a legion of commentators who argue the case for a leftward-leaning Republican leadership.

In 1964, for example, there was considerable talk about the mainstream of the GOP—a political Sweet Afton in which such people as Nelson Rockefeller, George Romney, and William Scranton were depicted as standing hip-deep. Conservative Republicans were portrayed as outcasts and mavericks who spurned the party's majority sentiments in order to pursue odd-ball conceptions of government. This was the premise on which Rockefeller waged his 1964 California primary campaign against Goldwater—capsuled in the Rockefeller campaign flyer asking, "Which do you want—a leader or a loner?"

The leaflet which posed this question went on to spell out its reasons for considering Goldwater a "loner" and asserted that Rockefeller represented the majority GOP position. It pictured the New York governor in phalanx with Lodge, Nixon, Romney, and Scranton and asserted that "in the California primary, Rockefeller represents them—in the kind of Republicanism that they and the overwhelming majority of Republicans believe."

The fact that Rockefeller went on to lose the California primary might reasonably suggest that his claim to represent the "overwhelming majority of Republicans" was mistaken, and that perhaps the GOP mainstream had not meandered so far to the left as the 1964 publicity implied. Liberal GOP spokesmen have, however, continued to advance this claim with regularity and vehemence in the succeeding years.

In a 1966 book on the shape of the Republican party, for example, liberal Republican authors Bruce Chapman and George Gilder state that "the right wing of the party represents a small minority of Republicans . . . a minority so small as to be negligible." Similar assertions have been made by countless columnists and other journalistic spokesmen, who contend that the rank and file of the Republican party, or its up-and-coming candidates, or a majority of its more promising leaders, are "moderates"—that is, liberals. This proposition has been advanced so often, in fact, that many journalists seem to have taken it for granted without bothering to check the facts.

Such a check is recommended to anyone who wants to expatiate on the nature of the Republican majority. For it will reveal quite clearly that talk of the Rockefeller sort is mistaken. By every available measure, from surveys of rank-and-file sentiment to the inclinations of its elected officials, the Republican party is overwhelmingly conservative. This fact may be obscured or confused by the play of rhetoric or short-term efforts to glamorize some particular liberal candidate; it is fact nonetheless.

In the matter of rank-and-file sentiment, the evidence is exceedingly plain. Every survey of grass-roots-Republican sentiment shows the "conservative" designation favored over "liberal" by sizable margins. A case in point was a 1964 poll conducted for the Republican National Committee by the Opinion Research Corp., which disclosed that 65 per cent of the Republicans questioned considered themselves conservatives, while only 14 per cent chose the liberal designation, the remainder saying they were "in between."

Similar results have issued from a series of polls conducted by Louis Harris, putting Harris in the curious position of having his political poll figures cutting strongly against his political inclinations.* Four different Harris polls between 1963 and 1967 showed both a strong conservative preponderance within the GOP and a net increase in Republican conservatism. The conservative-liberal percentages, with the remainder classified as "middle of the road," are as follows:

	Conservative	*Liberal*
1963	48	15
1964	53	11
June 1967	47	8
Sept. 1967	55	12

As might be expected, the numbers fluctuate, possibly from variations in the sample or minor nuances in the

* Harris is a Democrat who attained national prominence conducting surveys for the late President Kennedy. In commenting on one of his polls conducted in June, 1967, Harris argued that conservatism in the GOP was on the downgrade.

national mood. These polls show, however, that the conservative tag has consistently outpolled the liberal designation by a healthy margin. Moreover, the net tendency seems to be in the direction of increased conservatism. In the first poll, conservative preponderance over the liberal position was slightly over three to one. In the two 1967 polls, it was between five and six to one. Between the first poll and the last the conservative position was up by 7 percentage points, the liberal position down by 3.

If grass-roots Republican voters are conservatives, their local officials are no less so. This is not, indeed, a vigorously debated point. Many commentators hold it as an article of faith that the party "pros," for reasons best known to themselves, are considerably more conservative than the rank and file—an argument frequently resorted to as an explanation of 1964. Having demonstrated the essential conservatism of the rank and file, therefore, we may safely assume the party officials lean pretty heavily in the same direction.

There are, of course, no explicitly ideological ratings at this level, but there are a number of indices which suggest conservative-liberal inclinations. One of the most revealing is the periodic poll survey of GOP officials across the nation concerning their preference among presidential candidates. Year in and year out, these surveys show heavy strength for the more conservative presidential candidates, conditioned by the question of who at the moment seems to be a realistic contender. A 1963 survey showed Republican state and county officials preferred Goldwater to Rockefeller by the rather astonishing margin of 1,194 to 56. (This twenty-to-one imbalance against Rockefeller suggests his subsequent argument that Goldwater was a "loner" may have been a simple instance of transference.) More recent tests of candidate preferences among the county chairmen have yielded like results. In April, 1967, a Gallup Poll showed that Richard Nixon led

Romney among county chairmen by a margin to 1,562 to 423. And, although he had then been in office only three months, the survey showed Ronald Reagan was the chairmen's third preference, with 233 votes.

Moreover, the Gallup survey suggested, if Nixon were to withdraw from the race, the leading candidate would not be Romney, but Reagan. In that event, Reagan would get the support of 429 county chairmen, Romney 249, and a variety of other candidates would be strung out at some distance behind these two. By September, 1967, when Reagan had another five months as governor under his belt, these officials expressed an even stronger preference for him. A poll of the county chairmen by Frank Lee and Associates found 43 per cent of the respondents for Nixon, 26 per cent for Reagan, 12 per cent for Romney, and 10 per cent for Rockefeller.

In a December, 1967, follow-up on preferences among county chairmen, Gallup also found Reagan had moved solidly into second place. This survey yielded 981 votes for Nixon, 412 for Reagan, 268 for Rockefeller, and 101 for Romney.

Similar results have emerged from national and local polls of other party officials, including former convention delegates, precinct committeemen, and the like. In August, 1967, the American Broadcasting Company released the results of a survey taken among the 1,308 Republican delegates to the 1964 convention. The result of their answers was an overwhelming vote for the more conservative candidates—with Nixon first, followed by Reagan. Choosing their "personal favorite," the respondents voted Nixon first with 48.5 per cent of the responses, Reagan second with 17.1 per cent. On "best vote-getter," Nixon was again first with 39.9 per cent, Reagan again second with 25.9 per cent.

If we proceed to an examination of the party's elected officials, the ideological pattern remains the same. The chief difference is that, since we now have voting indices available to test conservative-liberal leanings, the pattern is a good deal clearer. Particularly in the national arena, conservative Republicans heavily outnumber their liberal counterparts. This was true prior to the 1966 elections and was equally true after them.

In the U.S. House of Representatives, the superiority of the conservative Republican forces is obvious and generally conceded by liberal GOP spokesmen. Thus, in a 1966 article, author George Gilder remarked: "In the House of Representatives, where the Republicans hold only 140 seats . . . the progressives in turn occupy approximately 40. . . ." The Ripon Society, for its part, alludes morosely to "the conservative weighting of the House Republicans." This analysis was roughly confirmed by a 1965 rundown of GOP House members conducted by *U.S. News and World Report,* which concluded that: " 'Conservatives' comprise the biggest group. They number about 75 Republican House members. 'Moderate' Republicans count a total strength of around 50. 'Liberals' among Republicans in the House number about 15."

A closer analysis of ideological leanings among House members is possible through use of the vote ratings published by conservative and liberal interest groups. For convenience' sake, we shall use the analysis published from year to year by Americans for Constitutional Action (ACA), since it is explicitly designed to test conservatism, and is more detailed than the vote ratings published by such liberal groups as Americans for Democratic Action and the AFL-CIO's Committee on Political Education.

ACA itself considers a 65-per-cent rating on its vote scale to be satisfactory, a measure which shows a legislator voting two thirds of the time on the conservative side of issues before Congress. For our purposes, we shall set a somewhat higher standard, making 70 per cent the cut-off point. Using this criterion, we find conservatives among House Republicans have over the past few years outnumbered their liberal colleagues by approximately a three-to-one ratio.

Thus, in 1963, when Barry Goldwater's cause was in the ascendant, the ACA ratings showed 132 out of 177 Republican House members had conservative ratings of 70 per cent or better. In the session following Goldwater's defeat, Republican numbers in general were reduced, so there were smaller totals on both sides of the ledger, but the proportion remained roughly the same. A 1965 check showed that, of 140 Republican House members, 107 had conservative ACA ratings. Of these 107, moreover, some 101 sought and gained re-election in the 1966 balloting—prima facie evidence that the conservatives would have a preponderance in the new GOP in the 90th Congress. And according to the interim ACA ratings published in September, 1967, no less than 42 of the 57 Republican freshmen also had ratings of 70 per cent or better. This meant that conservatives among the new congressmen were proportionately as numerous as they were in the previous session. Throughout, a ratio of approximately three to one prevailed.

The essential accuracy of the ACA ratings is underscored by *Congressional Quarterly*'s analysis of votes in support of the "conservative coalition" in the House. *CQ's* breakdown for 1966 shows 112 of the 140 House Republicans voting more than 70 per cent of the time on recorded roll calls to support the conservative position—a pro-conservative ratio of four to one.

Over on the Senate side, the proportions in favor of the conservative position are slightly reduced but the preponderance is marked. Using 1966–67 ACA ratings, we find there are, by a rather comfortable margin, more conservative Republicans in the Senate than liberal Republicans. The conservatives, 20 in number, include: Fannin, Murphy, Allott, Dominick, Williams, Jordan, Dirksen, Hickenlooper, Miller, Carlson, Pearson, Curtis, Hruska, Cotton,

Thurmond, Mundt, Young, Tower, Bennett, and Hansen. In addition, there are four other Republican senators with ACA ratings above the 60-per-cent mark: Boggs, Morton, Griffin, and Baker. That means more than 50 per cent of the GOP senators have ACA ratings above 70 per cent, while only a third have ratings under 60 per cent.

Again, the ACA analysis is borne out by *Congressional Quarterly*'s "coalition" scores. The latter once more reflect a slightly higher percentage of conservatism than do the ACA ratings, showing no less than 21 of the 36 senators casting their 1966 votes in favor of the coalition on 70 per cent or more of the roll calls for which their votes are recorded.

Other devices for testing the relative conservatism of Republicans in the Senate yield similar results. One such is the *Congressional Quarterly* computation of votes "for a larger or smaller Federal role." In the Senate, this tabulation shows the generally conservative position in the majority, with such liberals as Javits almost hopelessly isolated. The CQ analysis for 1965–66 shows that of the 33 Republicans who served in the Senate during this span, the overwhelming majority voted for "a smaller Federal role" more frequently than they did for a larger one. In fact, the proportion was exactly two to one—with 22 senators voting most of the time for a smaller role, and 11 voting most of the time for a larger one. Most liberal of all was Javits, who voted 20 times to increase Federal power, only once to curtail it. Even among the 11 who took the liberal position on a majority of issues, no one remotely approached this impeccably liberal performance.

These figures support the notion that Republicans in Congress are predominantly conservative. Moderates constrained to acknowledge this fact take solace, however, from the assertedly greater liberalism of the Republican governors. As portrayed to us by such people as Roscoe

Drummond, Theodore White, and Tom Wicker of the New York *Times*, the governors are the party's "problem-solvers," and *ipso facto* liberals. A typical statement of this view was offered by Wicker at the time of the 1967 Republican Governors' Conference in Jackson Hole, Wyoming. "With few exceptions," Wicker stated, "the governors either are in the moderate wing of the party or learned the lessons of 1964 well enough to be looking in that direction for a candidate."

The truth is that, as of the time Wicker wrote, most of "the governors" were *not* "moderates"—a development which goes far to explain the mystery that they could not "unite" to push a liberal candidate, the conundrum about which Wicker was writing. If most governors are liberals, it is indeed puzzling that they should not get together to push a liberal candidate; but if they are not in fact liberals, their failure to push a liberal candidate is altogether natural.

Methods for grading governors ideologically are, of course, rather imprecise and no doubt presumptuous; since so many commentators are grandly referring to them as adjuncts of the liberal GOP, however, some effort in this direction is clearly necessary. Perhaps the most careful attempt to provide such an ideological breakdown has been made by David Franke, in a report for the American Conservative Union. Franke summarized the line-up of Republican governors prior to the 1966 election as follows:

Conservative (4): Babcock (Mont.), Bellmon (Okla.), Boe (South Dakota), Hansen (Wyo.);

Moderate Conservative (2): Rhodes (Ohio), Avery (Kan.);

Moderate Liberals (1): Knowles (Wis.);

Liberals (10): Love (Colo.), Smylie (Idaho), Reed (Me.), Volpe (Mass.), Romney (Mich.), Rockefeller (N.Y.), Hatfield (Ore.), Scranton (Pa.), Chafee (R.I.), Evans (Wash.).

That deployment of forces justified the statement that the Republican governors were chiefly liberals. But when the election of 1966 had come and gone, the Republican gubernatorial picture looked very different indeed. As Franke analyzed it, the new line-up was as follows:

Conservative (10): Hickel (Alaska), Williams (Ariz.), Reagan (Calif.), Kirk (Fla.), Samuelson (Idaho), LeVander (Minn.), Babcock (Mont.), Laxalt (Nev.), Boe (S.D.), Hathaway (Wyo.);

Moderate Conservatives (3): Rockefeller (Ark.), Rhodes (Ohio), Bartlett (Okla.);

Moderate Liberals (2): Tiemann (Neb.), Knowles (Wis.);

Liberals (10): Love (Colo.), Agnew (Maryland), Volpe (Mass.), Romney (Mich.), Cargo (N.M.), Rockefeller (N.Y.), McCall (Ore.), Shafer (Pa.), Chafee (R.I.), Evans (Wash.).

These evaluations are highly subjective, of course, but other evidence suggests they represent a prudent rendering of conservative strength. For example, the *Wall Street Journal*'s Alan L. Otten, an experienced political reporter with no observable bias toward right-wing Republicans, puts governors Bartlett and Tiemann in the "conservative" column. Since Franke has made no effort to co-opt these chief executives for the ranks of explicit conservatism, it would appear he has not tried to overstate the conservative case.

Give or take a distinction, then, it seems that Franke's analysis of the change which had transpired is fairly accurate. He suggests the significance of that change when he remarks: "All of this does not mean . . . that the Republican Governors' Association now is a 'conservative' group. As the person-by-person breakdown shows, conservatives and liberals are almost evenly divided within the Association. The significance for conservatives is that the Association is no longer 'liberal'—and cannot be used by the liberals within the GOP as their vehicle in national and presidential politics."

The clearest indication that Franke's analysis was correct has been the altered leadership of the Governors' Association. In the wake of the 1966 elections, the group elected a new executive committee of five members—a majority of them acknowledged conservatives. The three conservatives were Reagan, Claude Kirk of Florida, and Tim Babcock of Montana. The Ripon Society, alarmed by this turn of events, complained that the GOP governors, "in an inexplicable move," had "yielded control" to men "prominently identified with Goldwater in 1964." The inexplicability, as we have seen, is easily explicated: The majority of the new governors, contrary to Ripon's own publicity, were conservatives, and conservative strength in the Association was correspondingly enhanced. The change in leadership merely reflected the change which had taken place in the organization.

In 1967, conservative representation in the RGA was increased still further with the election of Louie B. Nunn, a noted conservative, as governor of Kentucky. So persistent is the notion of gubernatorial liberalism, however, that even after Nunn's election columnist Roscoe Drummond popped up blandly asserting that "the governors" preferred Nelson Rockefeller as the next presidential nominee by a margin of 3-to-1 "over any other possible candidate." Drummond reported that "they" were convinced "Rocky could do the most to carry the needed Democratic and independent votes to the Republican column." No names were supplied in this analysis nor was any statistical breakdown offered to support the claim of 3-to-1 backing for Rockefeller.

The turnover at the Governors' Association made things pretty unanimous in the ranks of Republican leadership—in favor of conservatism. As with rank-and-file sentiment, the fact that the top Republican leadership is mostly conservative does not seem to be widely understood. Stirred chiefly by a changing of the guard at the Republican National Committee and some fuzzing of Republican thought and rhetoric, the idea is abroad that a new era of liberalism has commenced. Liberal Republican spokesmen looking into things have concluded, however, that nothing of the sort has happened, and the facts of record bear them out.

At the Republican National Committee, the replacement of Dean Burch by Ray Bliss was unquestionably a setback for conservatives, but not much of a victory for liberals. Although Bliss has proved himself in some cases congenial to liberal elements, he was not chosen because the national committee considered him a liberal, but because he was viewed as a technician neutral between party factions. And, as the laments of the Ripon Society make clear, he has performed in that fashion too often for liberal Republican tastes.

On Capitol Hill, the GOP congressional leadership features one, and only one, *bona fide* liberal, Senator Thomas Kuchel of California. Senator Dirksen, a "moderate" on some subjects, has taken a notably conservative stand on key domestic issues (14[b], reapportionment, prayer in the schools); was Bob Taft's leading partisan in 1952; was a defender of Senator McCarthy; and nominated Barry Goldwater in San Francisco. His 1966 voting record as tabulated by ACA, moreover, shows him to be among the more conservative Republicans in the Senate (85 per cent). The chairman of the Senate Republican Policy Committee is another conservative, Bourke Hickenlooper (97 per cent).

Over in the House, there is even less comfort for liberal Republicans. Representative Gerald Ford, the minority leader, had a 74-per-cent ACA rating in 1966; House whip Leslie Arends of Illinois (who defeated liberal GOPer Peter Frelinghuysen for the post) has an 81-per-cent rating; and Policy Committee Chairman John Rhodes of Arizona, a Goldwater protégé, has an 84-per-cent rating; Representative Bob Wilson, Chairman of the Republican Congressional Committee, 85 per cent; and Representative Melvin Laird, the House Republican Conference Chairman, 83 per cent.

In the aftermath of 1966, the liberal Republicans tried to make some changes in the Republican congressional leadership. And changes there were—in the conservative direction. The liberals had hoped to replace Thruston Morton (ACA 77) with Hugh Scott (ACA 35) as chairman of the Senate Republican Campaign Committee. The post went instead to George Murphy (ACA 82).

These developments were by no means lost on apprehensive liberals. As early as mid-1966, liberal GOP spokesmen began noting that the sea around them had a strangely conservative look to it. At that time the Ripon Society began raising alarm signals about the gubernatorial candidacy of Ronald Reagan in California and the possibility of a conservative push to nominate him for the presidency in 1968. A Ripon-operated group calling itself the "Council of Republican Organizations" was also concerned about liberal prospects in the party, and issued a statement saying:

> On the basis of the evidence of the last two years, there is little reason to believe that the Republican Party of 1968 and its national nominating convention will look much different from 1964. . . . Unless the performance of the next two years is dramatically improved, moderate Republicanism will have failed once again to bring leadership to their [sic] party and their nation.

Among the specifics were complaints that Republican liberals had brought forth no figure of "national stature" to lead their troops, that conservatives under Melvin Laird had consolidated control of the House leadership, that the liberal GOP was effectively shut out in the South, and that Ronald Reagan seemed to be looming up as a major figure in party circles. (Reagan-anxiety has been a principal theme of liberal Republican pronouncements since 1966.)

CRO's final lamentation was that "moderate" GOP groups had meager financial backing compared to conservative organizations and that "resources have been a critical limiting factor in almost all moderate Republican organizational efforts." This assertion was borne out in the fall of 1967 by the virtual collapse of a liberal GOP group which called itself "Republicans for Progress." Formed after the 1964 election for the purpose of liberalizing the party, this organization apparently never got off the ground. Chairman Charles P. Taft announced that "we've had great difficulty raising money. So we've decided to close the Washington office and conduct our operations from my office in Cincinnati."

In the fall of 1966, Ripon published a book bemoaning, among other things, the conservatism of the House Republican leadership. In the aftermath of 1964, Ripon complained, the House GOP liberals fumbled away even the slight resources they possessed and wound up out in the cold:

> When the smoke of battle had cleared, the moderates had nothing! . . . The Ford lieutenants decided they didn't need any agreements with the moderate forces. . . . As for [the] conference chairmanship [won by the conservative Laird], the [moderates] fielded a last-minute candidate, Congressman Peter Frelinghuysen of New Jersey. His near miss only underlined how ineffectively the moderates were using the leverage they had. The final blow came when Frelinghuysen, Ford's choice for minority whip, was defeated by incumbent Leslie Arends in a stunning reversal for the new leader. So demoralized were the moderates that there was not even token opposition to the election of John Rhodes of Arizona, a top Goldwater leader in the House, to the chairmanship of the Republican Policy Committee.

Ripon summarizes things by complaining that the post-'64 Republican leadership, across the board, "did not include *one* new moderate or liberal Republican face. In fact, the Goldwater conservatives had made important gains in the House. With Laird in control of the conference, and Rhodes as head of the Policy Committee, they had an even stronger power base than they had prior to November [1964]. They would find it very useful in 1966 and 1968."

Immediately after the 1966 elections the liberal Republicans experienced momentary relief from an otherwise consistent gloom. The media play given to Percy, Brooke, and Hatfield, created a sense of euphoria on the Republican left, and of course everyone was saying that George Romney was sure to be the next Republican nominee. But by midsummer 1967 the true shape of things was plain and the euphoria wore off. Two events in June 1967, strongly suggested the persistence of Republican conservatism: The conservative Young Republicans breezed to an easy win at their Omaha national convention, along the way whooping it up for Reagan and declaring him their favorite for 1968; and two gatherings of Republican governors in the states of Montana and Wyoming saw Reagan walk off with the honors while efforts to generate support for Romney sputtered in futility.

Ripon President Lee Huebner, writing in *The New Leader*, immediately reverted to the funereal mood of summer 1966. Discussing the Young Republican convention, Huebner reflected that he had seen the future and it worked. "The primary lesson of Omaha," Huebner said, "is that Reagan is for real. . . . Those who oppose Reagan would make a tremendous error if they attributed his success to style alone. In a way Goldwater never could, Reagan articulates and defends a beguiling set of conservative nostrums for our troubled times. . . ." To which Huebner added the observation that "these conservative leaders know what they want and they know how to go about getting it."

The way they felt about things over on the left side of the GOP was further suggested by columnist Carl Rowan in a July, 1967, dispatch. "The moderates in the Republican Party," Rowan said, "are falling into deeper disarray each month. With a helpless sort of fatalism, they are beginning to accept the notion that well-organized, well-financed conservatives could grab the 1968 presidential nomination for California Gov. Ronald Reagan." At about the same time, Washington *Post* political writer David S. Broder, a close if sometimes abrasive student of conservative Republican doings, came to similar conclusions.

In an analysis of the national GOP power-structure, Broder professed to find a kind of California conservative establishment in charge of the entire Republican party. Noting that Reagan's "stock has risen sharply" in the GOP, Broder concluded that conservative and therefore presumably pro-Reagan operatives were deployed at almost every level of the Republican apparatus. Among the assertedly pro-Reagan assets Broder cited:

1. Ready sources of campaign funds, from Eastern and Western contributors alike;
2. The competent presence of F. Clifton White, a staunch conservative and "top political manager . . . without peer";
3. Reagan's own position on the executive committee of the Republican Governors' Association;
4. Conservative control of the Young Republican National Federation;
5. Election of a "declared Reagan partisan," Mrs. Gladys O'Donnell of California, as head of the National Federation of Republican Women;
6. Election of California's Murphy to head the Senate Republican Campaign Committee; and

7. The presence of California Congressman Wilson as head of the Republican Congressional Committee.*

Broder was perhaps reading more into these things than they warranted. The omnipresence of what he deemed covert allies of Reagan in various influential sectors of the GOP was more nearly traceable to the conservative orientation of the party than to any specifically Reagan-oriented push for power. The point, however, is essentially the same: The Republican mainstream, contrary to Rockefeller's 1964 assertion, is uniformly and pervasively conservative.

* Most debatable of these conservative assets was the election of Mrs. O'Donnell, who had the backing of New York and other liberal states in her race against Goldwater conservative Phyllis Schlafly of Illinois. Mrs. O'Donnell ran as a conservative, however, and the liberal National Committee for an Effective Congress concluded she was "only slightly less conservative" than her opponent.

In a February 1968 report, NCEC confirmed the Broder analysis in other ways as well, naming off the same organizational elements and concluding that "the degree of real power resting with the Republican moderates in the national party tends to be exaggerated," principally as a result of media preoccupation with selected liberal GOP spokesmen. NCEC capped its analysis by quoting one New England Republican: "For all the Rockefellers, Javitses, and Lindsays in New York, the Republican Party across the land is conservative."

7:: THE NEW CONSENSUS

We have heard a great deal about consensus politics in recent years—not only from journalists who profess to see us bound to liberalism forever, but also from the presiding political genius of the welfare system, Lyndon Johnson himself. Under Johnson's Great Society, we are told, we have the grandest consensus for liberalism ever devised. And although Johnson did not invent the technique, we must grant that he has given it a special kind of twist.

The Johnsonian consensus is an effort to save the collapsing Roosevelt coalition by expanding it. Citizens beset by taxes and inflation can, in Johnson's view of things, also seek shelter beneath the Federal umbrella. They shall have subsidies of their own, just like everyone else —for medical care and college education, sewer lines and mass transit systems, trash collection and beautification. Through this device, an ever-expanding number of interest groups, finally embracing the whole of society, will be pulled into the coalition. Businessman and labor leader, stripling and pensioner, will join together in the peaceable kingdom of suborned agreement.

It seems, at first glance, an interesting idea. But it has two fatal weaknesses. The first is that the expanding benefits do not solve the economic problem but merely escalate it to a higher level. The middle-class voter who gets a college scholarship for his son, the pensioner who is provided with Medicare, soon finds he must pay for these "free" benefits even more dearly than before. The expanding Federal budget pushes both taxes and the inflationary cycle through another upward turn.

The second problem is in certain respects more difficult still. This is the development of a new consensus, until recent months largely unnoticed, in opposition to liberal programs. Cutting sharply across ideological lines, this new consensus is not a coalition of interest groups but a conflation of ideas. The participants are philosophical conservatives and disgruntled liberals, and the common theme is a concern for the integrity of the individual. Conservatives have been preaching the dangers and inadequacies of big government for years, of course, so their stance on this issue is not particularly novel. What is new is the emergence of a growing body of liberal scholarship and causerie vindicating the conservative position.

The net meaning of this development is, in its own way, quite as remarkable as the change recorded in the demographic tables. It clearly suggests that rebellion against the old liberal formulae is developing on two fronts simultaneously—in intellectual as well as economic terms. The motives involved are superficially different, but fundamentally alike: The suburbanite rebels against taxes and inflation, the dissenting intellectual against the apparatus of compulsion. Each is in fact protesting a different aspect of the same phenomenon—the encroachment of centralized power upon the sphere of personal autonomy. Should the two tendencies meet and combine, as they have in part begun to do, the result could be politically explosive.

So far has this development proceeded that it is no exaggeration to say the relative strength of conservatism and liberalism in philosophical combat is almost exactly the reverse of what is usually alleged about the world of politics. In virtually every sphere of intellectual or scholarly endeavor, the conservative position is on the attack, liberalism in retreat. Run down a list of major intellectual issues and you find that the advocates of the liberal view, once almost totally dominant, have in case after case yielded important ground, confessing their failures and giving increased recognition to the conservative alternative.

To take a prominent example, there is the field of American historiography, once in thrall to the crude determinism of Charles Beard and his coadjutors. For decades American college and high-school students have been instructed that our Constitution was the handiwork of greedy men trying to shore up their own financial interests. But in the past decade the Beard argument, by common acknowledgment, has been demolished through the researches of conservative scholars.

Similar results have obtained in the field of education, where the doctrines of John Dewey, once supreme, are now in general disrepute. Liberals like Hofstadter and Lawrence Cremin acknowledge this, and a number of liberals have participated in the anti-progressivist Council for Basic Education. To the list of discredited theorems we might also add the cult of progress, the notion that crime and other social disorders are caused by poverty, and the idea that whole communities can be made over by governmental fiat.

Most crucial of all the liberal casualties is the doctrine of central planning, long promoted as the only rational course for a modern industrial economy. Nowadays this conception is rejected not only by conservatives but by many liberals as well. The unhappy results of centralized power are obviously beginning to worry the people who brought it into being. Ironically, the point Senator Javits thinks has been definitively settled—the question of halting the trend to centralization by getting power back into the hands of the states and local communities—is precisely the point on which the liberal intellectuals are moving most notably toward the conservative position.

Much of this development is owing to the effective theoretical work done over the years by a number of conservative intellectuals—the seminal labors of Forrest McDonald and Robert Brown in the field of American history, Milton Friedman and George Stigler in economics providing only a few examples. It has in addition been promoted by the growth of conservative intellectual journals like *National Review, Modern Age, The Intercollegiate Review, Triumph,* and the emergence of such spokesmen for the conservative position as William F. Buckley, Jr., Russell Kirk, James Burnham, and Frank Meyer—again letting a few names do service for a considerable list. The presentations of these spokesmen and others like them seem to have had some effect upon more reflective members of the liberal community.

The common findings of the new conservatives and the new consensus liberals are well expressed by Richard Goodwin, a former aide to John F. Kennedy and an adviser to the late President's brother Robert. In an article for *Commentary* magazine (June, 1967), Goodwin discussed what he called "the most troubling political fact of our age": the fact that "the growth in central power has been accompanied by a swift and continual diminution in the significance of the individual citizen, transforming him from a wielder to an object of power."

Goodwin noted that "centralized bureaucracies tend to

become increasingly ineffective and coercive in direct proportion to the scope and intricacy of the problem they are established to solve. . . . One need only look at the fantastic labyrinth of welfare programs, the monstrous incapacities of the Department of Health, Education and Welfare—operated by some of the best teams of executives in government—as well as the foreseeable futilities of the new Departments of Housing and Urban Development and Transportation, to realize that something is wrong with the old approach."

All of which led Goodwin to observe that we must set about seeking methods of decentralization: ". . . the elaborate structure of American federalism," he said, "mirrored the judgment that a great deal should be left to local authority. For decades we have been moving in the other direction. Not only is this a dangerous, and, I believe, a mistaken course, but it is becoming clear that certain substantive objectives utterly depend on fashioning fresh techniques. Modern poverty, for example, cannot be abolished by friendly edicts from remote officials, and even if it could, the result would be sterile, vacuous, and purely material . . . the idea of decentralization is making its first timid and tentative appearances in political rhetoric. It is possible to predict that the first party to carry this banner (if buttressed by a solid program) will find itself on the right side of the decisive issues of the 1970s."

Statements of this sort from liberal sources have in recent months become increasingly numerous. Another former Kennedy aide, Daniel P. Moynihan, stirred a notable ruction in the late summer and fall of 1967 by offering some blunt opinion similar to Goodwin's. Among other things, Moynihan asserted in a searching article, liberal oratory and liberal programs in Congress had contributed to racial unrest because they had "raised hopes out of all proportion to our capacity to deliver on our promises."

He added that "in our desire to maintain public confidence in such programs, we have tended to avoid evidence of poor results. Somehow liberals have been unable to acquire from life what conservatives seem to have been endowed with at birth, namely a healthy skepticism of the powers of government agencies to do good."

Subsequently, in a speech before the national board of Americans for Democratic Action, Moynihan described America's troubles at home and abroad as "an especial problem of American liberals, because more than anyone else it is they who have been in office . . . and in large measure presided over the onset of" these difficulties. He noted that riots and disorder in American cities had occurred "in the aftermath of one of the most extraordinary periods of liberal electoral victories that we have ever experienced," and concluded that liberals "must divest themselves of the notion that the nation, especially the cities, can be run from agencies in Washington."

This is revolutionary talk indeed. Whatever else "liberalism" has come to mean in American politics, it has unquestionably meant, over the past thirty years, the centralization of political authority.* Why there should now be a falling away from the ancient doctrine is not entirely clear, although we have a number of clues. The modern liberal has always professed to believe concentrated power in Washington was compatible with the fullest plen-

* A suggestive formulation of the conventional liberal position was offered by Senator Joseph S. Clark (D-Penna.), in a 1953 statement. Clark defined a liberal as one who believes in "using the full force of government" at all levels of society and he rejoiced that, toward this end, "*spiritually and economically youth is conditioned to respond to a liberal program of orderly policing of society by government, subject to the popular will, in the interests of social justice.*" Similar statements about the need for policing, discipline, and chastisement of private interests have repeatedly come from such people as Arthur Schlesinger, Jr., and John Kenneth Galbraith—both, like Clark, members of Americans for Democratic Action. Goodwin and Moynihan, interestingly enough, are also members of ADA.

itude of "civil liberties," which liberals are also supposed to favor—a stance chiefly maintained by defining "civil liberties" in terms of things which the consolidation of authority had not as yet diminished. Thus, although centralization did constrict such freedoms as the right to hold and develop private property, to seek and accept employment freely offered, to be secure in one's home and the fruits of one's labor, many liberals ignored these things. These items, according to spokesmen for the American Civil Liberties Union, did not truly involve civil liberties and therefore need not concern us greatly.

But beneath the surface of bland assurance there was an undertow of doubt. During the 1950's a very few liberal spokesmen—Lionel Trilling, Edmund Wilson, Jacques Barzun, and David Riesman foremost among them—voiced some tentative misgivings about the direction in which liberalism was headed. When it developed that the new constrictions were beginning to squeeze the left as well as the right, to hurt liberal dissidents as well as conservative businessmen, the revaluation became widespread. Anxieties expressed in intellectual circles began making their way into politics and popular journalism.

One of the earliest, and best, statements of this gathering concern was offered by Irving Kristol, former editor of *Encounter* and *The Reporter*. Writing in *Harper's* for June, 1963, Kristol took a new look at the whole welfare state approach and decided it was not working well at all. He reported that "among New Frontiersmen in Washington today, the word 'bureaucracy' is used with the same bitter despair that used to be the hallmark of the reactionary. . . . The new men in Washington have discovered that in only rare instances can a large-scale plan encompass all the factors on which its success or failure depends."

Kristol cited a number of libertarian horror stories generated by the excesses of bureaucracy. "I can hardly pick up a newspaper," he wrote, "without my anti-bureaucratic nerve being given a shock. The Internal Revenue Service announces that it will not recognize the general validity of a tax court case decided against it. . . . Newbold Morris, New York City's Park Commissioner, denounces the suggestion that salesmen be allowed to carry merchandise samples in their private cars while driving on city parkways. . . . The Rural Electrification Administration announces that, with American farms electrified, its mission is now completed—and so it will henceforth be selling its electricity at a discount (courtesy of government subsidy) to suburbs, in highly unfair competition with private . . . utilities. . . ."

In 1966, related lamentations came from a group of Socialists, no less, writing in a book called *The Radical Papers*. Suggestive of the dilemma in which radical collectivists and other votaries of the left now find themselves are these statements:

> In recent years there has arisen a sophistication which understands that the abolition of private property alone will not guarantee the end of exploitation. The problem has been posed as: How does one check bureaucracy? . . . (Daniel Bell)

> . . . There is the virtual certainty that democracy will be the first and most lasting casualty of the revolution. For proof one need only run through the political alphabet from Algeria via Cuba to the Soviet Union. The resulting paradox—democracy without socialism on one side of the line, socialism without democracy on the other—is perhaps most plainly visible to a spectator perched on the Berlin Wall. . . . (George Lichtheim)

> Bureaucratism signifies a deformation, though not necessarily a destruction of the democratic processes. . . . The idea of a division of powers, which many Marxists have dismissed as a bourgeois device for thwarting the popular will, would deserve careful attention in planning a Socialist society. . . . (Lewis Coser and Irving Howe)

Even more frequent than general criticisms of centralized power are liberal attacks on specific governmental programs. Leading targets for this new hostility are such long-cherished Federal projects as urban renewal and public housing. Among the academic critics of these programs are Nathan Glazer, Scott Greer, Richard Cloward, Lee Rainwater, and several others—liberals all. Typical of their complaints is the assertion of Cloward that "the net loss in low-income housing" from government programs "is probably about 250,000 units," and of Glazer that "urban renewal has unquestionably reduced the quantity of low-cost housing and raised rents for the poor." In the political realm, similar utterances popped up in a speech by none other than Robert Kennedy, who said government relief programs were "inefficient and degrading" and that public housing "has conspicuously failed."

While disenchantment with renewal and housing has led the liberal march to conservative territory, other subjects have also played a role. Even liberal ideas about civil rights and "*de facto* segregation" have come under attack from columnist Joseph Alsop, in his syndicated column and in a long article for *The New Republic*. Most devastating of all, criticism has been directed at those two venerable sacred cows—TVA and the Post Office. Short years ago these were unbroachable subjects, the mention of which was guaranteed to elicit a charge of heresy. But in 1967 who should turn up suggesting the infusion of conservative principle into the Post Office operation but Postmaster General Lawrence O'Brien himself. He advocated that the agency be turned over to a government corporation to be run according to business precepts—just one step away from the long-standing notion of some conservative theoreticians that the mail might be handled a good deal better, if, like the telephone, it were a private rather than a public responsibility. Equally startling was the appearance, in *The Nation*, of an article taking the Tennessee

Valley Authority severely to task. Nothing would remain, it seems, but for some prominent liberal spokesman to come forward with a full-scale blast at Social Security.*

A final example in this category is the protest lodged by a number of leftist spokesmen against malfeasance in the "war on poverty." In some respects, the outcry of "new left" spokesmen concerning such things as the use of poverty funds to build patronage machines for the Democratic party sounds very much like the comment of conservative Republican congressmen. The motives are different, but the empirical findings are the same. Thus we find Clark Kissinger of Students for a Democratic Society saying: "What we don't like about the liberal welfare state is that all the decisions are made in Washington and handed down. We don't want to tell the poor what the solutions to their problems should be."

In all such statements, the strain between libertarian impulse and collectivist doctrine is apparent. For years American collectivists have proclaimed themselves champions of increasing centralization of power in government *and* the fullest exercise of personal freedoms by the citizen, characteristically evading the question of how the two goals are to be reconciled. Now, increasingly, the shoe is beginning to pinch. The libertarian left is reaching the point where it must choose.

Sensitivity to the conservative critique has brought other changes as well. A number of liberals are beginning to take up affirmative ideas previously advanced by

* *The Nation* article asserted: "Created in large part on the basic principle of relieving human misery, TVA has, with disturbing frequency, seemed to be adding to the problems of the people in its area of operation. As it has grown in power and influence, and as its projects in navigation, electric power and flood control have neared completion in the Tennessee Valley, the agency has begun to appear callous at home and covetous of fertile new fields to plow outside the valley." Virtually the same indictment had been leveled more than a decade previously by conservative economist Dean Russell of the Foundation for Economic Education in a book called *The TVA Idea*.

conservative spokesmen. Professor Walter Heller, former economic adviser to Presidents Kennedy and Johnson, has endorsed the tax-sharing idea long advocated by conservative Professor Roger Freeman, and advanced during the 1964 presidential campaign by Barry Goldwater. Similar liberal support has been evinced for Freeman's tax-credit proposals in the field of education and for the negative income-tax and rent-supplement proposals advanced by Milton Friedman—although the liberal application of these ideas, in both instances, is rather different from that favored by conservatives. Moynihan strongly urged the tax-sharing approach in his remarks to the ADA, reminding his listeners that liberals rather than conservatives had prevented this program from coming to fruition.

Not all the liberal disenchantment, to be sure, is the result of theoretical revaluation. Much of it has been traceable to the Vietnamese war. In 1966 and 1967 the Vietnam conflict was clearly pressing American liberals, by one route or another, onto conservative ground. And, ironically enough, this development was apparent on both sides of the qustion—among liberals who favored the war and among those who opposed it. Vice-President Hubert Humphrey, a former chairman of ADA, began talking a foreign-policy line on Vietnam which conservative anti-Communists found altogether congenial. On the other side of the issue, Senator J. William Fulbright, bitter antagonist of conservatives, was demanding that we get back to some good old-fashioned notions of balanced power in our Federal Government. Between them, Humphrey and Fulbright had the makings of a good conservative.

As befits an age suffused with dialectic and complementarity, the net benefit to conservatism in this strange double reversal lay in one direction tactically, another strategically. In the immediate context of Vietnam, American conservatives sided with Humphrey as opposed to

Fulbright. Yet in the long run it was the effect of the Vietnamese war on the left intellectuals which may have worked the deeper change for good.

This is so for a number of reasons, including the fact that the Vietnam commitment was precariously out of phase with the rest of the administration's foreign policy and was in consequence subject to so many modifications and restrictions that anyone who sought to project from it a long-range alteration of liberal foreign policy attitudes would have been a brave clairvoyant indeed. The net weight of the evidence did not suggest the conservative view of the foreign-policy function had found permanent lodgment in the high councils of the administration.

On the other end of the debate, however, there was evidence that the change in outlook would have long-term effects. The lesson which the dissident liberals have learned is, one should hope, impressive. President Johnson had, from their point of view, all too horribly gored the wrong ox. All that majestic power for good, heaped up with abandon in the assurance that the executive would use it for such things as negotiating disarmament, cutting off aid to Chiang Kai-shek, cherishing Tito and coddling Nkrumah—all was now being mobilized to combat a war of "national liberation" in Southeast Asia.

Moreover, there were spin-offs on the home front. For one thing, the President was claiming that the power to decide when and how to conduct such battles was inherent in the majesty of his office—quite a natural thing for him to think, in view of what had been said on this subject by countless liberal theoreticians. But the President found the same liberals were not so awed by majesty when it went counter to their policy on Vietnam.

The clearest example of reversal on this score is Walter Lippmann, long one of the nation's most influential advocates of a "strong" executive. Back in 1955 Lippmann had argued that the presidency by rights should be very strong, but had been denuded of its proper powers by an uppity Congress and contumacious electorate. The withered executive, he said, had "lost both its material and ethereal powers" to the legislature and the "misrule of the people." What was needed was to restore a strong executive government which could, among other things, "resist the encroachment of assemblies and of mass opinion."

Come 1966 and the entanglement of Vietnam, and Lippmann's opinions had notably changed. Angered by Johnson's policy of bombing in the North, and even more angered by Johnson's argument that such determinations were an inherent presidential right, Lippmann executed a sudden change of field. Johnson's assertion of executive powers, he said, was "heresy" against American constitutional doctrine—"a claim to arbitrary power, a claim that in making these momentous decisions, the President, once he is elected, is bound only by his personal views, not by any mandate or covenant with the people who elected him." In questions of power, that is, let no more be heard of confidence in Presidents.

It is obvious enough that, even in 1955, the American presidency was an immensely powerful agency in no danger whatever of being crushed by Congress or "mass opinion." Lippmann marshaled his arguments about a palsied executive and the need to strengthen it because he shared the common liberal view that Congress tends to conservatism and the executive to the liberal side of things. A decade later the calculus of advantage had rather vividly been altered. The immense power of the presidency was being deployed, not to serve liberal ends, but, as Lippmann believed, to disserve them. As the calculus changed, so did the principle.

An almost identical reversal was performed by Senator Fulbright, who in a 1963 pamphlet had stated that presidential powers in the foreign-policy field should be expanded to new dimensions. Congress was ill equipped to operate in this area, Fulbright stated, while "public opinion must be educated and led." For these reasons "we must contemplate the further enhancement of presidential authority in foreign affairs." During his 1967 split with Johnson over Vietnam, however, Fulbright suddenly blossomed forth as a champion of congressional privilege in the foreign policy arena, denouncing the president for usurpations of legislative authority.

The key to all this is provided by Goodwin, whose *Commentary* piece remains the most extensive statement of the new liberal disenchantment with liberalism. Among other things, Goodwin criticizes both the presidency and the Supreme Court, which he believes, as do most conservatives, to be an outpost of political improvisation. His comment on the latter is particularly significant. The entry of the Court into the arena of politics is, he says, "a transformation which almost certainly will come back to plague us as judicial personnel and social attitudes change, and as an institution which has become more and more political develops an even greater sensitivity to transitory shifts in political temper."

On the whole, the gnawing suspicion that concentrated power will indeed "come back to plague us" seems to be a common theme of the liberal disappointment—a fact which radical-liberal unhappiness over the war in Vietnam merely served to make flamboyant. "It is just possible," Goodwin says, "that conservatives have something to teach about the value of institutional arrangements, and the unwisdom of sacrificing them to immediate desires. At least we should understand that the hope for pure self-restraint in the use of power can be a very feeble guarantee, and often weakest in the temperament which wishes to accomplish the most for the country."

It is just possible, indeed, that conservatives have something to teach—on this subject and on others. And it is also possible that realization of that fact by an increasing number of liberals provides an opportunity for the unparalleled advance of conservative ideas in America, in the intellectual marketplace and the realm of politics alike.

8: : NEW LEFT, NEW RIGHT

It is an axiom of the old consensus that young people are always more radical than their parents. According to accepted notions about the steady liberal drift of everything, rebellion is thought to be exclusively a matter of outflanking the old folks on the left. If we may believe social critics like Paul Goodman and Edgar Z. Friedenberg, it is up to the young people to redeem our faltering society by stirring up still more leftism than we already have.

Whether this view of things is correct or not has become a matter of some importance. Signs that the liberal world view is raveling around the edges suggest a pressing need for alternatives, and nowhere is the need more obvious than on the college campus. Young people in America as elsewhere are stirred by the libertarian impulse and react strongly against systems which rigidify the conditions of life. Since liberalism is coming to be recognized as precisely such a system, the restiveness of the young becomes a major source of potential trouble.

But, if the conventional view of things is correct, liberalism is secure no matter what. No failure or inadequacy or disservice to freedom can bring it down. If the next generation is always more liberal than the last, then the leftward bias of our politics is permanently assured. Indeed, the very failures of today's liberalism will infallibly generate the more intensive fervors of tomorrow's.

Like other matters we have reviewed, this notion presents a number of difficulties. The most obvious of these is the fact that, when leftist politics is itself the orthodoxy, the shape and dimension of a leftist revolt against it are hard to envision. It is the same kind of conceptual problem one would encounter if he tried to conjure up a Papist uprising in the Vatican, a capitalist revolution on Wall Street, or a cheese *Putsch* in Wisconsin. The idea that orthodoxy should be challenged exclusively by ever more militant versions of itself suggests a curious view of human nature.

The problems inherent in this imagined revolution from the throne become plain enough when we note that its most recent incarnation is the so-called new left, a bearded legion of youthful activists who have set about to cast down the liberal orthodoxy by burning their draft cards, ingesting drugs, and protesting America's few residual commitments to Cold War rationality. The new left is, by all the available evidence, a very strange phenomenon. It has no discernible program and no apparent thought of devising one. On the testimony of its own principal spokesmen, the movement does not know what it believes, what it wants to do, or even why it exists. Its motto is "action" for the sake of action, with ideas considered *infra dig.* Unless the national destiny is conceived to be a final collapse into intellectual chaos (always a possibility), it is difficult to accept such an enterprise as a serious form of political augury.

It becomes even more difficult when we note that, despite the publicity lavished on it, the movement is a small one. Phillip Abbott Luce estimated the 1966 membership of all active new left groups at around 12,000, and the membership of the largest single organization, SDS, at around 2,000. More recent calculations suggest a slight expansion, but are along the same order of magnitude. It is, of course, true that numbers are not the best way of judging the effectiveness of youthful rebellion, or any rebellion. Far more important is the quality of the ideas expressed. But, as noted, the new leftists have virtually no ideas at all.

The liberal vision of America nonetheless requires us to believe that this, indeed, is it—the authentic shape of youthful insurrection. We have in consequence been treated to a long series of reports and analyses about new left beliefs and activities, telling us a good deal more about Students for Democratic Society and the Du Bois Clubs, the Student Nonviolent Coordinating Committee (SNCC) and the Free Speech Movement, than most people care to know. For a movement allegedly in hot rebellion against "the system," the new left receives strangely respectful and sympathetic coverage in the system's communications outlets.

As widely ignored by the media as the new left is promoted by them is the burgeoning young conservative movement on American campuses. By most accepted standards, this activity is a more important index to the political future than the conduct of draft-card burners and LSD enthusiasts. A review of comparative membership figures shows the young conservative groups are considerably more numerous than their left-wing opponents; an examination of the political track record reveals they are more effective in terms of practical results; and a survey of their literature reveals they are pre-eminently concerned, as the new left is not, with ideas. Yet they are seldom accorded the kind of attention that is routinely given the new left.

The obvious starting point in a discussion of young conservatism is an organization called the Intercollegiate Studies Institute (formerly Intercollegiate Society of Individualists). Founded in 1953 with only a few hundred students on its mailing list, ISI has expanded in geometrical proportions. By late 1967, the national membership of the group was estimated at 35,000—and still growing. It has become the largest explicitly ideological group on the American campus.

This becomes the more impressive when we reflect that ISI, devoted to scholarship and austerely nonpolitical, is not by intention a mass-membership organization. It does not aim to recruit new partisans by the thousands to send into picket lines, sit-ins, or demonstrations. Its object is to get people to re-examine some of the root issues of political philosophy, attend lectures, read books, write papers, go to seminars and summer schools, engage in debates. And in this respect it has been very successful indeed. In 1967–68 the group had 94 associated clubs. ISI and its associates sponsored 122 lectures on college campuses, superintended the production of 14 campus newsletters and magazines, distributed 3,268 books, published 6 issues of its journal, *The Intercollegiate Review* (press run of 45,000 per issue), and sponsored 8 seminars and summer schools.

Signs that the active and growing ideological force on the college campus today is not the radical left but the responsible right are numerous. ISI official John Lulves gave this 1966 summary of the conditions he encountered on major campuses in the midlands:

"New left" hoopla to the contrary, it can be reported that student conservatism is experiencing boom conditions and there is every indication that the immediate future portends growth rather than demise. There have been numerous indications that the temper of today's student body is not conducive to galloping liberalism. A recent survey at the University of Wisconsin, noted for *avante garde* leftism, revealed 72 per cent of the students favored American participation in the Viet Nam war, while only 16 per cent opposed such action. . . . The huge success of the blood for Viet Nam drives (Indiana University students, for example, donated more than 1,000 pints in three days) indicates students as a whole are not in step with the Vietniks. No less successful has been the movement to gather petitions supporting U.S. resolve in Viet Nam: from Michigan State University (more than 12,000 signatures) to Kansas State (2,000) students have signed up.

Lulves noted other indicia of conservative sentiment, including a rapidly ascending number of ISI-associated clubs on Midwest campuses, an augmented level of activity, larger club memberships, and big turnouts for club-sponsored speakers. "At the University of Wisconsin," he noted, "the Wisconsin Conservative Club attracted 70 students last September, a four-fold increase over last year; 150 signed the rolls of the Texas conservative club, 80 at Indiana University (where the Conservative Club won the student activities prize)." As for speakers: "Scattered attendance figures from the post-September [1965] experience of ISI speakers are revealing: 1,200 at Vanderbilt University, 80 at the University of Texas, 50 at Malone College (Ohio), 360 at Southern Illinois University, 400 for a film at Mankato State College in Minnesota."

Most telling of all are the membership figures. In the Midwest alone, more than 3,100 students and professors joined ISI during the first semester of the 1965–66 academic year. This number of new recruits was vastly in excess of membership increases during the two preceding years (998 in 1964–65, 476 in 1963–64)."It should not go unremarked," Lulves adds, "that this one-semester increase in one section of the country is greater than the claimed national membership of the Students for a Democratic Society, a campus left-wing group much examined by the *New York Times*."

At the national level, the membership has expanded correspondingly. During the 1966–67 school year, no less than 14,000 new members joined ISI—an increase larger than Luce's estimate for the new left movement as a whole.

While the growth of conservative ideas on the campus has accelerated notably in the past several years, it is not my argument that a majority of today's students are conservatives. They are not. An opinion survey on major issues would undoubtedly show most of them to the left of center most of the time, although to the right of center on certain key questions. A predominant, somewhat automatic liberalism is, under the circumstances, to be expected—if only because the reigning orthodoxy, on the campus and beyond it, is liberal. The truly significant fact about the conservative rebellion is that its members have the initiative and intellectual independence to go against the orthodoxy—to challenge the doctrinal preconditions of the compulsory state. It is this ability for independent *thought* which marks these young people as future leaders of American society.

The shape of the new left movement is markedly different—not because its members are less quick-witted, but because they have forsworn theoretical inspection of the going order. Many of these young people are both intelligent and sensitive, and they can see and feel many things wrong in our society; but because they are reluctant to traffic in ideas, their impulse toward resistance is aborted and channeled off into eccentricity. Their central complaints about bureaucracy, the pressures of mass society, the loss of individual integrity are valid. But since these things happen to be major consequences of liberal doctrine and liberal practice, they cannot be alleviated until liberalism itself is challenged.

It is precisely here that the chief distinction between the new right and the new left becomes most vivid: The young conservatives are engaged in battling liberal doctrine, while the young leftists are unknowing captives of it. Indeed, the new left promotes the central assumptions of the liberal orthodoxy more strenuously than do the liberals themselves. The root premises of the movement are a vague commitment to collectivism, permissiveness in morals, militant egalitarianism, hostility to patriotic sentiment, and strident pacifism. On all doctrinal matters, that is, the new left is merely American liberalism writ large, demanding that all the abstractions be enforced *instanter*, with no exceptions (as in Vietnam). That the "rebellion" is ideologically speaking at one with present conformity goes far to explain both the copious publicity and the new left aversion to ideas. Avoidance of thought is both a necessary precondition of the movement and a guarantee of its ultimate triviality. Rejuvenating liberal society with stiffer doses of liberalism is a form of homeopathy that obviously requires a blind eye toward doctrine.

The truth is that the new left, in serious terms, is not a revolution at all. The liberal media are attracted to it, not because it is different from them, but because it is essentially like them. The young people who deplore "corporate liberalism" and "faceless bureaucracy" think they are engaged in mortal combat with Time-Life and the governmental establishment. Yet they are diligently promoted by Time-Life, gloriously subsidized by the bureaucracy ($3.3 million from CIA to the new left-dominated National Student Association) and are recruited out of SDS and SNCC to serve in various government programs (according to new left mentor Paul Goodman, writing for Time-Life). While the new left may view itself as rebellion, the liberal establishment obviously views it as a kind of free-lance training program for junior executives. The new left is the officially certified and subsidized rebellion of the imaginary America.

It is this ideological problem, I think, which very largely accounts for new left eccentricities of dress and behavior—beards and boots, pot and promiscuity. If one is not distinguished from orthodox belief by the shape of his ideas, but still wants to be known as a rebel, the only recourse is to stylistic peculiarity. This provides an obvious kind of distinction, suitably scandalizes the squares, and gives everybody the message that you are rebelling. If you didn't look that way, didn't have that beard, how would anybody *know* that you are different? And in the age of the image, it is of course essential that others should know it—in order that you may know it yourself.

The long-range effectiveness of conservative ideation as opposed to new left idiosyncrasy has already become evident. The young conservatives have produced a host of youthful professors and instructors, authors and journalists, who have injected an entirely new element into the continuing battle of ideas. They have moved increasingly onto the faculties of colleges and universities, onto magazine and newspaper staffs, into the book-publishing industry and other crucial areas where, until a few years ago, there was little conservative representation. A rough count reveals about two dozen books published in the past few years by young conservative writers—as opposed to perhaps half a dozen which are identifiable products of the anticonservative youth program in all its modulations from new left to liberal Republican.

This aspect of the young conservative movement was brought out sharply by an Opinion Research Corp. survey in depth published in January, 1962. After interviewing a broad cross-section of the young conservatives, Opinion Research reached the following conclusions:

> Individual freedom is the unifying and galvanizing ideal of campus conservatism. . . . [The movement] is primarily intellectual. . . . The movement's vigor stems from the serious

motivation of its members. . . . When talking about motives for joining, leaders and members refer over and over to concepts, purposes, ideas, and the momentous problems facing the country. . . . Members devote considerable time to broadening their understanding of conservatism. . . . Because hard study is its hallmark, college conservative training quite obviously prepares students for leadership after graduation. . . .

This evaluation was written when the movement was considerably smaller than it is today, but it is equally applicable now. Indicative of the strong intellectual interests of these students is their eagerness to attend seminars and summer schools during holiday periods when other students are relaxing or making money. In the summer of 1967, for example, ISI held three summer schools able to accommodate some 150 students in all. It received applications from almost three times as many as it could accept.

Also noteworthy is the fact that so many of the ISI members go on to graduate school, intending to become teachers or professional specialists. A 1967 survey of the membership showed that 89 per cent planned advanced study. The implications for the future should be apparent. The vast majority of ISIers go on to become teachers, scholars, essayists, journalists.

The comment of liberal researchers Arnold Forster and Benjamin Epstein in *Danger on the Right*, taken as an admission against interest, should be considered definitive. These authors say of the young conservatives: "Their energy, their dedication, and their talent for the written and spoken word appear to overshadow anything that the more Liberal youth on or off the campus can offer. The Liberals of today do not appear to have produced leaders of stature and energy to do battle with them. These young rightists spawned in the last decade undoubtedly will make a substantial impact on American life."

Evidence that the impact has in part already been

achieved is the performance of the half-million member Young Republican National Federation, now so dependably conservative it is considered the strongest of conservative outposts in the national Republican party. This immense organization—the largest political youth group in the country and in fact the largest dues-paying political organization of any kind—has moved steadily in the intellectual direction suggested by the growth of conservative ideology on the college campus. It forms an obvious link-gate between the rise of the conservative intellectual community and the augmented conservatism of the Republican party.

The connection is underlined by the fact that the first explicit gestures toward GOP conservatism occurred on the campus. Many of the college Young Republicans who have gone on to hold office and to assume positions of influence in the YRNF and in the senior party have been members of conservative clubs on campus and/or taken part in conservative youth activities. The ideological stance of these youthful GOPers consists, typically, of traditional Republican doctrine spiced with formulations of the conservative position provided by the scholars and publicists of the right.

Significantly, the Goldwater movement bobbed to the surface in the ranks of the college Young Republicans before it appeared anywhere else. At a convention of the Midwestern Federation of College Young Republican Clubs in Des Moines, Iowa, in April, 1960, the delegates voted through a number of conservative resolutions and platform planks, and adopted a motion urging Goldwater to seek the party's vice-presidential nomination. So far as the record discloses, this was the first organizational expression of Goldwater sentiment in the national GOP. As a direct result of this meeting, the first national Youth for Goldwater organization was formed, out of which grew, in turn, the political action group, Young Americans for Freedom.

In subsequent years the conservatism of the College Young Republicans became even more pronounced. In 1961, the conservatives won outright control of the Midwest Federation, largest and most influential segment of the national college YRs. That victory was prefatory to the election of a Goldwater enthusiast, James Harff of Wisconsin, as the national college YR chairman (Harff was to become chairman of the 1964 Youth for Goldwater effort). Thus, as early as 1961, conservative forces were in charge of the national college Young Republicans—a direct result of the ideological ferment on the campus and a forerunner of other developments to come.

Conservative ideas have also made their influence felt in the parent YRNF. As early as the 1957 Young Republican convention in Washington, D.C., ripples of conservative belief began showing up in the group's platform and resolution statements. The 1957 gathering adopted platform planks opposed to Federal aid to education, cultural exchanges with the Soviet Union, "status of forces" treaties allowing U.S. servicemen to be tried in foreign courts, and trade with Communist nations.

At the 1959 convention in Denver the affirmations of 1957 were in all essential respects repeated—with the exception that the results were, if anything, more conservative. The YRs also turned back an abortive Rockefeller bid for influence in the federation and chose Nixon-backer Ned Cushing as their chairman. In 1961 the liberals staged their strongest counterattack, electing a candidate allied with the Rockefeller forces to the chairmanship as conservatives suffered an internal split. But the ideological leanings of the group were again made explicit in the platform, more conservative than any of its predecessors.

In 1963 the conservative sentiment hovering below the surface in the platform battles and the college YRs at last broke through to full public visibility. The conservatives, sobered by the '61 setback, regrouped and elected

Goldwater-backer "Buzz" Lukens at a tight convention in San Francisco. That victory marked the turning point. In 1965, Kansas state senator Tom Van Sickle, a former official of the Draft Goldwater committee, succeeded to the chairmanship. And in 1967, Jack McDonald of Tennessee, another Goldwater backer, followed Van Sickle in the chairman's post. Throughout all this, YR statements on national issues continued to be markedly conservative: e.g., the 1965 convention urged repeal of the Moscow test-ban treaty; the 1967 convention urged reconsideration of the consular accord with the Soviet Union.

What has been the impact of these developments on American young people at large? The answer is that, with the YRNF and the college group in conservative hands, and with that fact well publicized and relentlessly denounced by the liberal media, more college students are willing to declare themselves Republicans today than at any other time in recent years. According to a survey conducted by George Gallup, published May 30, 1967, there are now as many Republicans as Democrats among American collegians. Asked, "In politics, as of today, do you consider yourself a Republican, Democrat, or Independent?" student respondents gave the following replies: 29 per cent Republican, 29 per cent Democrat, 42 per cent Independent. A similar poll the preceding year gave the Democrats 35 per cent, with only 26 per cent saying they were Republicans.

Other surveys of youthful attitudes suggest increased emphasis on the traditional GOP philosophy of limited government could well gain the Young Republicans still more converts in the future. The Gallup poll figures of January, 1967 reflecting public concern over the growth of government showed this anxiety was particularly acute among younger voters. Gallup found no less than 61 per cent of his respondents in the 21–29 age group singled out big government as the "biggest threat." This compared with 47 per cent in the 30–49 age group and 44 per cent in the 50-and-over bracket. The AFL–CIO survey similarly showed strong concern over big-government-related subjects among younger members. Both sets of results suggest the GOP can break through to this hitherto Democratic group of voters by accentuating, rather than forsaking, its battle against the Federal leviathan.

Finally, YR political proficiency is not limited to intra-party battles. Contrary to liberal complaint, the YRs have proved themselves to be very effective in performing the brass-tacks work of politics; their alumni include numerous congressmen and state legislators, as well as countless office holders at the county and township level. This record of political success contrasts notably with the liberal Republicans and also, it might be added, with the hyper-publicized new left. On the latter point, an editorial in the *Young Republican News*, official publication of the YRNF, has made the apposite point. Noting that the new left offered no real alternative to Great Society liberalism and that YR membership outpolled the radical groups by a resounding forty-to-one margin, the editorial stated:

> The ultimate test of a movement is the dedication and commitment of its members, and the impact they are able to have on the course of history. New leftists riot and hold be-ins. Young Republicans ring doorbells, take the poll, conduct telephone campaigns, turn out the vote. It's harder work than sitting around a coffee house cursing the "system," but it gets better results.
>
> Look at the record; there is no figure in public office today who is a graduate of the "new left" movement, and not many in other positions of public leverage. Where, for example, is Mario Savio? But alumni of the YR movement in public office and other points of influence in U.S. society are legion.
>
> To cite only a few, and limiting the list to those in Federal office (there are dozens and even hundreds of others in state and local positions), there are Rep. John Ashbrook, Rep. Bill

Brock, Rep. D. E. "Buzz" Lukens, Rep. Bill Steiger, and Rep. James Gardner. These young Americans are more interested in doing something about keeping their liberty than in talking about it. Now they are in a position where their words and actions have national influence.

Just how much national influence the young conservatives were capable of wielding became increasingly clear as the political history of the 1960's unfolded.

9:: DEATH AND TRANS-FIGURATION

Much has been written about the Goldwater nomination and its effects, for good or ill, upon the Republican party. The interpretations differ widely, but in the liberal version there is a point that seldom varies: The assertion that Goldwater was a "minority candidate" who made off with the nomination through zeal and cunning while the "majority" liberals dozed.

One of the most direct statements of this view is offered by liberal Republican authors Gilder and Chapman, who tell us that the Goldwater forces, by methods unspecified, simply "seized control" of the party. "We believe that the Republican Party must be regained," they write, "by the Republican majority from which it has been seized. . . . The right-wing represents a small minority of Republicans. . . . We reject emphatically the view that the Goldwater nomination was either a true or a legitimate expression of the majority sentiment in the Republican Party.

We believe it was the product of the fanaticism and duplicity of a minority. . . ."

Given the liberal view of American politics, this is a natural reaction. If the "consensus" version of Republican sentiment is correct, there is no alternative to believing the Goldwater nomination was a brutal and duplicitous take-over, like the burning of the Reichstag or the storming of the Winter Palace. There obviously could be no other way to get the nation's vast legions of essentially liberal Republicans to accept so conservative a nominee.

But, natural or not, these intemperate statements are demonstrably in error. In point of fact, Goldwater's nomination was not a denial of rank-and-file opinion, but a crystalline expression of it.

To understand that this is so we need only look to the various indices of Republican sentiment from 1960 forward. The data clearly show the Republican party and the nation generally moving steadily toward conservatism. In consequence, while the Lippmanns and Restons of the world were doodling notes for a Rockefeller acceptance speech, the post-1960 Republican party was lining up behind Goldwater.

The economic and intellectual developments we have reviewed were to various degrees operative in the 1950's. But it took the political events of 1960 to release these forces from containment. That year's election opened the floodgates to the converging streams of conservative influence, replacing Nixon with Goldwater as the accepted spokesman for the Republican rank and file (a situation Nixon could conceivably have recouped, but did not, in 1962) and bringing to office a natural antagonist for conservatives in general and Barry Goldwater in particular —John F. Kennedy.

To cite Kennedy's election as a spur to conservatism may seem curious, but it was in many ways the most dramatic influence of all. With Kennedy in the White House, all ideological tendencies were sharpened. Congressional Republicans could assume a stance often denied them in the Eisenhower years. To take a conservative position on the issues was no longer an intraparty embarrassment but a matter of partisan pride. The result was a strong new rightward impulse in Republican congressional ranks.

Charles O. Jones encountered this theme repeatedly in interviews with Republican lawmakers. "It is more fun now," one asserted after Kennedy's election. "Now all we have to do is vote 'no,' " said another. "I always said that when Truman was President, my job was easy. All I had to do was vote 'no.' During the Eisenhower administration Republicans had to accept a policy even though it was against their principles." Still another put it that "under Eisenhower . . . your criticism of the administration had to be much more careful because it was a Republican administration. You had to keep your mouth shut if you opposed."

This change of mood occurred precisely as the conservative movement was beginning to surface, within the party and outside it. Conservative organizations of every description were being founded, and those already in existence experienced an upward surge in activity. Speakers on free enterprise, anticommunism, and the limited government philosophy criss-crossed the nation, addressing hundreds and sometimes thousands of people. The activities of the young conservatives, in the Young Republicans and in Young Americans for Freedom (YAF), helped to swell the expanding level of activity.

Symbolic of what was happening was a gigantic rally staged in March, 1962, by YAF, attracting a throng of 18,000 people to Madison Square Garden. Featured speaker: Barry Goldwater. Goldwater was the hero of the conservative legions, and drew those who were not already in Republican ranks to the GOP standard. He was also, significantly, the most sought-after speaker at party functions across the nation.

The departure of Eisenhower and arrival of Kennedy

served, that is, to release the Republican party from artificial restraints at a time when fresh infusions of conservative strength were entering the Republican bloodstream. The conservatives had a clear road, a receptive party, and a natural leader. Under that combination of circumstances, it would have taken a bemused or indifferent observer indeed to miss the implications for 1964; with few exceptions, the accepted oracles missed it.

Part of the problem may simply have been that the commentators weren't paying attention; but it also appears that they didn't know what to look for. Accustomed to describing conservatism as an amusement for troglodytes, they ignored what was perhaps the outstanding feature of the Republican movement to the right: its exceptional emphasis on youth. The men who organized the Goldwater push were, by and large, recent graduates of the Young Republicans; the most vocal advocates of Goldwater's cause in Congress were the younger conservative representatives like Donald Bruce and John Ashbrook; the stalwart Goldwater backers in the suburban precincts were, in case after case, youthful business and professional people; the most energetic of all the Goldwater legions were the Young Republican and campus conservative groups.

This is not to say the Goldwater drive was exclusively a matter of young people, or that it did not have many backers among older party leaders, congressmen, and rank and filers. It is to say the new conservative tendency came, not from the top down, as the stereotype would suggest, but from the bottom up. The Goldwater drive was as far from the "boss" charge as it is possible to get; it was a rare case of spontaneous ideological fervor, imposing its energies on a reluctant candidate.

The stages by which this steady upward filtration of thought occurred were clear and marked—but, until late in the day, unnoticed. What was happening in the

Young Republicans was happening, at a somewhat slower pace, in the senior party as well—with the difference that the senior party, between quadrennial conventions, seldom provides ideological markers for us in the form of clearly divided contests for power. The vast majority of the new Republican congressmen elected between 1960 and 1964 were conservatives, as were those elected in 1966. Equally significant, this group of Republican representatives included a large proportion of "new breed" conservatives of a sort seldom evident in previous years: Bruce, Ashbrook, Snyder, Brock, Gurney, Foreman, Roudebush, Bromwell, Clawson, Brotzmann, Battin.

In the Senate, a similar pattern prevailed. Between 1960 and 1964, every newly-elected Republican senator was a conservative Westerner—the easternmost states represented in the ballotings being Kansas and Texas. The most notably conservative of these was also the youngest, John Tower of Texas (thirty-five when he was elected). The seven GOP senators who came to Washington in this span (with 1966 ACA ratings), were: Tower (92), Peter Dominick (83), James Pearson (78), Len Jordan (95), Milward Simpson (90), Paul Fannin (88), and George Murphy (82).*

Liberal analysts who call the Goldwater nomination baffling or outrageous paid small attention to such things. It was altogether probable that the rising conservatism manifest in the House and Senate elections would achieve a national coalescence and attempt to move into the presi-

* The elections of 1966, bringing in three new liberal senators, moderated this tendency, but did not reverse it. Indeed, an evaluation of the fourteen new Republican senators elected in the period 1960-66 reveals a heavy gain for the conservatives over-all. The seven GOP senators newly-elected in 1966 were Percy, Brooke, Hatfield, Robert Griffin, Strom Thurmond, Cliff Hansen, and Howard Baker. Of the fourteen, nine are classifiable as conservatives, three as liberals, and two others as authentic middle-of-the-roaders. Since one of the conservatives replaced the other (Hansen replaced Simpson), the list reveals a net advantage of nine to five in favor of the conservative position.

dential arena, and that Barry Goldwater, the acknowledged conservative leader, would become the beneficiary.

By the spring of 1963, indeed, the relevant tests of presidential sentiment showed this clearly. Among the most important of these were the surveys conducted by *U.S. News*, *Newsweek*, and *Congressional Quarterly*, referred to in Chapter 2, showing most Republican leaders thought Rockefeller was going to get the nomination but *wanted* Goldwater to get it. In June, the Goldwater movement scored the first of its organizational successes to receive national attention—the victory of Goldwater-backer Lukens at the San Francisco convention of the Young Republicans. This event provoked outcries of chicanery from Rockefeller and his partisans, in the usual conspiratorial format, and that version of things received a considerable ride in those portions of the press which could not accept the idea of a conservative Republican majority. The unfolding evidence of Goldwater strength plainly revealed, however, the true shape of opinion within the GOP. By late summer and early fall, the Goldwater phenomenon had become too powerful to be ignored.

We have noted the contrasting Goldwater-Rockefeller visits to Illinois in September 1963. Such events were not confined to Illinois. In Los Angeles, 40,000 people turned out to attend a Goldwater rally at Chavez Ravine—on a night when the Dodgers were on the road fighting for the pennant. In Michigan, it was estimated, some 70 per cent of the county chairmen were for Goldwater. In Indiana, popular sentiment was so Goldwaterish that every major aspirant for the governorship let it be known, in one way or another, that he favored a Goldwater candidacy.

Out in the Rocky Mountain country, Idaho's Senator Frank Church flatly asserted: "It is the Goldwater brand of Republicanism against which we Western Democrats must prepare to wage the coming campaign." A spot check of Republican officials in Eastern Pennsylvania disclosed that Goldwater was favored for the nomination by four to one over Rockefeller, twelve to one over Scranton. And, most important, the New Hampshire polls placed Goldwater far ahead of Rockefeller in that state's first-in-the-nation primary.

Every conceivable kind of test showed Goldwater out in front. In a survey conducted at a meeting of the National Federation of Republican Women, 262 out of 293 respondents said they were for Goldwater. *U.S. News*, in a survey of Republican leaders, found 149 for Goldwater, 29 for Rockefeller, and 71 per cent of the state chairmen in Goldwater's corner. Gallup Poll surveys showed Goldwater sentiment constantly on the increase. In October, the results were: Goldwater 42 per cent, Rockefeller 26; in November: Goldwater 45, Rockefeller 23.

What was the reason for all this? If we are to accept the liberal interpretation of our politics, we can only conclude that the Republican party had, *en masse*, lost its reason. In a nation wedded to the liberal consensus, it would necessarily follow that an explicit conservative like Goldwater would be defeated by an explicit, and highly attractive, liberal like Kennedy. Or so, at any rate, we are instructed to believe. Kennedy biographer William Manchester asserts, for example, that the President, in the autumn of 1963, "had a strong hunch that the GOP would follow its death wish and nominate Barry Goldwater. . . . If Goldwater became the sacrificial lamb, so much the better. He would vanish in a historic landslide, carrying a handful of states. . . . " The "Barry boom," Manchester adds, "was becoming the biggest joke in politics."

In making these statements, Manchester presumes too greatly on the innocence of his readers and the sloth of his fellow journalists. Such assertions are in every respect misleading—an almost perfect example of the imaginary

America at work. The truth of the matter is that, in the autumn of 1963, John Kennedy looked like a very good prospect to lose the next presidential election—if his opponent were Barry Goldwater.

Indeed, Goldwater's potential strength against Kennedy was becoming so impressive that even the unwilling Reston felt constrained to notice it. While Kennedy was "lighthearted about the prospects of meeting Goldwater," Reston said, " . . . privately his associates are not so sure." In Pennsylvania, a prominent Democrat interviewed in the Pittsburgh *Press* said that "if the election were being held this year Goldwater would sweep Allegheny County—and furthermore I would vote for him." Eric Sevareid stated, October 13, that "the Goldwater phenomenon has reached proportions far beyond anything most serious observers, especially those in the Eastern centers, imagined it could attain a year ago, and the phenomenon is just hitting its stride."

What this meant in terms of electoral votes was suggested by *Look*'s Fletcher Knebel in a dispatch from the Southwest. "If Goldwater is nominated," Knebel wrote, "he will win Arizona and Oklahoma by landslides and probably will carry New Mexico and Texas—which John F. Kennedy won in 1960—by smaller margins. . . . Should any other Republican than Goldwater be nominated, the Southwest would belong to President Kennedy. . . . In the Southwest, conservative sentiment is running so deep that Goldwater might net the Republicans another governorship . . . another U.S. senator . . . four to six new congressmen . . . and perhaps 100 additional state legislators."

Nor was the phenomenon limited to the Southwest. Quizzing its political correspondents throughout the country on Kennedy's popularity and Republican prospects, *Time* (Oct. 8, 1963) came to the following conclusion:

"Until recently most political observers figured that Democrat John Kennedy was a sure 1964 winner, and that it did not make much difference who the GOP nominee would be. Now, many are changing their minds. To be sure, a President is historically at low ebb at the tag-end of a pre-election year, and between now and November 1964 a lot of things can happen—and probably will. But a state-by-state survey by Time correspondents indicates that at least Republican Barry Goldwater could give Kennedy a breathlessly close contest."

The *Time* correspondents reported a Goldwater edge in no less than 26 of the 50 states. They estimated that he was leading in most of the South, including Arkansas, Florida, Kentucky, Tennessee, and North Carolina; that his support in the Midwest was solid; that he would sweep all the Plains states without exception, and that in Illinois Kennedy "would probably lose to Goldwater today"; that Goldwater would take large segments of the West, including Idaho and Wyoming, with a small margin in Oregon and Washington; and that he or any other Republican could safely count Maine, New Hampshire, and Vermont in his pocket. Concerning politically crucial Texas, *Time* commented: "Kennedy could easily beat any other GOP candidate, but against Goldwater he can only be rated even."

These data show two things quite clearly. One is that the notion of Kennedy's overwhelming appeal during this period is a myth. All the contemporary evidence shows Kennedy was in great political difficulty. The second is that the notion of Goldwater's being propelled toward the nomination by sinister machinations is also a myth. Goldwater led in the nomination sweepstakes because he was the unquestioned favorite of the rank and file, and because he was in fact the strongest candidate the Republican party had—the only one who had a chance of beating Kennedy.

On November 22, 1963, John F. Kennedy was assassinated in Dallas, Texas, and American politics underwent a seismic upheaval. The Kennedy murder, fertile of many horrors, included a bonus horror as well: It became the occasion and pretext for the political maiming of Barry Goldwater. We are told that an acquaintance of Goldwater-backer Charles Barr, encountering him in a hotel lobby on the day of the assassination, remarked: "I'm sorry for you, Charlie, I'm afraid your man's all through." An observer quoted by the *Wall Street Journal* said: "Goldwater's house of cards has tumbled." Liberal journalist Richard Rovere says that when he was informed of the murder, "I was suddenly no longer much interested in Barry Goldwater. . . . I felt that he was finished in American politics." That was the nearly universal reaction.*

There were, of course, some obvious reasons for the anti-Goldwater fallout of the assassination, the most telling of which was the condign removal of Kennedy from the political equation. After two years of his term had run, Kennedy had become recognized as an archetypically liberal President; his policies, his geographical and educational background, his choice of subordinates, all symbolized the liberal East of big-city industrial states. In stark contrast stood Goldwater—businessman, Westerner, conservative. The clash of ideologies and styles helped Goldwater both within the party and without it.

The replacement of Kennedy by Johnson transposed all the psychological factors. Kennedy had been a Harvard liberal with a Back Bay accent. Johnson came over as a Texas middle-of-the-roader with a Southern drawl. The liberal President was replaced by a man of no certain ideology. The East-West contrast dissolved as Westerner

* That the reaction was widespread is not to say it was logical. *Why* should Rovere feel, when Kennedy was murdered, that Goldwater "was finished in American politics"? He does not tell us. Perhaps he assumed at the time, as many did, that Kennedy had been murdered by some crazed conservative. Oswald was, of course, not a conservative but a leftist, yet the reaction against Goldwater was strangely unaffected by this fact.

Goldwater was confronted by yet another Westerner. The liberal-conservative issues which had previously been so clear now seemed almost hopelessly blurred.

The implicit damage resulting to Goldwater's candidacy from the assassination was therefore apparent. But these things were perhaps of less importance than the *explicit* damage done to Goldwater, and the conservative cause in general, by the performance of so large a segment of the American liberal community. In the aftermath of Dallas the nation rocked with assertions that a general atmosphere of "extremism" was responsible for Kennedy's death; and, in case the point was not clear, it was repeatedly noted that Dallas was a center of "right-wing extremism," and that its sickly mental condition was a principal cause of Kennedy's murder. This version of things was recited by politicians, ministers, TV savants, newspaper columnists and everyone else who could get himself before a camera or microphone or immortalize his sentiments in print.

It was monstrous to suggest, as much of this rhetoric did suggest, that conservatives who had opposed Kennedy's policies were by virtue of their opposition responsible for his death—particularly monstrous in view of Oswald's specifically left-wing connections. The fact remains, as a point of political history, that the Kennedy murder was made the pretext for a massive assault on the conservative movement. And since Barry Goldwater was the embodiment of that movement, such a performance was inevitably damaging to his political aspirations.

From the assassination forward, Goldwater's effort to woo popular sympathies was a downhill ride to oblivion. Yet, ironically, the net result of this chaotic sequence was to demonstrate the strength of the conservative element within the Republican party. For Goldwater *did*, of course, go on to win the nomination. There could be no more effective testimony to the essential conservatism of the GOP than this astonishing datum—that the Goldwater intraparty struggle, despite the psychological horrors and the endless public lacerations, should actually have succeeded. He was so pre-eminently the leading Republican candidate that even when his strength had been cut in half he was the Republican front runner.

This point was made with some precision by the Associated Press survey of presidential leanings among Republican officials. In October, 1963, Goldwater had been favored by 1,194 respondents as opposed to 56 for Rockefeller and 44 for Nixon. In December, 1963, after the bottom fell out, Goldwater was favored by 601 respondents as opposed to 279 for Nixon and 101 for Rockefeller. The altered figures clearly illustrate the impact of the assassination on Goldwater's fortunes; but they also illustrate his truly enormous reservoir of support. *Even after his precipitous decline, Goldwater was a two-to-one favorite over his nearest competitor.* He had more fall-back strength than the other candidates could muster at the zenith of their popularity.

When one adds to all this the further damage done to Goldwater's candidacy by campaign mistakes in New Hampshire and elsewhere, the intense hostility of so many segments of the media, the efforts of Rockefeller, Scranton and other of Goldwater's intraparty antagonists to depict him as a dangerous and unstable man, the fact that Goldwater should actually have gone on to win at San Francisco becomes more impressive still. If Goldwater could secure the nomination under these circumstances, one can only imagine how easily he would have walked off with it had Kennedy not been murdered.

Goldwater won the 1964 nomination on his carry-over strength from 1963, because the residual authority of the conservatives was, even in its most crippled state, the most powerful element in the party. This was fully demonstrated by the Republican primaries, where, despite nonstop disparagement from the media, Goldwater actually did rather well. The aggregate results tell the story, as follows:

Candidate	*Popular Vote*	*Per Cent of Total*
Barry Goldwater	2,147,993	47.7
Nelson A. Rockefeller	1,262,539	28.0
Henry Cabot Lodge	341,841	7.6
Margaret Chase Smith	231,688	5.1
William Scranton	229,528	5.1
Richard Nixon	180,884	4.0
Harold Stassen	112,598	2.5

The liberal journalists have insistently played down Goldwater's showing in such important contests as the Illinois and Indiana primaries, where he faced the token candidacies of Margaret Chase Smith and Harold Stassen. They suggest that since Goldwater did not have serious opposition, these victories should be dismissed. This argument, however, ignores one pertinent question: If Goldwater was so hopelessly weak with the rank and file, why *didn't* he have serious opposition? Why didn't Rockefeller or Scranton come into these states and run against him? The answer, to anyone familiar with the Illinois or Indiana political landscape, is obvious. Rockefeller or Scranton would have been badly beaten, and so wisely decided to stay out. Five and six months after the assassination, that is, Goldwater strength in these key Republican states was still so great that no liberal dared risk his candidacy in either of them.

How far removed the liberal mythology on the primaries is from the facts of the case may be discovered by taking a somewhat closer look at the Indiana primary. In 1964, the Republican chairman of Marion County (Indianapolis), Indiana, was a confirmed opponent of Barry Goldwater and had, it was reliably reported, important links to Rockefeller. This formidable figure was confronted by a youthful group of Goldwater supporters who fielded candidates for Congress, state convention delegates and other offices in opposition to the organization's official slate. On primary day, Goldwater carried the county by a margin of five to one, a landslide so spectacular that it swept in conservative candidates at all levels. Rank-and-file sentiment for Goldwater, in sum, upset the local party hierarchy and carried to victory virtually anyone who was running on the pro-Goldwater ticket.

That episode, give or take a few details, was repeated in intraparty battles across the United States throughout 1964 —California, where most of the top Republican "bosses" were for Rockefeller but the voters went for Goldwater, providing the most obvious example.

In Oklahoma, Governor Henry Bellmon, although favorable toward Goldwater, did not want to commit the state's delegation early in the game. The rank and file wanted it otherwise, and Oklahoma became the first state to declare officially for Goldwater. In Kansas, Idaho, Iowa, the Dakotas, Washington, New Jersey, Kentucky, Missouri, the record, with variations in local detail, was essentially the same. It was not the bosses who were pressing for Goldwater; it was the grass roots. In several cases —Idaho, Kansas, Washington—incumbent Republican governors were actively against Goldwater. But party strength surging up from the precincts was simply too powerful to be contained.

That was the pattern which prevailed throughout the Republican party in 1964, and the reason that Goldwater triumphed over his liberal Republican adversaries. The convention win, so completely inexplicable in terms of the liberal hypothesis, merely demonstrates, after the fashion of unassimilable data, that the hypothesis is mistaken. The real reason for Goldwater's win may be found in the growth of conservative strength from 1960 forward, rising steadily to a peak in the fall of 1963, then falling off sharply after Kennedy's assassination to the low point of November, 1964.

The politically rewarding data, largely ignored in the ultimate liberal rejoicings, were chiefly two: 1. Goldwater had won at San Francisco on the downhill side of the arc —with conservatism able to muster only a portion of its potential strength; and 2. Even at the new low point, conservatism had reached a higher plateau of political attainment than any it had occupied in the preceding twenty years.

10:: EVERYTHING THAT RISES MUST CONVERGE

"Barry Goldwater not only lost the presidential election yesterday but the conservative cause as well. He has wrecked his party for a long time to come and is not even likely to control the wreckage." So wrote James Reston in the New York *Times*, November 4, 1964.

It appeared at the time—particularly to those who had devoutly hoped for the Goldwater defeat—a reasonable verdict. The hardships sustained by Goldwater and Company between November, 1963, and November, 1964, certainly seemed sufficient to have obliterated conservative influence from the nation at large and the Republican party in particular for years to come, if not, in fact, forever.

Yet it has become plain in the intervening months that Reston's analysis was mistaken. The conservative cause was not, it seems, lost after all. Conservative activity in the nation and conservative influence in political combat has, if anything, accelerated since 1964—a fact confirmed not only by the conservatives themselves, but, more important, by the witness of liberal spokesmen who make it their business to monitor activity on the right. These observers have reached conclusions directly counter to Reston's blithe assertions of the morning after.

One conclusion sifting its way up through a considerable quantity of evidence is that 1964, if it did nothing else, served to break the conservative movement's visibility barrier. Prior to the Goldwater candidacy, American conservatism was in many ways invisible; it existed, had corporeal dimension, a certain measure of untested political strength. But it couldn't be seen—at least not in terms of its true form and substance. In the land of McLuhan where media certification is the passport to political reality, the conservatives were hurting badly: They were either portrayed to the world as "sick" people whose views were pathological symptoms unrelated to this business of politics, or else ignored altogether, regarded as Un-Fact and Non-Movement.*

Such treatment had a severely limiting effect on the growth of conservatism, with respect to existing participants and prospective ones alike. It tended to demoralize and immobilize the former, keeping disparate centers of

* *E.g.*, Harry and Bonaro Overstreet in *The Great Enterprise*: "A man . . . may be angrily against race equality, public housing, the TVA, financial and technical aid to backward countries, organized labor, and the preaching of social rather than salvational religion. These intensive dislikes . . . add up to a kind of collective evidence that the man has identified himself, for his own ego reasons, with certain individuals and groups that have power and prestige; and that he is emotionally on the defensive against anything that would close the status gap between his group and 'lower' groups. In some people . . . we can scarcely open up a subject that does not tap their permeative, automatic 'againstness.' *Such people may appear 'normal' in the sense that they are able to hold a job or otherwise maintain their status as members of the society; but they are, we now recognize, well along the road to mental illness.*" It is noteworthy that a number of these symptoms of approaching "mental illness" have been popping up, as previously observed, among various members of the liberal community itself.

activity sealed off from one another, and to scare off the latter by convincing them conservatives were lunatics or else preventing them from knowing that such a thing as "the conservative movement" existed to begin with.

It was in this respect, more than any other, that the 1964 campaign advanced the conservative cause it was so widely reported to have buried. The public notice given to Goldwater was hardly favorable, and much of it served to turn away potential backers of the cause who might have responded to an orderly and reasoned presentation of the conservative position. The campaign nonetheless succeeded, in strangled tones, in getting some important issues before the people—crime in the streets being the most obvious—which have subsequently become Grade A topics for all respectable politicans.

In addition, Goldwater and such of his supporters as Ronald Reagan managed to secure prime television time to drive home some plain truths which had seldom been ventilated on the national networks: and although the audience for political programs is relatively small, it is certain that more people heard conservative presentations of the issues as a result of these broadcasts than had ever heard them before. Finally, Goldwater's convention triumph taught some of the liberal reporters and editors who had slighted his candidacy that a repeat performance in future contests could be hazardous journalistic practice: The media did not look good when they played up all the Republicans who did not get the nomination and averted their gaze from the one Republican who did.

In sum, through a rather painful process which left its scars on Goldwater personally and the conservative movement in general, 1964 succeeded in transporting conservatism from the realm of un-fact to that of fact. It is a toehold position, to be sure, just across the border, but to those who have wandered in the wilderness of media oblivion, even a refugee encampment on page 57 of the *Times* is a welcome change of scenery. This modest celebrity makes it possible for conservatives to obtain some kind of national forum for their views; not as good as the liberals, but considerably better than it used to be. They can in consequence project their message to untold numbers of people who might otherwise never have had the opportunity of hearing it.

This very conclusion about the Goldwater campaign has been circulating for quite a while in the more esoteric journals and memoranda of the left. A close reading of this material, making allowance for the hostility of the language, shows that the oft-pronounced death of conservatism has never been accepted by the left wing's more cautious trend-spotters. Consider, for example, the impassioned cry of Hollywood Ten alumnus Dalton Trumbo in *The Nation*, contradicting liberal complacency about 1964. Trumbo proclaimed the Goldwater campaign "the greatest victory *their* side"—*i.e.*, the conservatives—"had ever seen." Never before, he said, "had the far American right [*i.e.*, conservatives] been able to carry its program to the whole people from the platform of a national party; never had a candidate of the right been so attractive, or aroused such profound devotion; never before had hundreds of thousands of dollars—perhaps even millions—flowed to its cause from the 'grass roots.' " Trumbo concluded with a melancholy reflection on "the vigor and variety and burgeoning health" of the awful conservative movement.

A similar interpretation issued from the Anti-Defamation League of B'nai B'rith, which dourly opines that "the real accomplishment of the radical right [conservatism] in the 1964 campaign was in the exposure of millions of Americans to its message, in new recruits to its membership, and in a reservoir of potential recruits being built up . . . through their efforts in the Goldwater campaign." As a result of this breakthrough, ADL adds, the 1964 contest "left the radical right [conservatism] stronger than ever and poised for new propaganda and recruitment drives which are already under way."

Among the most important results of the new conservative visibility has been its effect on the already committed votaries of the cause. When one is beneath the visibility barrier, it is extremely difficult to maintain a national movement, to build *esprit de corps,* to concert various centers of activity. Under these circumstances, the normal human reaction is a sense of futility. If one is hopelessly alone, unaware that there are other people who share his concerns and aspirations, he is obviously in no position to take effective political action. But if conservatives in Iowa discover, via the national press, that conservative Republicans have won the chairmanship in Maine or a congressional primary in Ohio, or made intraparty gains in the state of Washington, that intelligence has an inspiriting effect; it tells the Iowa partisan his comrades are in the field; the battle is going forward; if he continues to attack his sector of the front, he will be making an important contribution to an on-going national campaign that has reasonable prospects of success.

The Goldwater enterprise helped create this kind of intercommunication, both by making the press more sensitive to such developments and by fostering among conservatives their own circuits of communication. The upshot is that the conservatives, once rather isolated, not knowing each other very well or even being aware of one another's existence, now form something like a coherent movement. The interior lines of communication, which did not exist to speak of in 1960, are now established; the common discussion of ideas is an accepted and welcome practice; and the common presentation of themes and nuances of opinion is becoming more apparent in those areas of the public media where conservatives have obtained some kind of entry.

This phenomenon has been most clearly described by liberal editor David Danzig, writing in *Commentary*. The signal achievement of the Goldwater campaign, Danzig says, was to unite in a single national effort the energies of countless conservative groups which had thitherto been confined to state or local activities. "From having been local and sporadic," he says, "this movement was becoming organized and self-conscious . . . the extreme conservatives [conservatives] . . . have reappeared on the national political scene after a period of submergence during which their influence was confined to scattered local communities."

From this coalescence, Danzig believes, the conservative movement has drawn new strength and new bargaining power in the national political arena—a development he describes as a "turning point" in American politics: "The idea that serious account must now be taken of the extreme conservatives [conservatives]—that they have become for the first time an identifiable bloc with demands to make on the *national* scene, and with the power and organizational skill to press these demands—constitutes a recognition of a truly important change in national politics." He concludes that "the organizational strength of the right-wing bloc [which] has been concentrated in the community, state and regional networks, if anything, was strengthened and *not* weakened by the opportunities provided during the campaign."

Symptomatic of the post-Goldwater sense of conservative community was the founding of several new conservative organizations—among them the American Conservative Union, the Free Society Association, the Conservative Book Club, Arlington House Publishers, the Philadelphia Society, Constructive Action, Inc., the Constitutional Alliance, *Triumph* and *Rally* magazines and other groups. All these came into being and/or reached major organizational status after 1964 supposedly obliterated the conservative movement of which they are a part. The effect was altogether different from what had been anticipated. As the Research Institute of America put it: "Something new is happening in the conservative movement. Conservatives have not only refused to play dead following their 1964 defeat, but are making a vigorous comeback."

Essentially the same conclusion was reached by the principal liberal agency in charge of conservative surveillance—a political intelligence organization called "Group Research, Inc." In a year-end report for 1965, Group Research disclosed that conservative performance since the Goldwater defeat, rather than diminishing, had experienced a marked upward movement and had staked out new positions of political strength.

Delivering this verdict at a January, 1966, conference in Washington, GRI Director Wesley McCune stated that "established right-wing groups stepped up their political activity (in 1965). . . new groups have sprung up in the political arena . . . the right wing has shown surprising success in elections since 1964. . . ." McCune added that "the Goldwater defeat in 1964 did not dismay his adherents; on the contrary, they have turned their talents to community organizations of a less partisan nature," and that "the conventional right-wing groups, varying from ultra-conservative to radical right, generally had a good year."

As the last comment indicates, GRI's method in reaching these conclusions is eclecticism itself, dumping everybody from the late George Lincoln Rockwell to liberal Democrat Thomas Dodd into a single pot called "the right wing." And although this makes it difficult to tell how much of the McCune verdict is intended to apply to authentic conservatives, enough is apparent between the lines to suggest GRI sees the conservative movement as a powerful and growing force rather than an expiring has-been. Its focus on such things as William F. Buckley's showing in the New York mayoral election (directly contrary to the public liberal interpretation of this contest—see p. 185) in particular indicates the conclusions are relevant to the main body of conservative opinion.

An additional benefit conservatives derived from the 1964 campaign was a sorely earned lesson in political sophistication. Some of the people involved in present-day conservative activity had not been much interested in politics prior to 1960, had never taken an active role in a presidential campaign or any political campaign whatever. They were new to the business and liable to make errors, both rhetorical and substantive. Having been through the tempering and chastening experience of 1964, many of them have learned from their successes and their failures equally; from the Goldwater nomination victory, they learned some of the things one does to achieve political success; from the bitter defeat in the fall, they learned some of the things one does not do.

A new tactical dexterity was clearly evident, for example, in the 1965 and 1966 battles over section 14(b) of the Taft-Hartley Act. In those encounters, conservative forces were impressively marshaled in an all-out battle to prevent imposition of a new layer of coercion on American workingmen. Under the leadership of the National Right-to-Work Committee, which showed itself more than capable of matching the labor-liberal forces step for step, the friends of voluntary unionism staged an effective antirepeal campaign in support of Senator Dirksen's filibuster. Considering the existing balance of political forces, conservative victory had at first seemed improbable; but, through concentration on a specific point with determination and attention to the virtues of an attractive rhetoric, the job was done. This effort succeeded in translating the conservative sentiment of the nation into a notable political success, without throwing away the victory in a moment of pique or exaltation.

Within the Republican party, the strengthening of the

conservative position as a result of the Goldwater race was equally notable, and Reston's conclusions even more widely off the mark. True, Goldwater's personal dominion at the Republican National Committee was abruptly ended. But the ceremonial exfoliation of a chairman personally chosen by a defeated candidate was to be expected, and meant, as we have seen, relatively little in terms of ideological inclination. Developments on other fronts made it plain that the Goldwater run actually strengthened rather than weakened the conservative position in the GOP.

This fact was grasped readily enough by the liberal Republican Ripon Society, which observed that "the very *fact* of a Goldwater nomination produced long-term changes in the Republican Party, most of which strengthened the hand of the 'conservatives' for the post-November leadership struggle. . . The November results will mean increased voting strength for Southern Republicans in the Republican National Committee, the Young Republican National Convention, and ultimately the National Convention. . . ."

Equally important has been the expanded strength of the Republican conservatives in intraparty contests, a phenomenon which emerged with consistent clarity in the 1966 primaries for major nominations as conservatives impressively downed their liberal GOP opponents. The pattern was so obvious and emphatic that *Congressional Quarterly* asserted that conservatives in the 1966 primaries had "emerged triumphant in virtually every contest where moderate or liberal Republicans opposed them." That conclusion is borne out by a survey of representative contests for party leadership.

The most celebrated of these confrontations was, of course, the clash of Ronald Reagan and Mayor George Christopher in the California gubernatorial primary. Despite the dour projections of liberal journalists, Reagan won a smashing two-to-one victory. Reagan pulled 1,385,550 votes—a plurality of some 722,351. This astonishing victory, totally unanticipated by the liberal commentators, established the fact that conservatism was growing steadily in California.

The Reagan-Christopher primary was the most publicized conservative victory, but it was not the only one. Across the nation, when the forces of GOP conservatism and liberalism were put to the test, the conservatives repeatedly came out on top. Some sample results:

Maine: Former Representative Peter A. Garland, described by *Congressional Quarterly* as "an outspoken conservative," won renomination to the House over six primary opponents. CQ commented that "the strength of the conservatives in the district was demonstrated by the ability of Garland and another conservative in the race to win 49 per cent of the vote between them, while the strongest running Liberal polled only 21 per cent."

New York: Liberal forces within the party went all out to secure the primary defeat of former Representative Steven Derounian, a conservative and a 1964 Goldwater supporter. Derounian won going away, downing self-proclaimed "moderate" William J. Casey by a vote of 22,542 to 15,956.

In another New York congressional primary, conservative Republican John Pillion upset the organizational choice. Pillion charged that the "moderate" candidate was selected "in New York City by the Rockefeller machine and big banking and money interests."

New Hampshire: A hard-fought senatorial primary was won by conservative General Harrison Thyng, a "hawk" on Vietnam. Thyng was strongly supported by the influential Manchester *Union-Leader*, and this support was considered to be an important factor in his victory. Similarly, in another New Hampshire race, conservative former Representative Louis Wyman easily won renomination.

New Jersey: Two Goldwater supporters, Charles Sandman and John Hunt, won key primary races for Jersey congressional seats. Sandman had been the state Goldwater chairman in 1964.

Pennsylvania: Former Representative George Goodling, a Goldwater supporter in 1964, overcame the opposition of party chieftains and five primary opponents to win renomination to the House.

Ohio: Youthful Republican leader Donald E. "Buzz" Lukens, who had been elected chairman of the national YRs in 1963 as a Goldwater backer, took on the local organization choice for Congress and won handily. Lukens had been a particular object of attack among "moderate" Republicans and in the liberal media.

Wisconsin: Former Representative Henry Schadeberg, a staunch conservative, overcame opposition from some party bosses to secure renomination for the November balloting.

Minnesota: After a fierce contest, Minnesota Republicans chose as their nominee for governor Harold E. LeVander, testily described in the New York *Times* as a "relatively unknown conservative." In so doing they rejected the bid of former Governor Elmer E. Andersen, who, the *Times* noted, "was strongly criticized for having refused to back Goldwater in 1964."

Idaho: Republican voters, in an upset, nominated conservative state senator Don Samuelson for governor, defeating the incumbent "moderate" GOP governor, Robert Smylie.

Kentucky: Conservative M. Gene Snyder, running against a large field and strong moderate opposition, won nomination to Congress, defeating his principal opponent by a vote of 9,332 to 5,534. (This Kentucky trend was continued into 1967, when conservative Louie B. Nunn bested "moderate" Marlow Cook in a contest for the GOP gubernatorial nomination.)

Elsewhere in the South: Conservatives continued to gain ascendancy in the Southern GOP, with strong efforts in

South Carolina, Alabama, Florida, and Texas leading the way. Tom Wicker of the New York *Times* commented that "the lingering Goldwater cast of the party will not be shaken in the South, either, where several conservative Republicans will make strong bids for statewide office."

Such was the general Republican track record in 1966. Here and there, countervailing tendencies developed. In New Mexico, for example, the GOP somewhat unexpectedly came up with a liberal candidate for governor. On the whole, however, the trend to conservatism was clear, confirming the drift of party sentiment made manifest in the victory of Ronald Reagan.

Concerning the significance of Reagan's win, it is perhaps best to call in the testimony of Louis Harris, who on other occasions has warned us of the decline of conservative Republicanism. Assessing the California results, Harris was constrained to come to some altogether different conclusions, as follows:

> . . . for all its accent on the new and the young, California is going conservative. Both the Republican and Democratic primaries of 1966 revealed a heavy conservative tide. . . . Fully one-third of the total Democratic votes cast in this primary can be considered conservative. . . . Six out of every ten Republicans in California are conservative. . . . What made it clearly a conservative victory . . . was that Reagan impressively topped Goldwater in hitherto moderate areas. . . . With this election, the GOP moderates in the state, headed by Sen. Thomas Kuchel, have been routed and reduced to a permanent minority for the foreseeable future.

Harris concluded that new forces crystallized in a losing political effort sometimes carry over into succeeding elections as the central element in a new majority. "In 1928," he wrote, "Al Smith lost for President but brought out the big-city Catholic vote that provided a central pivot for Franklin Roosevelt's new majority in 1932. In 1948, Tom

Dewey lost but brought into being new suburban Republican power which largely formed the basis of victory for Dwight Eisenhower in 1952. Now conservatives are hoping that when Barry Goldwater lost in 1964, he crystallized a new right-of-center vote in America."

That new bloc, Harris says, could lead on to national conservative victories in the years to come. Whether this is so we shall consider in the succeeding chapters.

11:: A CONSERVATIVE CONGRESS

On the record and the concession of the liberal analysts, the conservative hand in Republican councils and in the nation at large was strengthened by the Goldwater nomination. In the liberal presentation, however, this is not a compliment but a reproach. The conservative advance, it is alleged, has come at the expense of the party as a whole, securing a larger percentage share of a diminishing Republican base.

What is the truth of this assertion? Has the augmented conservatism of the party been accompanied by a decline of Republican strength? Or has the GOP as a whole reaped benefits comparable to the conservative expansion?

The record shows that the second of these alternative suggestions is the correct one. It can be demonstrated, indeed, that 1964 opened the way to sources of Republican strength which can and very probably will transform the GOP from a minority to a majority party—a fact which will emerge rather clearly if we examine certain peculiarities of our political landscape.

The quest for congressional and presidential majorities by either of the two political parties is essentially a problem in arithmetic. In its finer elaborations, of course, it becomes a number of other things as well. But in the first instance, it is an exercise in numbers. With respect to congressional majorities, the GOP must somehow figure out a method of electing at least 218 members of the House of Representatives and 51 members of the Senate. With respect to presidential majorities, it has to devise a formula for securing at least 270 votes in the Electoral College. In the present chapter, we shall consider the nature of this problem as it applies to Congress. In the next as it relates to the presidency.

Over the years, the Republican search for a congressional majority has been a frustrating business, as indicated by the fact that there have been Republican majorities in only two Congresses since 1932—the 80th and the 83rd. The Democrats controlled both houses of Congress for six of the eight years of the Eisenhower administration, and won majorities in 1956 while Eisenhower rolled to a record victory over Adlai Stevenson. If a Republican congressional majority was unattainable in that boom year, it must be a very elusive article indeed.

The reason for the elusiveness becomes apparent if we analyze the way in which the Republican party has been compelled to function. During this long span of almost forty years, the GOP has been like a prize fighter with one hand behind his back, or a football team that agrees to restrict its operations to the area within its own 20-yard line. Considering the ground rules under which the party has been playing, it is not surprising that it has won only two congressional majorities. It seems a miracle that it won any.

The ground rules hold that the GOP must concede to its Democratic opposition some 100 or so of the 218 seats needed to control the House of Representatives, and some 20 or so of the 51 senators. These automatic pick-ups for the Democrats have been located in the so-called Solid South, which for historical although not ideological reasons has persistently cast its ballots for the Democrats. For most of this span, there has been no Republican party in the South—no local organization, no local candidates, no congressional candidates to speak of, only an occasional senatorial or gubernatorial candidate. The Republican party, to all intents and purposes, was shut out—and the Democratic opposition was halfway toward control of Congress before a vote was cast.

This state of affairs placed an almost impossible burden on the Republicans. In order to come up with the requisite number of votes in the House or Senate, GOP candidates had to sweep the non-Southern portions of the country by an enormous margin. They were contesting only about 330 of the 437 congressional seats, and had to win 218 of them. They had to take these races, that is, by a margin approximately two-to-one in order to gain a simple congressional majority. As Dr. Gallup put the matter in 1966: "The real congressional battlefield lies in the 37 states outside the South . . . nearly 100 of the 119 [Southern] congressional seats are safely Democratic—many of them not even contested . . . the Republican Party must win nearly two-thirds of the seats outside the South to take control of the House."

A uniform two-to-one majority from Maine to California is difficult to achieve. Even the most massive of electoral landslides seldom reach such proportions. That the GOP has not under these circumstances obtained congressional majorities does not mean it is inherently weak; it does mean that, within the limited area of its operations, it has not been superhumanly strong.

In seeking to overcome this 100-seat deficit, the GOP has two alternatives: either to make itself so massively the majority party within its regional limitations that it can infallibly beat the Democrats by two-to-one in congressional races; or else to stop giving the Democrats the head start to begin with. The first of these goals is of course desirable, but unlikely. Such a fortuitous landslide may occur once in a decade or a generation; but that it will occur with any regularity over the course of the years is, at best, highly improbable.

It becomes obvious that, if the Republican party wants to obtain congressional majorities, it must break the Democratic grip on the South. This is not a matter of speculation, hope, or academic theory. It is simple reality. The laws of political arithmetic show that unless the Republican party can make inroads in the South, it is doomed to be a minority party for the foreseeable future. If it wants to gain a majority in Congress, it must stop conceding its irrelevance to a third of the nation, and start transforming itself into a truly national party.

By fits and starts, Republicans have made attempts in this direction. For a number of years the party has conducted an enterprise called Operation Dixie, aimed at electing GOP congressional candidates in the South. Until the Goldwater movement began to make its impact, however, Operation Dixie was slow going. With the rise of Goldwater, it became very fast going indeed. In the years since 1960, the GOP has been making rapid strides toward the development of a two-party South, and thereby making impressive progress toward the requisite votes for a majority in Congress.

The Goldwater presidential run brought in a large number of Southern Republican congressmen, of course, but this was merely an incidental factor. Even more decisive than the presidential race itself was the Goldwater influence on the construction of Republican organizations;

presidential sweeps of some southern states had occurred before—Eisenhower's 1956 win, for example, in Louisiana and other Southern states. But those victories helped the congressional Republicans very little since they were purely personal triumphs seldom backed by organizational development.

Since 1960, the Goldwater influence has resulted in the building of Republican organizations in almost every Southern state. The prime example is the high-powered GOP put together in the state of Alabama by James Martin and John Grenier, which despite the 1966 Wallace landslide has obviously worked a permanent revolution in Alabama politics. These organizations are not simply interested in presidential and congressional races; they are interested in building the infrastructure a political party needs to maintain itself as a functioning institution, and to elect the city councilmen, state legislators, county trustees and other local officials upon whom the life of the party ultimately depends.

Throughout the early 1960's, the rising tempo of this activity was apparent. Republicans began winning local elections, mayorships, and state legislative seats all over the South—in North Carolina, Florida, Texas, Alabama. The party began to lay the groundwork which could lead on to the election of congressmen, governors, and senators. The results, in terms of congressional races, became almost immediately apparent. With each succeeding congressional election, Southern Republican ranks in the U.S. House of Representatives have expanded in geometric proportion.

In 1960, the GOP had only 8 congressmen in the South, most of whom represented unusual suburban (Arlington, Va.; Dallas, Texas) or historically Republican (East Tennessee and Kentucky) districts, and had been representing them for years. To all intents and purposes, the Southern GOP was on dead center. But in 1962, when the first ripples of Goldwaterism were being felt in the party, the GOP picked up 5 new Southern congressmen —Brock, Gurney, Foreman, James Broyhill, and Snyder— giving it a total of 13. In 1964, with Goldwater at the top of the ticket, 3 Republican Southerners (Snyder, Alger, and Foreman) lost, but the party picked up 7 others for a net gain of 4 and a total of 17. In 1966, the party lost 4 Southerners (Walker, Martin, Andrews, and Callaway), but picked up 13 more for a net gain of 9 and a total of 26.

The stepladder pattern is as obvious as the net result: After years of relatively little progress in the South, the party in the space of three congressional elections more than tripled its Southern representation—from 8 to 26. And almost all of this net gain was traceable to the influence of the Goldwater-conservative movement within the GOP. Which means that the Republican party has the conservative movement to thank for its most impressive congressional gains in years.

Nothing is more illustrative of this fact—or of the power shift within the party—than a regional breakdown of the 1966 elections. These results show, with surgical precision, the Southern and Western shift of Republican power and the consequent strengthening of the party— accompanied by a drastic shrinkage of the Eastern GOP.

Republican congressional gains in 1966 were massive everywhere throughout the country—everywhere, that is, but the stronghold of the liberal Republicans. "Only in the East," *Congressional Quarterly* notes, "did the Republicans fail to capture a significant number of House seats." In all, the Eastern GOP picked up only six of the new House seats, and some of these (Wyman of New Hampshire, Goodling of Pennsylvania, Hunt of New Jersey) were clearly of the conservative variety. The worst performance was in New York, where the Rockefeller-captained GOP failed to unhorse a single one of the freshman Democrats elected in 1964.

In the Midwest and West, however, the party did very well indeed. In the midlands, the GOP scored a net gain of 21 seats, while the West rang in with 10 new Republican representatives. This constituted a healthy comeback for the party, and served to restore the GOP to the congressional levels it had attained in 1962. The figures showed that the Republican heartland was essentially as sound as ever.

In the South, however, the congressional races demonstrated a good deal more. They demonstrated that the party, if it conducted itself in appropriate fashion, was well on its way toward capturing that long-sought but elusive majority. The Southern GOP came up with a net gain of 9 new seats which were, in the final analysis, the most important gains of all. For these were not simply Republican seats restored to their rightful place in the GOP column; they were brand-new seats, taken away from the opposition. *They were seats which had historically been Democratic and were now being transferred to the Republican party.*

It was this fact which accounted for Republican net gains over 1962, and for the emergence of the GOP in a congressional position stronger than any it had occupied since the elections of 1956. Two years after the Goldwater strategy assertedly put the Republican party on its back, it was the Goldwater strategy which delivered the goods. It was the South, and the South alone, which represented the net difference between 1962 and 1966. It was the South which yielded the party the long-sought increment of votes which could propel it in the direction of a congressional majority.

That the net gains of 1966 were owing to the conservative effort to open up the South is statistically demonstrable. The regional breakdowns show that, in 1962 and 1966, the Republicans and Democrats outside the South fought to consecutive draws. In the earlier election, the GOP did slightly better than the Democrats outside the South, winning 165 seats to 164 for the opposition. In the later one, the Republicans outside the South lagged some three seats behind the 1962 showing—while racking up a total net gain of 10. *The reason that the GOP had 187 seats instead of the 177 of 1962 was, quite simply, the improved performance in the South.**

The implications of the Southern *démarche* are plain. There are more seats where these came from—and they are obviously accessible to a generally conservative Republican party. If the GOP continues to advance at the pace it has maintained since 1960, it can elect a House majority in a few years' time. And when that occurs, it is obvious that similar inroads can be made in the less volatile Senate and in an increasing number of governors' mansions.

Needless to remark, the liberal analysts are not enthusiastic about all this. They have for years ignored the GOP potential of the South, assuming it was beyond the reach of the Republicans—although failing to explain how the party could otherwise obtain majority status. When Republicans such as Representative William Miller and I. Lee Potter promoted Operation Dixie, they came under bitter attack for allegedly catering to racists, and a similar attack was of course leveled at Goldwater's presidential strategy in 1964. (We shall consider the merits of these charges in a subsequent chapter.) The liberals also maintained that it couldn't work, and that in the absence of Goldwater himself at the top of the ticket, the Southern congressmen would quietly expire.

Thus, according to George Gilder's pre-election sum-

* Less dramatic, but also indicative, was the redistribution of Republican congressional strength outside the South. Although the pattern is not as consistent as the breakthrough in Dixie, the general and unmistakable trend is from East to West. Thus, in 1962, there were 21 GOP congressmen from New York, 13 from California. In 1966 there were 15 from New York, 17 from California.

mary in *The New Leader*, the 1966 balloting would see the GOP lose its "Goldwater coat-tailers" in Alabama and Mississippi, a prospect Gilder obviously viewed with satisfaction. In the event, however, the implied destruction of Goldwater's Southern gains did not occur. The party did lose its 1 congressional seat in Mississippi, 2 in Alabama, and 1 in Georgia; but in 3 of these 4 cases, the Republican incumbent retired to seek a higher office. *In only 1 case (Andrews of Alabama) was an incumbent Southern Republican congressman defeated.* And, as we have noted, the party picked up 13 other new seats while this single incumbency was being lost.

This fact becomes the more astonishing when we reflect that the GOP managed to hold 3 of its 4 incumbencies in Alabama despite the Wallace landslide of 1966. That performance, in which Alabama voters obviously had to split their ballots between Democrat Wallace and the Republican congressmen, is the best possible testimony to the fact that the party has sunk its roots deep in Southern soil. If those seats could be held despite the Wallace avalanche, what might not be accomplished in future years when a more liberal and less popular Democratic name is at the top of the ticket?

It is worth adding, in this connection, that the Southern GOP in 1966 also triumphantly re-elected its two conservative senators, Tower of Texas and Thurmond of South Carolina, elected another in Tennessee, elected governors in Florida and Arkansas, and won the popular vote for the governorship of Georgia (47.8 per cent to 47.4 per cent). All of these achievements, with the obvious exception of Winthrop Rockefeller in Arkansas, were in one way or another traceable to conservative Republican penetration of the South. (It is arguable that even Rockefeller's win was in part owing to the same development, since he takes a much more conservative stand on the issues than does his more celebrated brother.)

When the Southern Republicans refused to dry up and blow away, the liberal analysts came up with another explanation of developments in Dixie. Although hardly as satisfying as the anticipated wipeout would have been, it was meant to accomplish the same essential task—proving that conservatives had somehow lost out in the 1966 elections. The argument this time, advanced by Paul Duke in *The Reporter*, was that the newly elected Republicans, all too indubitably there and impossible to ignore, were "moderates," an appellation which made their otherwise unbearable presence easier to take.

Again, however, the relevant data do not bear out the liberal argument. Congressional voting statistics show that Southern Republicans in Congress have historically been conservative; that they remained so during and after the Goldwater run of 1964; and that the new crop of Southern Republicans—with rare exceptions and the possibility of marginal change in future computations—are conservative as well. The first ACA scorecard for the 90th Congress showed all but two of the new Republicans from Dixie had conservative ratings higher than 80 per cent, and that the two exceptions (Bush of Texas and Wampler of Virginia) were scored at 79 per cent.

These provisional ACA tabulations for Southern Republicans suggest a remarkably homogeneous conservatism. The list, with the new members indicated by an asterisk, appears on page 155.

It should be apparent that, as the Republican party gains strength in the South, so does the conservative position gain strength within the GOP. It would be surprising, indeed, if the majority of the new Southern Republicans were not conservatives, since it is conservatism which allows them to defeat the incumbent Democrats. As CQ notes, the Democratic casualties in 1966 were, almost without exception, the strongest supporters of Johnson's Great Society within their respective delegations. It

Alabama	
Edwards	100
Dickinson	100
Buchanan	100
Arkansas	
Hammerschmidt	87*
Florida	
Gurney	100
Cramer	95
Burke	100*
Georgia	
Blackburn	86*
Thompson	85*
Kentucky	
Cowger	81*
Snyder	82*
North Carolina	
Gardner	100*
Jonas	95
Broyhill	100
South Carolina	
Watson	100[a]
Tennessee	
Quillen	92
Duncan	88
Brock	91
Kuykendall	86*
Texas	
Bush	79*
Price	100*
Virginia	
Poff	96
Scott	92*
Wampler	79*
Broyhill	88

[a] Changed registration from Democratic to Republican in 1965. Elected as a Republican in his own right in 1966.

is by contesting this liberal tendency that the GOP can score points with the Southern electorate.

That Republican leaders other than Goldwater and the Operation Dixie staff have paid attention to all this was suggested in May, 1967, when House Republican leader Gerald Ford of Michigan delivered a controversial speech on the subject of the "conservative coalition" in Congress. The speech stirred up a good deal of dispute which obscured the true—and revolutionary—significance of what Ford was saying.

The coalition is an interesting topic which clearly suggests, among other things, that there is a potential conservative majority in Congress and elsewhere in American politics. According to an analysis by the Associated Press and NBC, for example, the 1966 elections brought in 196 conservatives in the House, compared to 163 liberals and 59 middle-of-the-roaders. Subsequent analyses by *Congressional Quarterly* suggested a conservative majority of 217 to 177 on Great Society bills in general, and even larger majorities on specific topics of prospective liberal legislation.

If this conservative preponderance seems strange, it merely serves to underline the fact that there are, as the poll statistics indicate, more *conservatives* in America than there are Republicans, and the further fact that since the excess of conservative over GOP votes in Congress consists almost entirely of Southern Democrats, a goodly number of these are situated in the South. Responding to this fact in legislative terms, the Republican party under Joe Martin and Charlie Halleck frequently struck up alliances with the Southern Democrats and brought a good deal of liberal legislation to a screeching halt.

In 1967, Ford made headlines by announcing that he was forsaking the coalition strategy. He stated that "we won't win as many legislative fights as we could if we resorted to the old coalition, but it's the big prize that counts." The big prize was a future majority in the House of Representatives—which Ford said he intended to get by forcing Southern Democrats, whenever possible, to take their stand by the side of the Johnson administration. His objective was to drive them "into the arms of the administration, where they belong, on votes that will hurt them in their home districts."

Conservative outcry about this statement was understandable, particularly in view of the rhetoric about constructiveness in which Ford presented it. Nevertheless, the clear logic of Ford's position is to push the Republican party precisely in the direction we have been discussing

—to seek a congressional majority by winning additional Republican seats in the South.

It should be apparent that, in several senses, this must be a conservative rather than a liberal strategy: conservative first of all because, far from rejecting the South, it clearly recognizes that Republican hopes for the future repose there; because, to be successful in such an approach, the Republicans must line up consistently to the right, not the left, of the Southern Democrats; and because, as the previous results suggest, a continued influx of Southern Republican congressmen will shift the power balance of the House GOP increasingly to the right.

If the GOP handles the matter properly, then, the conservative position should benefit from Ford's Southern strategy in a number of ways. When the Republican party stakes out a solid position in favor of limited government, fiscal responsibility and economy, then lets the Southern Democrats decide whether or not they want to come aboard, the conservative position cannot lose. When the Southerners do come on board, the coalition exists *de facto* and is able to defeat liberal legislation. When they do not, the GOP scores points toward further congressional wins in Dixie.

These developments are dependent on a number of variables, most obviously on the performance of the Southern Democrats. There has been some speculation in recent years that tendencies within the Dixie Democratic party, where liberals have been making some headway, would speed the development of the two-party South. But Democratic survival instincts have, on a number of occasions, derailed this pat analysis. In cases where the liberal Democrats have triumphed, Republican inroads have indeed been notable, as when Claude Kirk defeated the late Robert King High for the Florida governorship and William Scott bested a liberal Democrat who had in turn beaten the venerable Virginia conservative, Judge Howard Smith.

But Dixie Democrats have not been anxious to commit suicide. In several states they have managed to stem the Republican advance by reverting to an arch-conservative position. Similar right turns by congressional Southerners could conceivably slow the pace of the Republican advance. But even in this case the GOP Southern strategy will have performed a useful purpose, since it will serve to keep the Southern Democrats—many of whom do not have conservative records on anything but "civil rights"—considerably more honest than has been the case in previous years.

Republican *rapprochement* with the South, then, is good for the conservative cause, and good for the Republican party. And what is true in the matter of congressional majorities is true in other areas as well.

12:: A CONSERVATIVE PRESIDENT

Republican gains in Congress through the employment of a conservative strategy provide an obvious rebuttal to the notion that conservatism is politically hapless. And the fact that a conservative majority can and does exist in Congress at a time when liberalism is presumed to be at its political zenith suggests that inclusive statement about the liberal consensus is considerably off the mark.

There remains, however, the subject of the presidency. That Congress is in many cases conservative and may well become more so is a prospect which some liberal spokesmen occasionally acknowledge. They assert, however, that such congressional tendencies merely illustrate the unrepresentative nature of our representatives, the untrustworthiness of so antiquated and parochial a body as a measure and servant of the popular impulse. More reliable in both respects, they say, is the presidency, which combines plebiscitary sanction with appropriately centralized authority. And this branch of government is, we are informed, unfailingly liberal.

The merits or demerits of this exaltation of the executive cannot be canvassed here—although recent liberal misgivings on the subject, noted in Chapter 7, suggest some obvious flaws in it. The fact is that, right or wrong, the drift of governmental power over the past three decades has made the presidential office the supreme focus of our political system. The power of the presidency is so immense that no political formula will gain a hearing if it does not offer some reasonable prospect of attaining it. And it is precisely here that the conservative case is presumed to be at its weakest.

That no conservative can hope to reach the White House is considered axiomatic by a number of reigning political theoreticians. The idea is that the presidential elements in both political parties must be liberal, and that there is not very much that anybody can do about it. A typical statement of this view tells us: "A presidential candidate has to campaign for vital votes in states that are closely contested, such as New York, Michigan and California. Since winning or losing one of these states may hinge on a relatively small number of votes, it is more important for a presidential candidate to influence votes in these states than in the 'one party' states of the South and Southwest that tend to vote conservative."

Or as another authority opines: "In their efforts to win fiercely competitive national elections, the presidential parties in this century have had to arouse and respond to the waxing city and suburban vote across the nation. They have had to support liberal social and economic programs. The presidential 'gerrymandering' and 'winner take all' arrangement of the Electoral College, as a result of which the presidential candidates tend to vie for the big, closely contested heavily urban states with their big labor unions and ethnic groups, has forced both presidential parties to the left."*

Congress, according to these theorists (including such disparate spokesmen as James MacGregor Burns and the late Willmoore Kendall) is intrinsically conservative; but the executive branch, as a result of the Electoral College arithmetic if for no other reason, is intrinsically liberal. This argument draws *prima-facie* support from obvious features of our political discourse and political practice—such as the fact that liberals have historically magnified the presidency, that conservatives have favored Congress, that the executive concentrates power while Congress diffuses it, and so forth.

Yet, on the whole, the demonstration fails. There is in fact nothing in the nature of the American system which says the presidency *must* be liberal or that Congress *must* be conservative, the Vietnam debate between Fulbright and Johnson offering an obvious example to the contrary. As so frequently occurs in politics, "inevitable" and "necessary" are pseudonyms for custom and convenience. We are told that the presidency must be liberal because for thirty years it has been, and because for an even longer period many of the people who pontificate on such matters have wanted it to be.

The opinions quoted above are very good statements of the way in which our two-party system, for several decades, *has worked*. But they purport to be descriptions of the way it *must* work—as if there were something in the character of the presidential nominating system or the Electoral College which dictates the liberal approach to the exclusion of any other. And this is transparently not the case. For

* Nelson Polsby and Aaron Wildavsky further elaborate that our present system "tends to give greater power to the large, urban states . . . consequently, presidential nominees . . . tend to run on platforms likely to appeal to big-city interest groups. . . ." This further means, the authors assert, that the nominees will tend to ignore one-party areas like "the Deep South, which will probably go Democratic. . . ."

reasons touched on in our study of American demography, it is obvious that statements about one-party states in the South and Southwest, or the overwhelming power of liberal-minded interest groups, are hopelessly obsolete.

The impact of the demographic revolution is most immediately evident within the Republican party, where the asserted power of the liberal big-city states has already gone into eclipse. The 1964 GOP convention showed this clearly, as a massive nationwide alliance of Midwestern, Southern, and Western states piled up a towering majority. That alliance has grown stronger in the intervening years. The conservatives who nominated Goldwater can effectively control the choice of Republican presidential candidates for the foreseeable future—if they become aware of their own strength.

The Midwest-Far West-Southern axis which won for Goldwater has long been theoretically able to command a majority of convention votes, but was prevented from doing so prior to 1964 by lack of common goals and the almost total absence of an authentic Republican party in the South. For years the Southern GOP consisted largely of "post office" Republicans whose allegiances were secured by patronage and who were oriented to the Eastern wing of the GOP. (Thus several conservative Southern states wound up in 1952 opposing the aspirations of conservative candidate Robert A. Taft.)

For these reasons among others there was no coherent nationwide conservative Republican effort prior to 1960. And since the Eastern liberals had the additional advantages of money, press, and prestigious connection, they were able to direct Republican conventions virtually at will. Those days are past. The westward drift of the American population, growing concern over the enormous increase of Federal power, the rise of an articulate conservatism with its own channels of communication—all have contributed to a radical transformation of Republican power relationships. Most decisive of all has been the development of the two-party South, breaking the hold of the "post office" stalwarts and transferring upwards of 250 GOP delegate votes from the liberal to the conservative column.

In GOP conventions prior to 1964, the back-room strategists had been mesmerized by the strength of New York and the other Eastern states. If one could merely get the support of these states, so the reasoning went, the nomination battle was won. And since New York and other Eastern states were chiefly liberal, the obvious way to go about getting this support was to adopt the liberal position. Recent events have chipped away at this analysis until there is virtually nothing left of it.

To see what has occurred in arithmetical terms we need only examine the strength of the various delegations in the 1968 Republican convention, dividing them, on a present reading, into "conservative," "liberal" and "undecided" categories. The results, in large part self-explanatory, appear on page 164.

This list has been compiled to reflect minimum rather than maximum conservative strength. States where rank-and-file Republicans are clearly conservative—Ohio, Illinois, Missouri, Iowa—have for various reasons been excluded from the conservative column despite the fact that Goldwater made heavy 1964 inroads in each of them. These states might well go with the conservative candidate again. On the other hand, it is conceivable certain states listed as conservative might defect in the other direction. Since it is impossible to calculate such things months in advance, and since shifts of this sort have a way of balancing out, the prudent course is to take the over-all balance on the historical tendency of each state.

On this basis, we find the conservative element beginning with 292 delegate votes in the South; 136 delegate votes in the Middle West; and 162 votes in the Far West—for a

1968 DELEGATES

Conservative

South

State	Delegates
Alabama	26
Florida	34
Georgia	30
Louisiana	26
Mississippi	20
North Carolina	26
South Carolina	22
Tennessee	28
Texas	56
Virginia	24
Subtotal	292

Midwest

State	Delegates
Indiana	26
Wisconsin	30
Kansas	20
Nebraska	16
North Dakota	8
South Dakota	14
Oklahoma	22
Subtotal	136

West

State	Delegates
Arizona	16
California	86
Idaho	14
Montana	14
Nevada	12
Utah	8
Wyoming	12
Subtotal	162

TOTAL 590

Liberal

East

State	Delegates
New York	92
Pennsylvania	64
New Jersey	40
Massachusetts	34
Connecticut	16
Rhode Island	14
Maine	14
Subtotal	274

Other

State	Delegates
Michigan	48
Maryland	26
Oregon	18
West Virginia	14
Hawaii	14
Alaska	12
D.C.	9
Puerto Rico	5
Virgin Islands	3
Subtotal	149

TOTAL 423

Undecided

State	Delegates
Illinois	58
Ohio	58
Minnesota	26
Missouri	24
Kentucky	24
Washington	24
Iowa	24
Colorado	18
Arkansas	18
New Mexico	14
Vermont	12
Delaware	12
N. Hampshire	8

TOTAL 320

total of 590 out of 667 needed to nominate. The liberal element, thanks to the Eastern giants, starts off with a bigger bang than do the conservatives, but ends up with less. Giving the liberal GOP candidate everything in the 16 delegate constituencies listed above, we come up with 423 delegate votes—167 short of the conservative total.

The nature of the liberal dilemma is apparent. The conservative candidate needs only 77 more votes to achieve nomination. The liberal candidate needs 244. The conservative needs only to carry, say, Illinois and Iowa. The liberal, on the other hand, would not have the nomination even if he did win these states; he would have to take Illinois and Iowa plus all of the other major disputed areas like Ohio, Missouri, Kentucky, etc. And, as recent history has demonstrated, his chances of doing this would not be particularly promising. It becomes apparent that the task of the liberals is extraordinarily difficult and that the basic advantages in terms of simple arithmetic are on the side of the conservatives.

The key to this development, precisely as with the shift of power in Republican congressional ranks, is the South. The growth of Southern delegate strength at Republican national conventions since 1952 has been nothing short of phenomenal—with the result that the South today has the largest single bloc of votes at these national gatherings. The Southern share of the total vote has risen from 19 per cent in the 1952 convention to 26.7 per cent in 1968. Since delegate votes are apportioned according to votes for the Republican presidential candidate, senators and governors, this increase is largely traceable to the Goldwater campaign and the associated growth of Republican strength in Dixie.

It is clear, in sum, that the presidential element within the GOP need not be liberal, and in fact is much more likely these days to be conservative. That shift in power relationships, although evident in the Republican party earlier than elsewhere, is equally true of the nation at large. The Republican transformation accurately reflects the transformation which has come over the whole spectrum of American politics.

Electing a President, like winning a majority in Congress, begins with a problem in mathematics. For the Republican party, the problem boils down to a matter of moving out from its base of 120 or so electoral votes in the Midwest to secure another 150 or so votes in other parts of the country. The liberal strategy, employed by every Republican candidate from Willkie to Nixon, has been to seek votes in the liberal East. New York, Pennsylvania, and New Jersey, after all, represent the nation's most concentrated groupment of electoral votes; if a Republican could win these and add them to his Midwestern base, he would be well on his way to becoming President. So the liberal Republican reasoning has gone. The historical record suggests, however, a number of difficulties in this approach—the most obvious being the fact that the new votes solicited in New York and elsewhere are not, by and large, votes conformable with the existing base of Republican strength. In order to woo them, the Republican party must abandon its traditional notions of government, with erosive effects on its original support. The experiment, after a twenty-year period of trial and error, has not proved much of a success.

President Eisenhower, of course, was elected, and overwhelmingly. But it seems doubtful that Eisenhower won because of the election strategy employed by his campaign managers so much as because of his stature as a popular hero. At all events, the feat he was able to perform was not duplicated in any of the other elections in which Republican candidates tried to use the same approach. It has proved impossible for *national* Republican candidates to appeal to the essentially conservative constituency of the midlands and plains while simultaneously being left-wing enough to gain the votes of Eastern liberals.

The Goldwater campaign of 1964 began from the premise that the New York strategy, having failed so many times out, should be replaced with something else. The recommended alternative was generally called "the Southern strategy," although it might more accurately have been called the "Southern-Western strategy." In trying to make this strategy work, of course, Goldwater lost; yet paradoxically enough he proved what he set out to prove—and in so doing pointed the way to possible Republican victories in the future.

The Goldwater strategy was to suggest that the obvious source of new Republican votes was in the conservative sectors of the country, principally the South. The Republican party was conservative; the South was conservative; why therefore leave the South, by default, to the Democratic opposition? Why not stick to one's conservative principles and simultaneously develop a whole new source of electoral strength?

The underlying logic of this proposal was identical to the reasoning behind the Republicans' Southern push in Congress. If the Republican party is to become a majority force in national politics, it must not start off an election by conceding to the Democrats an entire third of a nation and better than 120 electoral votes. To survive, the party must get outside the regional strait jacket it has been wearing for so long and break the Democrats' hold on the Solid South.

When this Southern strategy was first suggested, Goldwater's opponents said such an effort could by no stretch of the imagination succeed. There was not a prayer that a Republican could penetrate the Solid South and add its electoral votes to the GOP base in the Midwest. And when Lyndon Johnson became President this commentary was redoubled.

As Goldwater's sweep of the Deep South demonstrated, these arguments were badly in error. The one thing Goldwater did achieve, while losing everything else, was precisely the thing his opponents said he never could achieve. And in attaining that supposedly improbable goal, he brought about the single most revolutionary development in American politics during the past generation—he succeeded in transferring from the Democratic column an entire bloc of electoral votes which had historically gone against the Republican party; *he succeeded in breaking through to precisely that source of new electoral votes the Republican party had been seeking, without success, in the big-city states of the East.*

The implications of this breakthrough were, of course, completely obscured by Goldwater's defeat everywhere else throughout the nation; principally, they were obscured by the fact that, while picking up the new electoral votes, Goldwater lost the Republican base—the Midwest and the plains. The inundation successfully blotted out the fact that the only new, the only thoroughly unprecedented occurrence of the 1964 election was the Republican victory in Mississippi, Alabama, South Carolina, Georgia, and Louisiana, *en bloc.*

What does this breakthrough imply for the future? As 1966 demonstrated, the Republican loss in the Midwest and plains states was not premised on a sudden casting off of traditional Republican principle; the Midwestern bastion is obviously still there. The West, as Reagan has shown, is increasingly accessible to the conservative appeal. And the South is there to be had as well by a Republican candidate who stands forth for conservatism and limited government. Which means that, despite the Goldwater defeat, his losing effort proved the Southern strategy is indeed capable of achieving Republican success.

Again, it will help us to gain perspective if we sort out the states, not according to the New York-plus approach, but on the basis of relative liberalism and conservatism. If we do this, we find the states which may be reasonably expected to take a conservative stance in national elections outnumber in total electoral votes the states (including the supposedly decisive Eastern states) which can be reasonably expected to take a liberal stance:

1964 Electoral Votes

Conservative		*Liberal*		*Undecided*	
Alabama	10	Alaska	3	Arkansas	6
Arizona	5	Connecticut	8	California	40
Colorado	6	D.C.	3	Delaware	3
Florida	14	Hawaii	4	Kentucky	9
Georgia	12	Maryland	10	Maine	4
Idaho	4	Massachusetts	14	Nevada	3
Illinois	26	Michigan	21	New Hampshire	4
Indiana	13	Minnesota	10	New Mexico	4
Iowa	9	Missouri	12	Vermont	3
Kansas	7	New Jersey	17	Washington	9
Louisiana	10	New York	43		
Mississippi	7	Oregon	6	TOTAL	85
Montana	4	Pennsylvania	29		
Nebraska	5	Rhode Island	4		
North Carolina	13	West Virginia	7		
North Dakota	4				
Ohio	26				
Oklahoma	8	TOTAL	191		
South Carolina	8				
South Dakota	4				
Tennessee	11				
Texas	25				
Utah	4				
Virginia	12				
Wisconsin	12				
Wyoming	3				
TOTAL	262				

Again, it must be acknowledged that the analysis is purely rule of thumb and provisional. Yet I think any reasoned assessment of political tendencies in the various states will indicate that those listed in the first column have proved themselves, in a variety of ways, accessible to conservative appeal, that those in the second generally have not, and that those in the third are of an ambivalent character.

In essence, our list of conservative states consists of three groups: The traditional GOP base in the Midwest, the newly Republicanized Rocky Mountain states, and the still more recently Republicanized South. These three areas supply most of the votes needed to achieve an Electoral College majority: the Midwest and Rockies, 140; and the South—the biggest single bloc—122.

A candidate who could begin with this base would need to pick up only eight more electoral votes—*e.g.*, Maine and New Hampshire—to be elected President. If he carried California, he would be well over the 300-vote mark. The key, as in the congressional races and the delegate battle, is the South. If the Republicans could hold their base in the Midwest while carrying the South, they would be within striking distance of the presidency.

The New York approach, in sum, has failed, not once but five times, to achieve its stated objectives. It has been able to score some local victories where Republicans can unabashedly go all the way in their leftward flanking maneuver, but it has proved incapable of uniting in a single phalanx the conservative Midwest and the liberal East. The conservative strategy offers a realistic alternative: Why not seek victory for the more conservative of the major parties by uniting the conservative Midwest with the conservative South?

The secret of liberal success in presidential elections has been precisely in forestalling this coalescence of the Midwest and the South. The two analyses we have quoted take it as a premise that the liberal big-city states are up for grabs and therefore worthy of Republican effort, but that the South is not. It is assumed that the South is a "one party" area, which is not "closely contested." This is an obvious anachronism which ignores recent election results.

The state of Alabama today is far more accessible to a Republican presidential candidate than are the liberal bastions of the East. Moreover, the voting records of Alabamians in Congress are far closer to those of Republicans from the Midwest, and more closely attuned to majority GOP sentiment generally, than are the voting records of many New York or New Jersey GOPers.* Added to all of which is the fact that the South as a whole contains more electoral votes than do the Eastern states.

There is, in short, no great likelihood that a liberal Republican candidate can put together an Electoral College majority. But the chances for assembling a conservative presidential majority are very good indeed—if, that is, the real America becomes aware of its own reality.

* The best "party support" voting record (votes with the majority position of the party) among House Republicans in 1966 was established by an Alabama Republican, Representative John Buchanan. Four of the top ten Republicans in the support rankings were from the South. All six of the Republicans with the worst "party support" records were from the Northeastern United States—and three of these were from New York. See p. 210.

13:: THE GOP AND THE SOUTH

There are, it appears, a number of different conservative majorities, actual and potential. So many of them, in fact, that almost any political graph of the United States, drawn on one or another of the relevant bases, shows conservative elements to be in the ascendant or rapidly approaching it. How does it happen, then, that the liberal view has remained so dominant in our politics? Why haven't the essentially conservative elements been able to elect Presidents, control Congress, shape the direction of national policy?

By far the most important answer, testimony to the asymmetry of our politics and the rhetorical powers of the Eastern Republicans alike, is that the component elements of the different conservative majorities have been divided into warring political camps. They have not been able to win because they have not been able to get together. Separated by historic barriers that are no longer apposite, the conservative areas of the nation have been unable to unite on critical matters of mutual concern.

As our inquiry into congressional and presidential strategies makes plain, the key to this enigma is the South. The shifting about of the American population indicates that the Republican party needs to build its strength in the Western and Southern regions, while maintaining its essential bastion in the Midwest. The West, with a prior history of Republicanism in most states, does not present any unusual problems—witness the presence of 11 Republican governors there after the 1966 elections. But the South is another matter altogether.

Since the Civil War, the South has voted consistently in the Democratic column. Even in the days of Franklin Roosevelt, the essentially conservative South stayed hitched to the essentially liberal Democratic party, and it for the most part stayed hitched for Adlai Stevenson and John F. Kennedy as well. So long as this conservative section of the nation persisted in voting for liberal Democratic candidates, hopes for a national conservative victory were doomed to disappointment. We have observed, however, that recent elections show this illogical alignment under stress. Signs of a Republican breakthrough in the region have multiplied since 1960 and the advent of a demonstrably conservative GOP.

Given the fact that such a breakthrough is imperative if the party is to achieve the appropriate majorities, it would seem logical that Republican spokesmen who have insisted that the GOP must "win," and commentators who proclaim the virtues of the two-party system, would welcome a Republican advance on the one-party South. But welcome it, of course, they have not. Liberal spokesmen have, on the contrary, denounced the notion of Southern Republican gains in the most vehement terms imaginable. The assertion of the Goldwater strategists in 1963 and 1964 that they were going after the electoral votes of the Southern states evoked unanimous anger in the liberal Republican and journalistic communities; only slightly less incensed have been the denunciations of Republican efforts to elect additional Southern congressmen.

GOP strategies aimed at winning Southern votes, according to the liberal spokesmen, threaten to turn the GOP into the "white man's party"; Governor Scranton declared it was Goldwater's asserted appeal to "racism" which finally provoked him into his mission impossible of 1964; Richard Rovere portrays the 1964 campaign as a cunning attempt to surface racial hatreds; Gilder and Chapman say the Goldwater campaign and the congressional "Operation Dixie" were sellouts of the Republican heritage for a mess of racist pottage. And so forth and so on, at considerable length.

On this presentation, the Republican party *should* not win in the South even if it can; it would be morally tainted by achieving a majority in Congress or electing a President if the increment of votes which made victory possible came from the states of the Old Confederacy. It must avoid trying to elect congressmen or win electoral votes there by running conservative candidates. Which means, since the party has no realistic hope of getting a congressional majority otherwise, and only slightly better chances of an Electoral College majority, that it must resign itself to permanent minority status as the price of ideological hygiene.

Thus liberal journalist Rovere asserts that, "even if Goldwater had managed to win a simple majority of both popular and electoral votes, he would nevertheless have been a minority president—one who owed his victory to disfranchisement"—that is, to the fact that he had received the votes of the South. A Republican conservative who won with Southern backing would be *ipso facto* an illicit President. The proposition is simply immoral and that is all there is to it.

The implication that the GOP should reject a Southern-based victory on grounds of moral rigor forms an interesting contrast to the usual rebuke leveled at conservative Republicans—that they are too much interested in doctrinal purity and not enough interested in "winning." The conventional liberal position is that the GOP must be "pragmatic," not stuck in the mud with outmoded principles, and that conservative zealots fail to appreciate this fact. The very same Richard Rovere, in the very same essay quoted above, blandly asserts that, to Goldwater conservatives, "doctrinal rectitude is vastly more important than the spoils of victory." Within the space of three pages, that is, he upbraids conservatives (a) for cherishing victory above principle, and (b) for cherishing principle above victory. The suspicion dawns that there is very little conservative Republicans can do to meet with the approval of Richard Rovere—except, perhaps, to stop being conservative Republicans in the first place.

Similar contradictions impair the counsels of the liberal Republican Ripon Society. This organization claims to be opposed to conservative Republicans on the grounds that they can't win—and that therefore a conservative stance for the national GOP will weaken the party; but its choicest epithets are reserved for the newly successful Southern Republicans who have been winning very well indeed. In such cases, one would suppose the previous argument would prove to be a logical embarrassment. The "moderates" take such matters in stride, however, and proceed to pile still other confusions on top of this one.

There is, for example, that argument about the intrinsic immorality of seeking Southern votes for the Republican party. It is curious to note that, when liberal Republican Hugh Scott was national chairman, he did not hesitate to solicit Southern support—unsuccessfully, as it happened—for Thomas Dewey. Nor is there any record that liberal Republicans demanded that Eisenhower reject the votes of Louisiana or Virginia, when thousands of segregationists in these states obviously cast their ballots for him in preference to Adlai Stevenson. Evidently it was permissible for a "moderate" Republican to carry some of the Southern states, but not permissible for a conservative Republican to do so.

The contradiction in the liberal GOP position is even more noticeable in the case of the liberal journalists. The people who denounced Goldwater for assertedly creating a "white man's party" in quest of Southern votes have managed to maintain a fairly equable temperament while viewing the historic misalliance of the Democratic party and the South. It was all right, apparently, for Franklin Roosevelt to carry all of the Southern states, when the prerogatives of the Negro were considerably less secure there than they are today. And it was equally all right for Stevenson and Kennedy to receive their full measure of tainted segregationist votes, for Stevenson to have a Southern segregationist as his 1952 running mate, and for Kennedy to sit down in harmonious conclave with a segregationist governor in order to woo Alabama's convention votes (he got 3½ of them, the bulk going to—Lyndon Johnson).

Most all right of all, it seems, is Arkansas Senator J. William Fulbright, who has voted consistently against civil-rights bills during his long tenure in Congress, but who nonetheless enjoys excellent standing with the liberal press. Fulbright votes the segregationist line on racial matters, but takes an arch-liberal stance on everything else, particularly in the field of foreign policy. He is therefore considered a fine fellow and his segregationist performance is quietly ignored. Goldwater, on the other hand, was not and is not a segregationist, but a consistent conservative on domestic and foreign-policy issues whose stance against big government led him to vote against the 1964 civil-rights bill. That the liberal journalists admire Fulbright and detest Goldwater tells us something about the depth of their antisegregationist passion and their notions of candor as well.

During the 1964 campaign, Goldwater made no appeals to racial feeling and uttered not one segregationist sentiment. In fact, as Theodore White observes, he deliberately moved, to his own disadvantage, to eliminate the subject of racial animosity from the campaign. The record clearly reflects all this, and in an attempt to prove otherwise Rovere is reduced to arguing that Goldwater sought to elicit racial feelings by using a "code" in which, during his Southern campaign forays, mentions of either *Johnson or Humphrey by name* were implicit attacks on "integrationists."* Evidently, to avoid such encoded racism, Goldwater should have conducted his campaign without referring to the Democratic candidates at all.

The liberal position, in sum, boils down to a statement that it is moral for liberals to win segregationist votes in the South, to make political bargains with segregationists, or in fact to be segregationists themselves. But it is immoral for a conservative, by taking a consistently conservative stand while eschewing all semblance of segregation, to win those same votes. The apposite point seems to be not where the votes come from, but *who gets them*; not that the ballots are tainted, but whether a conservative or a liberal is the beneficiary.

As for the Southern Republican gains in Congress, it is apparent that these are closely related to conservatism *per se*, rather than to racial feeling. Basic Republican support in the South comes, not from the rural areas where racial feeling is the strongest, but from the suburban areas

* ". . . in the Old Confederacy, 'Lyndon Baines Johnson' and 'my opponent' mean 'integrationist.' 'Hubert Horatio' (it somehow amuses Goldwater to drop the 'Humphrey') means 'super-integrationist.' 'Federal judiciary' means 'integrationist judges.'" Rovere grudgingly concedes that such things as the TFX controversy and McNamara's defense policy were not "code," but says criticism of Bobby Baker was useful "because of his embarrassing connections with the integrationist in the White House." (Richard H. Rovere, *The Goldwater Caper*, New York, 1965, pp. 143-144). One devoutly hopes that these passages are themselves a kind of code, since their significance when taken literally suggests American political journalism has reached hitherto unfathomed depths of imbecility.

where there is considerable concern, as there is in the North, over the economic aspects of the liberal program. It is not the racial issue which supplies GOP leverage against the Southern Democrats—just the opposite. The Republican talking point is that the Southern Democrats in many cases have not in fact stood forth for the limited government position on anything *but* racial matters. A Fulbright or a Sparkman is vulnerable to Republican challenge, not on the "civil rights" issue, but on the general issues of conservative-liberal philosophy.

In a final twist of the argument, the liberal analysts revert once more to *realpolitik*—asserting that the Republican Party in the South must be "moderate" in order to secure the newly-enfranchised Negro vote. Recent election results do not do much to support this argument. Some Negro candidates have been elected to local offices in the South, but by and large the "Negro vote" has been neither so predictable nor so powerful as the liberal conspectus would indicate. To the surprise of many political observers, Negroes in Alabama voted heavily in favor of Mrs. Wallace in 1966; some conservative Republican candidates have received a healthy proportion of the Negro vote; and in still other cases—the Mississippi gubernatorial campaign of 1967 being the most prominent—Republican campaigns publicized as efforts to secure Negro votes in accordance with the liberal analysis have resulted in electoral disaster. The voting statistics suggest that the Southern constituency as a whole is going to be overwhelmingly conservative for the foreseeable future, and that a left turn in the South will net the GOP almost nothing. The stance which can maximize Republican strength there is a consistent philosophical conservatism which avoids the fallacies of Kluxism and liberalism alike.*

* It is necessary at this point to violate my self-imposed rule about moralizing; some notice should be given to what the GOP view on this question, as a matter of justice, ought to be. In general, I think Republi-

The liberal argument is, moreover, as bad an exercise in history as it is in logic. Neither the legacy of Lincoln nor the accumulated precedents of Republican history dictate that the party must smolder with antagonism toward the South or endorse any and every centralizing measure put before Congress under the rubric of "civil rights." What liberal spokesmen like the Ripon Society seem to have in mind is a latter-day Reconstruction, a scourging of Dixie with whips and scorpions in which the national government, driven by zealous egalitarian Republicans, wages total war upon the prostrate South. This is portrayed as the Republican heritage.

In fact, the Republican heritage is nothing like this. Reconstructionist passions are not the legacy of Lincoln, or of the historic Republican ascendancy either. They are to some extent the legacy of Thaddeus Stevens—although the 1964 civil-rights bill happened to go far outside the boundaries established by the Reconstruction amendments Stevens grudgingly accepted as sufficient medicine for

---

cans should affirm the stance that Goldwater took and that Reagan has taken: That it should be the duty of government to insure that every citizen is guaranteed every right given him by the Constitution—*e.g.*, the right to vote—but that efforts to create artificial economic rights like "open housing" or FEPC at the expense of other people's rights are both wrong and self-defeating. As it happens, the failure of compulsion to assuage Negro distress and the movement of the "civil rights" controversy from the South to the North have served to underline the fallacy of the liberal approach. Compulsory unionism, minimum wage laws, urban renewal, public housing, and school "busing" have harmed the Negro rather than helping him (augmented Negro interest in right-to-work laws is an interesting recognition of this development), while efforts to compel brotherhood have stirred rather than quieted racial antagonisms. The cause of the Negro will be served, not by imposing further rigidities on the American economy but by eliminating rigidities. The rise of countless Negro self-help programs, job-training projects, and employment programs like that promoted by Reagan in California contain more hope of a successful answer than do compulsions handed down from Washington. The evidence shows that the private market economy has done more to improve the position of the American Negro than all government programs combined.

Dixie. The Stevens legacy was directly opposed to Lincoln's view and equally opposed to the policies upon which the long ascendancy of the Republican party was built. To suggest that the heritage of the GOP or the memory of Lincoln mandates a Reconstructionist vendetta is provable error of the most obvious sort.

There is, to begin with, no evidence whatever that Lincoln favored a *revanchist* policy toward the South and the consensus of scholarly opinion is that, had he lived, he would have pursued the conciliatory line of his successor, Andrew Johnson. He was not an abolitionist and signed the Emancipation Proclamation only under political stress. As for Lincoln's views on the subject of civil rights as currently construed, it is to be presumed there are few Republicans, liberal or conservative, who would endorse this particular legacy, since Lincoln was an out-and-out segregationist who advocated separation of the races and Negro colonization—a view more closely resembling South African *apartheid* than any one of several American variations on the theme of attaining harmonious and just relations between the races.

The Reconstruction legacy itself was, as it happened, a rather short-lived business. The modern Republican ascendancy is not dated from the postwar assault on the South, but from reconciliation with the South. The Republican party in the Reconstruction era was, in fact, woefully weak, and national revulsion against Radical excesses contributed importantly to that weakness. As Paul Buck observes, the Radicals' policy served to make the GOP "a sectional party only," which "operated to split asunder the fabric of national life." This is, of course, precisely the stance which the latter-day Reconstructionists urge upon the Republican party now.

The result was not politically beneficial to the GOP. In the 1868 election, the Democratic popular vote was only 300,000 short of the vote for Grant. Had it not been for systematic suppression of Democratic votes in the South, Buck observes, "a Democrat, Seymour, would have beaten the Republican Grant three years after the latter had stood under the famous apple tree at Appomattox. It was an alarming situation for Republicans."

How alarming was amply demonstrated by the elections of 1874, when the Democrats won majorities in both houses of Congress. In the 1876 presidential election, Republican Hayes lost the popular vote to Democrat Tilden. The Republican party's first President after Grant was elected, precisely, through *rapprochement* with the South. Hayes came to office through the famous compromise whereby Federal troops were withdrawn from the remaining Reconstruction states in return for Democratic acquiescence in his election by a special presidential commission. It was only after this healing of postwar wounds that the party began to build itself toward authentic majority status.

The aftermath of this policy was eminently successful, and led to the repeated election of Republican presidents between 1876 and 1928. During this span the GOP could claim no less than 10 of the nation's 12 presidents (9 elected in their own right), and lost elections only to the eccentric candidacies of Cleveland and Wilson. The Republican string included Hayes, Garfield, Arthur (succeeded upon the death of Garfield), Harrison, McKinley, Roosevelt, Taft, Harding, Coolidge, and Hoover. The party which in 1874 was swept under in the congressional elections and in 1876 lost the popular presidential vote compiled a streak of political victories which may never be surpassed. To equal it, present-day Democrats would have to carry five more Presidents into office as against a single Republican.

If it is conceded that it is no more immoral for a conservative to carry the South than it is for a liberal to do so, and that the Republican party is not prohibited from such an effort by its ancient traditions, the liberal Republicans have other objections at the ready. Such an approach, it is asserted, amounts to "writing off" the Northeastern states, and embarrassing the liberal Republicans by teaming them with a conservative presidential candidate. Moreover, because the Southern states are implacably hostile to the GOP, it can't be done. Any Republican strategy predicated on carrying the South will be derailed by an inevitable third-party candidacy. This was argued prior to the 1964 campaign and has been repeated, with less vehemence and more illogic, in the intervening years.

With respect to the writing-off and embarrassment charges, a conservative *tu quoque* seems entirely in order. These lamentations come with peculiar grace from Republicans who are themselves even now writing off a third of the nation and who have never been particularly troubled by the embarrassment of conservative congressional candidates who have had to run in tandem with a liberal presidential nominee. The principal point, however, concerns neither of these items, but the fact that a Southern-Western strategy can maximize Republican strength in congressional and presidential races while an Eastern strategy cannot. It is not a question of writing off any section of the country—since it is obviously desirable that the Republicans win everywhere they can; it is a question of what the party can reasonably *expect* to win while maintaining its existing strength intact.

The third-party issue, moreover, would appear to militate in favor of the conservative Republican approach rather than against it. The notion that the South would shy away from *any* Republican and go for unpledged electors in a third-party movement was effectively torpedoed in 1964, when the projected candidacy of George Wallace dissolved following Goldwater's nomination. The lesson of 1964 was reinforced by opinion surveys preliminary to the 1968 balloting which showed a Wallace candidacy would do well in the South if a liberal Republican candidate were chosen but not so well if the GOP nominee were a conservative.

A January, 1968 Gallup Poll, for example, found Lyndon Johnson and Nelson Rockefeller running even in popular favor when paired off in a two-man race, each obtaining 43 per cent of the vote. But with Wallace in the race, Johnson led Rockefeller 41 per cent to 37 per cent, with 12 per cent going to the former Alabama governor. Robert Donovan of the Los Angeles *Times* commented that "the polls indicated that Wallace would hurt not only a so-called liberal Republican, like New York Gov. Nelson A. Rockefeller or Michigan Gov. George Romney . . . but even a more conservative one, like Richard M. Nixon. California Gov. Ronald Reagan, on the other hand, might be able to make heavy inroads into Wallace's strength with the old Goldwater following."

Nineteen-sixty-four demonstrated that the votes of the South are accessible to a conservative Republican, while subsequent surveys have demonstrated that a liberal Republican would make a third-party candidacy a virtual certainty. By adhering to its conservative principle, the GOP can head off third-party movements and rally new voters to its cause. If the GOP takes the liberal tack, it will lose these votes and damage its chances in national and statewide elections.

Precisely how this kind of development can make trouble for Republicans was suggested by the 1965 gubernatorial contest in Virginia. In that election, Democrat E. Mills Godwin defeated Republican Linwood Holton by a few thousand votes, securing less than a majority. The comment of liberal pundits was that, had the GOP gone further left, it would have garnered more liberal-oriented votes and won the election. That analysis neglects the fact that a Conservative candidate running in the same election drew no less than 70,000 votes—more than enough to have elected Holton. If the Republican party had been *more* conservative rather than less, it could have won. GRI's Wesley McCune notes that the Virginia results established the leverage of the third-party tactic, observing that "the Conservative candidate polled more than enough to tip the balance."

Although the third-party question is thought to be principally a matter involving the South, it has ramifications in the North as well. Republican liberalism can serve to generate third-party efforts which have nothing whatever to do with segregation, but everything to do with the desire of many Republican rank and filers for a conservative party to represent their opinions. In some ways this development is even more serious than the Southern third-party impulse, since it means the GOP is losing votes to which it could previously lay claim. In New York state, for example, where the rise of the Conservative party has caused groans from various Republican leaders, it is clear that the third-party effort (it is in fact a fourth party, counterbalancing the Liberals) is premised exactly on the derangement of the GOP from traditional principle, and that the chief participants are people who, on the national scene, would be considered Republicans and who so consider themselves. The New York Conservatives say the Rockefeller-Javits-Lindsay brand of Republicanism is indistinguishable from the Democratic party, and that their own enterprise is an effort to give the traditional Republican outlook a voice in New York politics.

That there is a market for such activity if and when the Republican party heads irrevocably left is indicated by the rather phenomenal success the Conservative party has enjoyed during its brief existence. In the 1965 New York City elections, Conservative mayoral candidate William F. Buckley, Jr., drew 341,226 votes, tripling the party's previous high mark in the city. This result was made the subject of disparaging comment by liberal analysts in *Life* and *Newsweek,* who said it represented merely the vote total previously achieved by New York splinter candidates. In a postelection statement, the Conservative party gave this interesting rebuttal:

> The liberals immediately claimed that the Buckley vote was "only" in the same range that Lawrence Gerosa achieved in 1961, and that in view of Buckley's conceded rhetorical superiority over Gerosa, Buckley's campaign had flopped. This analysis conveniently overlooked several facts—that Gerosa was widely known, incumbent Democratic controller in 1961, that he had beaten Wagner on a citywide bond issue in 1959, and that he had led the Democratic ticket, including Wagner, in 1957. The real miracle was that Bill Buckley had achieved a larger vote in 1965 than Gerosa did in 1961. . . .

This analysis was confirmed by McCune, who declared that "the right wing has shown surprising strength in elections since 1964," and cited Buckley's race as the premier example, noting that the Conservative candidate "came very close to deciding the winner." Buckley probably aided Lindsay rather than hurting him, McCune opined (as did Buckley), "but he set out to swing a bloc of votes and he did do that. Lindsay failed to get a majority and won by only 136,000 votes. Meanwhile, the Conservative Party hit a new high."

In 1966, the Conservatives improved on this showing by drawing more than half a million votes statewide and displacing the veteran Liberal Party on Row C of the New York ballot, a coveted position from which the Liberals had long exerted a "swing" influence on both Democrats and Republicans. In achieving this, the Conservative gubernatorial candidate, Dean Paul Adams, outdrew the revered name of Franklin D. Roosevelt, Jr. Along the way, the Conservatives also spearheaded a successful campaign to repeal one of Lindsay's major liberal initiatives

—a civilian Police Review Board. It appears that the New York Conservative party is going to be an increasingly powerful factor in Empire State politics so long as the Rockefeller Republican party continues to steer its course down the left side of the road. The lesson for Republicans elsewhere in the nation should be apparent.

Quite clearly, such developments show the old liberal Republican counsel that "the conservatives have nowhere else to go" is sadly mistaken. They do have somewhere else to go, and when they go there, North or South, they can subtract crucial votes from the Republican column. Such movements are generated by Republican forays into liberal territory; they can be prevented by Republican adherence to traditional principle.

The logic of the third-party issue brings us around to a final question. If Republican efforts to penetrate the South are neither immoral nor impossible, if the liberal Republicans and liberal Democrats alike have been happy to receive all the Southern votes they can get, and if it is demonstrable that a breakthrough in the South can produce a Republican victory—why do the people who talk so much about "strengthening the GOP" oppose Republican success in Dixie? The answer, I think, is relatively plain: The liberal Republicans oppose this strategy, not because it can't win, but because it can.

The objection to the Southern flanking maneuver is not that it will prevent a traditional Republican from reaching the White House, but that it could all too possibly put one there. The linking up of the South to the Midwest and West would, after all, be the most decisive of all possible steps toward the surfacing of the conservative majorities, an event which liberal Democrats and liberal Republicans alike devoutly want to prevent. The point of the argument is to make sure that no such coalescence occurs—that the conservative areas of the country so long divided by circumstance remain divided by design.

14: : THOSE 27 MILLION

Before leaving the subject of the 1964 campaign and its possible meanings for the Republican future, there is one other item which merits consideration: The question of what, if anything, Goldwater's vote implied about the strength of explicit conservatism in America as of November, 1964.

From the statements of Reston and Hofstadter and other such spokesmen, you would certainly have thought the Johnson landslide was satisfactory. But some of the analysts were not so easily appeased. Goldwater had been badly beaten; but he had also secured 27 million votes, and it was vaguely troubling to reflect that there might actually be that many people around who agreed with his position. The number is not large enough to win a presidential election; but it is a lot of people nonetheless—far more than we are accustomed to thinking of as dissenters from the liberal consensus, far more than the number usually imputed to the extreme right wing (conservatism).

When the matter is viewed in this light, it becomes clear that Goldwater's having lost the election is not, after all, enough. It is not sufficient that his total should have been a losing one, 16 million votes short of Johnson's. If the conservative poltergeist is to be fully exorcised, it becomes necessary to start subtracting votes from Goldwater's abbreviated total. The conservative element must be whittled down to more manageable dimensions.

So it was that Roscoe Drummond and Louis H. Bean, in the March 23, 1965, issue of *Look*, set out to scotch the idea that Goldwater's vote had really been a vote for Goldwater. The vast majority of the 27 million, Bean and Drummond argued, were not conservatives and didn't like Goldwater at all. They had simply cast their ballots for him in a routine gesture of Republican party support. The notion that Goldwater "owned" these votes was therefore mistaken. "Goldwater's 27,000,000 votes," they said, "though reduced because of his extreme conservatism and other positions was [sic] obviously made up mostly of the historically unwavering party supporters. It clearly reflects the basic Republican Party strength." They then ran through a demonstration purporting to show that the true Goldwater vote "lies between 2,500,000 and 3,000,000 votes."

There are several observations one can make about this argument, the first of which is that nobody, to my knowledge, has said Goldwater "owned" the votes cast for him, either literally or in the figurative sense that he could personally dispose of them by flashing political signals. The relevant point, obviously, is whether the Republican voters in question were *conservatives*, generally in agreement with Goldwater's position, or whether they were nonconservatives who pulled the lever for Goldwater anyway. The answer to this question is a matter of some importance; if the first alternative is correct, then the 27 million figure takes on a certain significance; if the second is correct, then it would probably be advisable for conservatives to forget about politics and head for the catacombs forthwith.

Inquiry into the subject of the 27 million suggests a number of reasons for questioning the Bean-Drummond analysis. To begin with, they have entirely omitted the traumatic aftermath of the assassination—the psychological and political maiming of Goldwater, the sanctification of Johnson and the Democratic program, the strenuous campaign to leperize the American conservative community. Is it reasonable to suppose that all this had no effect on less-than-conservative Republicans? An even more important omission is the performance toward Goldwater of so many of his fellow Republicans. Since the argument centers on the alleged behavior of "historically unwavering party supporters," this would appear to be a rather crucial point.

When this powerful factor is considered, it seems doubtful indeed that Goldwater was the beneficiary of a routine Republican turnout. One might as convincingly argue that William Howard Taft garnered the basic Republican vote in 1912. There were obviously many pressures creating massive Republican desertions in 1964, slicing Goldwater's total even in the arch-Republican strongholds. Foremost among these was the campaign of various liberal Republicans branding the candidate as an extremist, political cutthroat, and nuclear madman—charges which were made repeatedly and never retracted or papered over. If assertions of this kind did not drive a proportion of the normal Republican vote away from Goldwater, then we may safely assume the American electorate has become emotionally insensate.

The rhetoric the liberal Republicans employed against Goldwater demonstrates, among other things, how fervently immoderate these moderates are capable of becoming. And it also demonstrates, in a very explicit way, that their purpose was to split the Republican party in two, to subtract from Goldwater the support Bean and Drummond say he got. Consider, as only one of several examples, Governor Rockefeller's attack on the Goldwater conservatives following the 1963 Young Republican convention. The Republican party, Rockefeller said,

> . . . is in real danger of subversion by a radical, well-financed and highly disciplined minority. . . . It has now become crystal clear that the vociferous and well-drilled extremist elements boring within the party utterly reject [the] fundamental principles of our heritage. They are, in fact, embarked on a determined and ruthless effort to take over the party, its platform and its candidates on their own terms. . . . Every objective observer at San Francisco has reported that the proceedings there were dominated by extremist groups, carefully organized, well-financed and operated through the tactics of ruthless, rough-shod intimidation. These are the tactics of totalitarianism.

What was the reason for this violent statement? As the present writer knows from personal observation, there was no color of fact to Rockefeller's charges about the Young Republican convention; the authentically scandalous tactics at that gathering were employed by Rockefeller's own youthful partisans. The truth is that the intrinsic merits of the Young Republicans' performance—apart from the fact that they had rejected Rockefeller's chosen candidate—had nothing to do with it. The purpose of his statement was, quite simply, to revive his sagging presidential candidacy—and to do so by splitting the Republican party.

"The furore over the rightist antics by the Young Republicans," Robert Novak observes, "was the pretext, not the reason. . . ." The real reason was that, without a major Republican blowup, "Goldwater seemed the sure nominee." Thus: "*Party discord now was necessary for Rockefeller to stage a comeback. He needed to stir up ancient animosities, to purposely reopen the schism he had spent two and a half years trying to close. He needed to become the champion of the party's 'Eisenhower wing' against the right. Without the internal bloodletting, Rockefeller was dead.*"

Resort to such vituperation as an intraparty tactic was to become the moderate rule, rather than the exception. William Scranton, for example, repeatedly invoked similar language when he made his belated bid for the nomination, as did numerous other Republican liberals. Perhaps the most famous example was the "letter" Scranton sent to Goldwater on the eve of the San Francisco convention. Scranton subsequently said he had not seen this letter and disapproved of some of its wording. It nonetheless sums up, all too clearly, the nature of the Scranton attack on Goldwater and is a good specimen of the moderate rhetorical style. This missive to Goldwater stated:

"Your supporters . . . admit that you are a minority candidate, but feel that they have bought, beaten, and compromised enough delegate support to make the result a foregone conclusion.

"With open contempt for the dignity, integrity, and common sense of the convention, your managers say in effect that the delegates are little more than a flock of chickens whose necks will be wrung at will. . . . We have calculated an important element you are not capable of comprehending. That is the element of respect for the men and women who make up the delegations to this convention. . . .

"They are not breaking commitments to you; you have broken commitments to them.

"You have too often casually prescribed nuclear war as a solution to a troubled world.

"You have too often allowed the radical extremists to use you.

"You have too often stood for irresponsibility in the serious question of racial holocaust. . . .

"In short, Goldwaterism has come to stand for a whole crazy-quilt collection of absurd and dangerous positions that would be soundly repudiated by the American people in November."

Here was moderation indeed—language of a sort which

the alleged extremist Barry Goldwater, to this writer's knowledge, never employed against his intraparty adversaries. What could prompt the liberal Republicans to say such terrible things? What were they trying to accomplish? The answer, as Theodore White details it, was that Scranton and those supporting him had quite cold-bloodedly set out to destroy the Republican party's certain nominee for President.

When Scranton issued his various statements, of which the "letter" was merely the last of a series, he had no realistic chance at the nomination. The question had been settled before he entered the race. The only purpose which could be served by his eleventh-hour harangue was to destroy Goldwater's slender chance of being elected in the fall. Describing Scranton's frame of mind when he jumped into the race, White tells us: "It was *his* party: and if, to save it, he had to punish Goldwater, an old friend, and *destroy, in 1964 the value of its nomination,* then so it had to be." And so, throughout that long campaign, from the snows of New Hampshire to the pyrotechnics in the Cow Palace, it was.

White's reflections on this subject, and on the Scranton letter in particular, are instructive—especially so in view of White's liberal inclinations and high regard for Scranton. The strategy incapsulated in the "letter," White says, "had made the Republican Convention the stage for the destruction of the leading Republican candidate. What Rockefeller had begun in the spring, Scranton finished in June and at the convention: the painting for the American people of a half-crazed leader indifferent to the needs of American society at home and eager to plunge the nation into war abroad. . . . Rockefeller and Scranton had drawn up the indictment, Lyndon Johnson was the prosecutor. Goldwater was cast as the defendant."

Added to all this, and obviously related to it, was the explicit desertion—and even more widespread implicit dumping—of the Goldwater ticket in the fall. Not since the Mugwump movement of the 1880's had there been anything in the Republican party to equal it. (Even Teddy Roosevelt, after all, was straightforward enough to shed the Republican label when he broke with the party.) Among the leading Republicans who refused to support the Goldwater-Miller ticket were Nelson Rockefeller, Kenneth Keating, Jacob Javits, John Lindsay, Edward Brooke, and George Romney.

A representative sample of the liberal Republican campaign style is the transcript of Romney's remarks at a Michigan AFL-CIO question and answer session, as follows:

QUESTION: "Do you or don't you support the national Goldwater-Miller ticket?"

ROMNEY: "My position is quite clear. The Republican Party has made its decision on the platform and the candidates. I accept these decisions. I accept them, but I don't endorse them."

Shout from the floor: "Answer the question, George!. . . "

QUESTION: "Will you support and vote for the Republican national presidential and vice-presidential candidates?"

ANSWER: "I will not vote for candidates other than the candidates of my party."

Shout from the floor: "Answer the question, George, you bum!"

ROMNEY: "That's my personal privilege, and I don't expect to answer that here. . . "

Romney's supporters surpassed even this show of nonsupport, instructing voters on ways in which to split their ballot. A 1964 election flyer distributed in Michigan, bearing pictures of Johnson and Romney, contained the following "directions for voting":

"1. Move the red handle to the right to close curtain.

"2. Pull down the lever over the name of Lyndon B. Johnson and leave it down.

"3. Pull down the lever over the name of George Romney and leave it down.

"4. Pull down the lever over the names of other candidates of your choice.

"Move the red handles back to the left and open the curtain. (Take this with you when you vote.)"

The techniques employed by and for Romney were used in other places as well—and were supported by less flamboyant but equally effective procedures such as failure to promote the national ticket through advertising or refusal to distribute its literature. The repetition of such things on a nationwide basis can and probably did involve the loss of hundreds of thousands of votes.

The point of these reminiscences is not to criticize the behavior of Romney and the other Republican liberals—although it certainly merits criticism—but to suggest the extraordinary conditions under which the Goldwater race was run. With important Republican figures flaying their presidential candidate as a madman or worse at every possible turn, then undercutting the ticket in the fall, the conditions were about as adverse as it was possible for them to get.

Which brings us back to the assertion of Messrs. Bean and Drummond, that Goldwater rode into the election on "basic Republican Party strength." Can it be seriously maintained, in view of the massive party-rending of so many prominent Republican leaders, the verbal whiplashing, the ticket-splitting instructions, the well-publicized refusals to support the candidate, that Goldwater simply waltzed into the November balloting as the beneficiary of a routine Republican vote?

Among other things, this is an interesting reflection on the mental processes of the hypothetical nonconservative Republican voter. This voter, evidently, sees a man nominated as the candidate of his party who is not only opposed by leading figures in the GOP, including figures to whom the nonconservative voter pays his own allegiance and would rather have seen nominated, but who is depicted by those leaders, without subsequent retraction, as a maniac who will plunge the nation into nuclear holocaust. So observing, this average nonconservative Republican walks into the polling booth like a zombie and casts his vote for the man anyway.

That hypothesis does not say very much for the Bean-Drummond average voter. Nor does it say very much for the persuasive powers of Rockefeller, Keating, Javits, Lindsay, Romney and Co. The more obvious conclusion is that any Republican who was not reasonably partial to conservatism would take the cue provided by his moderate leaders and refuse to vote for Goldwater. Which, in many cases, is exactly what happened.

Alternatively, the voters who did in fact vote for Goldwater must have had strong reasons to resist the Rockefeller-Javits-Romney effort to dump the ticket. They must, obviously, *not* have been followers of these men. That the average Goldwater voter outside the South was indeed a party regular in most cases goes without saying; but it is also apparent that he was to some important degree a conservative—the two things not, as we have seen, being mutually exclusive.

The Bean-Drummond analysis becomes even more curious when we note their assertion that the total conservative vote in the GOP is not more than 3,000,000. This is very interesting, in view of the fact that, in the 1964 primaries, Goldwater received some 2,147,993 votes—accumulated in only ten states. This means that, in all the other forty states of the union—including the six states Goldwater actually carried in the election—there were *at most* only 850,000-plus Goldwater supporters. Bean and Drummond, clearly, are speaking to us from the mythical America rather than the real one—in this case an America where Goldwater had 2,147,993 supporters in ten states and only

850,000 in the remaining forty. It is no doubt a mark of Goldwater's superior cunning that he picked the states where his plus 2 million votes were concentrated to wage his primary campaigns, after first having arranged, decades ago, that these states should adopt the primary system in the first place.

It is clear enough that the basic strength of American conservatism is well above the level suggested by Bean and Drummond. There is good reason to suppose it is roughly equivalent to the 27 million votes Goldwater received. And there is some reason to suppose it is even larger than Goldwater's total vote.

That this is so may be gleaned from an examination of the issues which ravaged Goldwater in November: the idea that he would somehow plunge the nation into nuclear holocaust, and the idea that he would seek to destroy Social Security. Goldwater's partisans, of course, maintain that these charges were unfair. The present writer agrees, but again the question of fairness is not at issue. The essential point is that Goldwater's opposition, both within the party and in the general election, set out to portray him as an *irresponsible personality*, to brand him as an unstable man who could not be relied upon as Rockefeller, or Scranton, or Johnson, could.

Robert Donovan observes that "the fear that a Goldwater administration might somehow lead to war was the most powerful single factor Johnson had on his side. Everywhere reporters and polltakers found voters worried about what Goldwater would do abroad. This was especially true in the suburbs where parents worried about their children's living close to prospective target areas in time of war. This worry was undoubtedly the main reason why many men and women who might otherwise have been expected to vote Republican deserted Goldwater." The result of such fears, Donovan concludes, was that "all questions . . . became subordinate to the question of Goldwater's fitness for the presidency."

That both the liberal Republicans and Lyndon Johnson chose to conduct the campaign on this *ad hominem* level is suggestive. We may grant that the point of departure for all of these charges—the nuclear business, Social Security, the "civil rights" bill—was located somewhere in conservative territory. But it was precisely the strategy of the GOP liberals and of Johnson to refuse all debate about such subjects on their merits; in each case, the topic was used as the pretext for emotional opportunizing, for the bandying about of demagogies suggesting Goldwater's personal unfitness.

It is no debate of liberal-conservative issues, after all, to cry "nuclear death" or, as Johnson phrased it at one point, "the world you save may be your own," when serious issues of foreign policy are raised, when the merits of the test-ban treaty are discussed, or when the complex question is broached of what kind of delegated authority should exist respecting tactical nuclear weapons in the event of massive Communist attack. Nor is it debate of the overarching tendencies of the welfare state to equate any critical mention of welfarism with the destruction of Social Security, or to brand discussions of the burgeoning indebtedness and inequitable features of this program as an attempt to deprive the elderly of their livelihood. The hurling about of such charges is not an effort to engage the root issues of liberalism and conservatism, but to evade them.

The evasion, as we have seen, was highly successful. The image of Goldwater as a bomb-crazed maniac—fastened on him, as White observes, "first by Rockefeller, then by Scranton, then by Johnson"—was decisive. The result was that Goldwater wound up running his campaign, "not only against Lyndon Johnson and against the Democratic record, but against fear itself."

That the 1964 campaign was conducted in terms designed to mask rather than clarify liberal-conservative issues was further suggested by the utterances of the various liberal candidates and of their supporters in the media. Both

Rockefeller and Scranton strove to argue that *they*, not Goldwater, were the true "conservatives." Johnson, in the fall election, delivered a number of speeches which could well have been prepared for him by the research staffs of the NAM or the American Legion. In some instances, the conservatizing of Johnson and deconservatizing of Goldwater was made explicit.

Thus Walter Lippmann found himself able to write that "there is no more unfounded claim than that Barry Goldwater is a conservative. . . . Sen. Goldwater is in fact a radical opponent of conservatism who, under the banner of personal freedom, would compound that moral disorder which is the paramount problem of the modern age." Johnson himself put it that, "conservatism may be written on their banner, but radical is written in their hearts. . . . They are not conservatives in the American tradition. . . . Their outlook is neither conservative nor Republican."

The result of all this was to complete the befuddlement of the issues that began so precipitously with the death of Kennedy. Conservatism versus liberalism, which was to have been the point of 1964, never succeeded in getting itself discussed. In consequence, as Edward Folliard of the Washington *Post* observed, the election "was not a measure of the relative strength of conservatism and liberalism in the United States. President Johnson, seeing the middle of the road wide open, would not call himself a liberal, and would not acknowledge that Sen. Goldwater was a conservative." Richard Scammon pushes the thought one step further. He tells us that "the 1964 figures only highlight the feeling of some voters that Senator Goldwater was the 'radical' in that contest, President Johnson the more conservative." Donovan similarly notes that "millions of voters regarded Johnson as a middle-of-the-road conservative and Goldwater as a radical or extremist"—a verdict confirmed, as we have seen, by the Harris poll results.

To paraphrase John Stuart Mill: Whence this fear of

conservatism? If the conservative position is as politically disastrous as we are told, how did it happen that the liberals, confronted with the first conservative presidential candidate in thirty years, labored so hard to demonstrate that he was *not* a conservative? If the American consensus is overwhelmingly liberal, the best possible strategy against a conservative candidate would seem to be to prove that he *is* a conservative. While the best possible strategy for a liberal would of course be to present himself in full ADA regalia.

Yet the Republican liberals, Johnson, and their supporters in the media resolutely avoided confrontation. They stuck to the technique of personal attack, promoting the idea that Goldwater was an untrustworthy individual, a "radical," and that Johnson was a stable, prudent person who could be trusted as Goldwater could not. The Johnson campaign avoided, throughout, any effort to ballyhoo the explicit ADA-style liberalism at the heart of the Great Society program. All of which suggests that Senator Javits' conception of 1964 as a national referendum on the welfare state is badly in error.

That Johnson's strategy was a wise one is indicated by the ruminations of David Danzig in *Commentary*. Danzig notes the Harris Poll figures referred to in Chapter 5, derived "just before the election . . . when the Johnson tide of moderate progressivism was running at its full." He observes that, "to the extent that these findings are at all representative, the election did not test the strength of the conservative appeal; far from engaging the above issues, it failed even to sort them out." Precisely so. To which Danzig might have added that, from the liberal perspective, the campaign was conducted to avoid engaging these issues and sorting them out. It was all aimed at generating fear of Goldwater as a personality.

That Goldwater's poor showing was in large measure attributable to the successful effort to brand him as personally irresponsible, rather than to his conservative stance as such, is further suggested by a comparison of his electoral performance with that of Republican officeholders in conservative areas who were quite as conservative as Goldwater himself, but who uniformly ran ahead of him. The only significant difference between these candidates and Goldwater was that they were not subjected to the kind of demoralizing personal attack that was his daily lot.

Thus H. R. Gross of Iowa, Richard Roudebush of Indiana, and John Ashbrook of Ohio—they are chosen for their explicit conservatism, but otherwise more or less at random, since the same pattern held true across the nation—all ran far ahead of Goldwater in their respective districts. Goldwater trailed Gross by 13,000 votes, Roudebush by almost 10,000, Ashbrook by almost 11,000. Obviously, if Goldwater's *conservative ideology* had been the reason for his poor showing, these three congressmen would have run more or less even with him, since their ideological position was in all major points virtually identical to his. But they in fact garnered many votes from people who cast their ballots against Goldwater. These results make it clear that Goldwater was not only not the recipient of a routine Republican vote; he was not even the recipient of a routine *conservative* vote. Not only did many moderate Republicans desert Goldwater; many essentially conservative ones—the kind who vote for Gross or Roudebush or Ashbrook—deserted him as well. These citizens clearly were voting, not against conservatism, but "against fear itself."

Danzig, although placing the blame for this outcome on Goldwater rather than his adversaries, comes to essentially the same conclusion. He states that the Goldwater campaign alienated farmers, trade unionists, Negroes, ethnic minorities, advocates of public power, the aged, and the unemployed, "as well as those who have lost the courage to die in a nuclear holocaust" (he might more accurately have said that such people, particularly the last-named, were "alienated" for him), and that his political base in the stock terms of interest-group appeal was incredibly narrow. Danzig concludes that "the fact that so negative an approach to bi-partisan American politics could still gain more than 27 million votes must surely be attributed to more than party loyalty, for the Republicans who voted for Goldwater were either affirming or, at the very least, acquiescing in this approach."

None of this is meant to suggest that had the election been run on a straight ideological basis—more welfarism *vs.* more free enterprise, more "accommodation" *vs.* greater firmness—the conservative alternative would necessarily have won. Our elections aren't conducted that way, and the numerous plus factors operating for Johnson would still have entered into the equation. It *is* meant to suggest that the mass defection of normally Republican and relatively conservative voters confers a special kind of significance on the remaining 27 million who weathered the storm and pulled the lever for Goldwater anyway.

It seems altogether likely that most voters who stuck with Goldwater through the confusion and billingsgate of 1964 were conservatives indeed, and particularly committed and obstinate ones at that. The evidence indicates that Goldwater's vote was something like a measure, not merely of generalized conservative sentiment, but of conscious, articulate, and strongly motivated conservatism.

15:: In REPUBLICAN MASQUERADE

In the age of the image, I have suggested, the predispositions of the media are a subject of the first importance. There is no likelihood that one will understand the struggle for control of the Republican party, or the political landscape in general, if he does not understand the TV networks, the national magazines, the influential daily newspapers, the columnists and commentators.

Because of their powerful effect on our conceptions of ourselves and others, it is a mistake to view the media simply as interpreters of political data. Their performance is major political datum in its own right. And nowhere is that performance more suggestive than in the demonstrated partiality of the daily press and other communications outlets for the liberal branch of the Republican party. This attitude tells us something, of course, about the media themselves; but it tells us something about the liberal GOP, too. Indeed, it provides us with a significant means of understanding an important aspect of the whole liberal Republican movement, and its appointed role in the drama of American politics.

What makes the media interest in the liberal Republicans so intriguing is the fact that, by an overwhelming margin, the media are staffed by Democrats. This fact has been consistently reflected down through the years by every survey of journalistic attitudes available to us. Thus Seymour Lipset writes:

"In the mid-thirties, a study of 104 Washington correspondents . . . reported that . . . the large majority had backed Roosevelt . . . straw votes conducted among reporters on the campaign trains of presidential candidates of both parties in later years suggested that, as a professional group, journalists have remained sympathetic to the Democratic party and to liberal causes. A more recent study of . . . foreign correspondents in Western Europe reported that in the winter of 1953–54, 58 per cent of those interviewed favored Stevenson, while 36 per cent supported Eisenhower for re-election."

More recent data yield similar results. Commenting on a 1963 survey of political preferences among journalists, Professor James MacGregor Burns notes: " . . . the correspondents continue to be heavily liberal and Democratic. In a . . . poll of Washington correspondents . . . 32 per cent styled themselves Democrats, 10 per cent Republicans, and the rest independents. More than 55 per cent of the correspondents called themselves liberal, 27 per cent conservatives. Perhaps the most revealing figure here is the number of correspondents in 1963 who refused to state their affiliation with either of the regular parties but who called themselves liberals or conservatives—mainly the former."

More recently still, an article in the spring 1964 issue of the *Columbia Journalism Review* described the characteristics of foreign correspondents for American newspapers. Checking the political predispositions of these journalists, the magazine found an eight-to-one preponderance of Democrats over Republicans, with 49 per cent choosing the former designation and only 6 per cent the latter. The remaining 41 per cent called themselves "independents," and one said he was a Fabian Socialist.

These figures, it should be noted, concern the one segment of the media where there is some fairly strong conservative influence—conservative owners, nationally famous papers like the Chicago *Tribune* and *The Wall Street Journal,* etc. The mass-circulation magazines are for the most part similar in tendency to the daily press, since they draw upon essentially the same pool of talent for their employes. The difference is that there are fewer of them, and of those which engage in week-to-week political coverage only one, *U.S. News and World Report,* has displayed much sympathy toward the conservative position. In the field of network television the options are more severely constricted still.

There is nothing intrinsically sinister about this preponderance of liberal and Democratic views in the daily press and in other segments of the communications media. These are occupations toward which liberal members of our society have historically been drawn, and the typical college education which prospective journalists receive is often heavily weighted toward the liberal and Democratic position. The Democratic overloading is a reflection of long-term cultural drift among the professional intelligentsia, only now partially being corrected by the growth of the conservative intellectual community.

Whatever the reasons for it, however, the preponderance of liberal Democrats in the media presents some obvious difficulties when the subject up for discussion is the *Republican party.* What does it mean, for example, when various Democratic journalists wax so authoritatively on the "mainstream" of the GOP? What are these journalists about when they profess such a fervent interest in building a "strong" Republican party? Why do they take it upon themselves to exalt certain Republican candidates and to disparage others?

Let us grant that these are men of intelligence and noble purpose, who want to achieve what they think is right. But can we seriously accept the proposition that, as liberal Democrats, they render their political judgments on the basis of *what is good for the Republican party*? The proposition seems doubtful. It is as difficult to believe that a press corps heavily staffed with ADA-style Democrats is equipped or entitled to sermonize on the nature of the Republican "mainstream," as it would be to assume that an archly conservative Republican is equipped or entitled to hold forth on the Democratic "mainstream." It is questionable whether liberal Democrats are any more interested in building a "strong Republican Party" than, say, the Chicago *Tribune* or William F. Buckley, Jr., is interested in building a "strong Democratic Party."

Democrats who would appeal to the *Trib* or to Buckley —Frank Lausche, Richard Russell—would be, of course, precisely those Democrats who are *least* typical of their party, not most typical of it, and the same holds for the Republicans who get themselves so routinely admired by liberal journalists. We are entitled to suspect, in fact (although not to assume), an inverse ratio between the insistence of the liberal media that so-and-so is a mainstream Republican and the actual relationship of so-and-so to the majority sentiment of the GOP.

Consider, as the obvious example, the case of John Lindsay, a Republican officeholder who, as we have seen, is strenuously favored by the media. An examination of Lindsay's record discloses that he is not merely a liberal Republican, but a Republican so thoroughly liberal that he is indistinguishable on any ideological point from the most leftward of possible Democrats. Although a figure beloved among the nation's Republicans—if we are to credit *Life* and *Newsweek*—Lindsay obviously does not reciprocate. While a member of Congress, he steadfastly voted with the Democrats (amassing a party-opposition score of 60 per cent in 1964); and, as a candidate for mayor, he eagerly embraced figures from the opposition party while sedulously avoiding representatives of his own. Among his campaign vows was a promise that, if elected, he would under no circumstances use his office to advance the interests of the Republican party. A campaign flyer used in his behalf summed up Lindsay's Republicanism quite well when it stated: "For seven years he has represented New York in Congress, where he has supported the programs of Presidents John F. Kennedy and Lyndon B. Johnson."

What are we to make of the effort in the media to portray Lindsay as the knight gallant of the Republican party, and to recommend him to the GOP as the candidate it needs to salvage its political fortunes? The prevalence of all those Democrats in all those editorial offices provides, I think, an intelligible clue: The fact is that Republicans of the Lindsay stripe simply are not Republicans at all in any serious meaning of the word. According to every known test of party congruity, including his own campaign literature, Lindsay is simply a Democrat who for reasons of his own has decided to operate under the Republican label. To a greater or lesser degree, this is the secret of liberal Republican allure—the alignment of the GOP with the Democratic program.

There are occasions, indeed, where this implicit Republican loyalty to the Democratic cause becomes overt, and in this event the commentators are happier than ever. The mainstream is never flowing more certainly through the great broad channel of the Republican tradition, it seems, than when the Republican candidate in question is, in point of relevant fact, a Democrat.

We need only recall, for example, that archetypical

mainstream Republican Wendell Willkie, who not only made his mainstreaming proclivities plain by seconding the New Deal in most of its particulars but who was listed as a Democrat in *Who's Who* the very year that he was nominated as the Republican presidential candidate. And, it should be noted, Willkie called himself a "liberal Democrat" into the bargain. The Democratic columnists and commentators could hardly help concluding that here, indeed, was the man to redeem the Republican party and carry on its great traditions.

Although adherence to the Democratic label is not always explicit as in Willkie's case, there have been other examples provided us. A generation after Willkie's unsuccessful run for the presidency, the Republican party of Philadelphia nominated as its candidate for prosecutor a member of the Democratic party and a member of Americans for Democratic Action as well. During the Eisenhower administration, one of the asserted Republicans sitting in the seats of power was Emmet John Hughes, speech-writer for the President and subsequently for Governor Rockefeller. In a memoir about his experiences in the Republican administration, Hughes revealed that he had favored all Democratic presidential candidates from 1932 to 1952, and evidently was rather proud of it. Hughes now performs as a columnist for *Newsweek* magazine, where he regularly holds forth on the duties and heritage of the Republican party.

There is reason to believe, therefore, that the Democratic media like Republicans who most closely resemble Democrats—and the closer the resemblance, the greater the affection. This helps to explain the otherwise curious fact that a microscopic organization like the Ripon Society can and does get excellent coverage in the media, while authentic Republican groups like the Republican Congressional Committee are largely ignored. The Ripon Society has a small membership, can claim no constituency within the party, nominates and elects no candidates. Yet its pronouncements are given very respectful coverage, indeed, in the New York *Times* and by the TV networks.

Like Lindsay, whom it greatly admires, the Ripon Society is ideologically at one with the Democrats—or, more precisely, with the most leftward element of the Democrats. Its notion of a bold Republican initiative is a suggestion that the United States relax its opposition to United Nations membership for Red China—a stand opposed not only by the overwhelming majority of Republicans, but by most Democrats and the nation at large. On domestic matters, Ripon asserts that the nation is in fundamental agreement with Great Society programs and that Republicans should therefore not oppose them, adding: "The fact that we meet on common ground is not 'me-tooism.' It is time to put away the tired old notion that to be real Republicans we must be as different as possible from our opponents. . . ."

"Republican" thought like this usually excites the Democrats in the media. Thus it is hardly surprising that both Ripon's Red China statement and the book which contained the assertion about the necessity of halting GOP opposition to Democratic programs should be written up respectfully in the New York *Times*, even as a report about the Ripon Society itself, published by the American Conservative Union (under the name of Republican Representative John Ashbrook of Ohio), was ignored.

A continuing approximation of Republican personnel to Democratic positions is also discernible in the activities of some of the politicians to whom the Ripon Society has attached itself. A write-up of Senator Charles Percy of Illinois and some of the young men working for him tells us that many of the latter are in effect Democrats and quotes one of them as saying: "If the Democratic Party still had a Kennedy, I suppose a lot of us would be calling ourselves Democrats." This young "Republican" and his immediate superior, the story tells us, are both members of the Ripon Society.

Perhaps the boldest statement of this theme has been advanced by newspaper columnist Carl Rowan, commenting on the 1966 Senate campaign of Edward Brooke of Massachusetts. Rowan, who served in high appointive capacities with the Democratic Kennedy and Johnson administrations (and therefore presumably knowledgeable in such matters), reported that leftward forces in Massachusetts "regard Brooke as one of their own—infiltrating the enemy camp—and making the enemy like it. *They regard the Massachusetts Senate race as a contest to see whether an ideological Democrat can go all the way to the top in a Republican masquerade.*" It would be impossible, it seems, to state the matter more clearly than that. (The research chairman for Brooke's campaign committee turned out to be the president of the Ripon Society.)

The clearest indication that the mainstream accolade is conferred in proportion to Democratic rather than Republican characteristics is the liberal Republican performance in Congress. "Party unity" scores as compiled by *Congressional Quarterly* reveal the ideological assimilation of the liberal GOP into the Democratic program and the corresponding estrangement of these Republicans from the prevailing sentiment of their own party. In both houses of Congress, and without exception, the lowest "party unity" and highest "party opposition" scores have been achieved by precisely those Republicans who are advertised as being in the mainstream.

Thus, the Senate Republicans with the highest percentage of votes in opposition to the majority of their colleagues (with 1966 ACA ratings) are:

Name	*State*	*Opposition Score*	*ACA Rating*
Javits	New York	64	19
Case	New Jersey	61	26
Smith	Maine	49	41
Griffin	Michigan	42	67

Name	*State*	*Opposition Score*	ACA *Rating*
Aiken	Vermont	41	40
Fong	Hawaii	37	43

Conversely, the best records for party support among Senate Republicans were established by conservatives. The research organization gives these percentages for votes cast in support of the stance taken by the majority of Republicans during the 1965–66 session:

Name	*State*	*Support Score*	ACA *Rating*
Williams	Delaware	91	93
Fannin	Arizona	88	88
Hickenlooper	Iowa	87	97
Mundt	South Dakota	86	86
Hruska	Nebraska	85	100
Cotton	New Hampshire	85	96

Exactly the same relationship holds true in the House. There the worst records of party support were held by the following congressmen, all liberal Republicans:

Name	*State*	*Opposition Score*	ACA *Rating*
Tupper	Maine	68	11
Reid	New York	63	35
Kupferman	New York	58	38
Conte	Massachusetts	49	43
Schweiker	Pennsylvania	44	59
Horton	New York	43	59

On the other hand, the best records of party support were uniformly held by conservative congressmen. The CQ ratings for 1965–1966 give these figures for votes in favor of the GOP majority position:

Name	*State*	*Support Score*	ACA *Rating*
Buchanan	Alabama	96	100
Reid	Illinois	94	96

Name	*State*	*Support Score*	*ACA Rating*
Hutchinson	Michigan	94	88
Langen	Minnesota	94	89
Latta	Ohio	94	92
Poff	Virginia	94	100
Duncan	Tennessee	93	96
Jonas	North Carolina	91	89
Chamberlain	Michigan	90	77
Dole	Kansas	90	93

What is true on the broad question of all party-line votes is equally true in terms of the key roll calls which decide whether or not a piece of crucial legislation is passed or defeated. The record—as spelled out in an American Conservative Union (ACU) document called "The DMV Report"—makes it clear that the liberal Republicans have repeatedly bailed out on their party when their votes meant the difference between victory and defeat.

The DMV stands for Democratic Margin of Victory, an item which, as the report documents, has been provided again and again by a handful of liberal Republicans. About two dozen of these GOP congressmen have made it possible for the New Frontier and the Great Society to win a long series of legislative victories. Had these representatives remained faithful to their party, the Democrats would have sustained an equally impressive series of defeats.

Among the issues on which the DMV was thus provided were the 1961 packing of the House Rules Committee, Area Redevelopment legislation, raising the Federal debt limit to $300 billion, purchase of U.N. bonds, "war on poverty" funds, various foreign-aid bills, "demonstration cities," and other programs of Federal intervention in the domestic economy. In each of twenty-four such selected votes, the bulk of the Republican membership in the House voted against the liberal program, while a minority GOP element averaging between twenty and thirty members repeatedly defected.

The DMV Report yields much the same pattern as do the *CQ* figures. The report shows that some two dozen Republicans, from 1961 through 1967, sided with the Democrats on eight or more critical occasions. The list of these DMV voters, and their 1966 ACA ratings, is as follows:

Name	*State*	*Votes with Democrats*	*ACA Rating*
Halpern	New York	22	33
Dwyer	New Jersey	18	61
Reid	New York	16	35
Corbett	Pennsylvania	15	63
Cahill	New Jersey	15	57
Morse	Massachusetts	15	48
Mathias	Maryland	15	50
Horton	New York	15	59
Conte	Massachusetts	14	43
Fulton	Pennsylvania	13	59
Stafford	Vermont	10	59
Frelinghuysen	New Jersey	10	48
Schweiker	Pennsylvania	10	59
McDade	Pennsylvania	10	52
Pirnie	New York	10	60
Fino	New York	9	57
Maillard	California	9	50
Widnall	New Jersey	9	63
Bates	Massachusetts	9	65
Ayres	Ohio	9	68
Saylor	Pennsylvania	9	67
O'Konski	Wisconsin	8	67
Keith	Massachusetts	8	67
Mosher	Ohio	8	72

On the other hand, the DMV analysis found there were forty House Republicans who, during this same period, had cast no votes at all with the Democrats on crucial roll calls.* All of these congressmen, without exception, had 1966 ACA ratings above 70 per cent. The lowest rating was 75 per cent, and only three had ratings under 80. No less than 29 had ACA ratings above 85 per cent, and 19 scored between 90 and 100 per cent. The congressmen who do *not* provide the Democratic opposition with votes on crucial roll calls are, uniformly, conservatives.

In both cases—the *Congressional Quarterly* analysis for "party support" in general, and the ACU analysis of party regularity on key selected roll calls—the statistical correlation is virtually complete: Conservatism equals fidelity to the Republican party, and the greater the conservatism the higher the fidelity; Liberalism equals flirtation with the Democrats, and the greater the liberalism the more frequent the indiscretion.

Indeed, so outright is the demonstration that it becomes a kind of tautology: It is apparent that the Republican-party stance in Congress is, time after time, a conservative stance, with the majority of the GOP taking an antiliberal position on critical issues. Votes in favor of that position therefore yield, simultaneously, a high conservative rating and a high party support rating, while votes against it achieve the opposite results. A congressman who stands consistently with the majority of his colleagues will have a high ACA rating, the congressman who opposes his colleagues will have a low ACA rating.

Finally, the liberal Republicans have established a not-

* These Republicans were: Adair, Ind.; Anderson, Ill.; Ashbrook, Ohio; Battin, Montana; Belcher, Okla.; Berry, S.D.; Bow, Ohio; Brock, Tenn.; Brotzmann, Colo.; Buchanan, Ala.; Cederberg, Mich.; Clancy, Ohio; Clawson; Calif.; Collier, Ill.; Cramer, Fla.; Derwinski, Ill.; Devine, Ohio; Dickinson, Ala.; Dole, Kansas; Edwards, Ala.; Goodling, Penna.; Gross, Iowa; Gurney, Fla.; Hall, Mo.; Hutchinson, Mich.; Johnson, Penna.; Kyl, Iowa; Laird, Wis.; Langen, Minn.; Latta, Ohio; Martin, Neb.; McEwen, N.Y.; Mize, Kans.; Nelson, Minn.; Reid, Ill.; Roudebush, Ind.; Schadeberg, Wis.; Skubitz, Kans.; Talcott, Calif.; Thomson, Wis.; Watkins, Penna.; and Watson, S.C.

able record of refusing to support the leadership and candidates of their party. The Ripon Society and members of the so-called Wednesday Club in the House of Representatives (formerly headed by Lindsay) have conducted a long guerrilla campaign against the Republican congressional leadership, in keeping with the vote patterns established in the CQ and ACU tables. According to press reports in early 1967, the Wednesdayers were exhorted to explicit rebellion at a private meeting addressed by Senator Hugh Scott. A congressman in attendance was quoted by the Washington press corps as saying, "I never heard a more open invitation to revolt."

In the matter of failing to support Republican candidates, as we have seen, the liberal record is distinguished. Nor has this sort of performance been limited to the Goldwater campaign. In October 1966, Governor Romney refused to endorse the gubernatorial candidacy of Ronald Reagan, and instead, according to one press account, "slapped at Reagan's policy on civil rights." California's Senator Thomas Kuchel, another highly acclaimed mainstreamer, refused to back the statewide Republican ticket with respect to no less than four different candidates—Nixon in 1962, Goldwater and Murphy in 1964, and Reagan in 1966.

The emerging pattern, I think, is clear. The media presentation has given us the Republican situation almost exactly backwards. We are told that John Lindsay is a joy and comfort to the nation's Republicans, and find he has in fact abandoned the Republican party at every conceivable opportunity; we are told that Thomas Kuchel is a model of enlightened Republicanism, and find he has consistently failed to support his party; we are told that Jacob Javits is a "Trustee for Tomorrow" highly deserving of a place on the national Republican ticket (*Time*, June 24, 1966), and discover that he has the worst record of party support of any Republican now in Congress

(Representative Tupper, his only superior in this respect, having retired).

Conversely, the conservative Republicans who have down the years faithfully supported the party even when they did not get their way in national conventions, who have the highest party support records, and whose views clearly reflect the broad majority of Republican sentiment—these Republicans are portrayed as misfits, extremists, or venal politicians indifferent to the fate of their party. Or, what is even more usual, simply allowed to go their way in silence, while another cover story is cranked up proclaiming the virtues of Lindsay or Javits. We are obviously through the looking glass; the liberal mavericks get depicted as inhabitants of the mainstream, the party regulars as eccentrics.

The remaining question is: Why? What motivates this effort to magnify Republicans who are most distant from their own party and most closely attuned to the Democrats? The argument that it takes a Kuchel or a Javits to strengthen the two-party system is singularly unconvincing. It is difficult to see how, *e.g.*, Kuchel's refusal to back four different Republican candidates in his state "strengthened" anyone but the Democrats. Nor can it be said that he was simply dissociating himself from losing candidates, since two of the men he refused to back—Murphy and Reagan—scored stunning victories.

It becomes apparent that the argument about conservative Republicans being unable to win is a diversion. As in the case of the South, the liberal Republicans are equally as hostile to conservative Republicans who *win* as they are to those who lose—indeed, a good deal more so. The objection is, purely and simply, to conservative Republicans as such; the principal concern is not to shore up the two-party system, but to insure that, whatever the relative condition of the two parties, both are committed to liberalism.

What is in effect demanded is a *one-party* system, in which the nation's politics are ruled by a single opinion, divided for dumb-show purposes of quadrennial entertainment into "Democratic" and "Republican" factions, rather like the "Red" and "Blue" contingents of an army on maneuvers. The two contingents would compete for power and the gauds of office, and bemuse the public with their excitingly diverse claims to administrative competence, but would otherwise be indistinguishable.

The value of this approach in the eyes of doctrinaire liberals is self-evident. If the Republican party becomes a consortium of Javitses and Kuchels, all ideological debate will be at an end. The liberal view will be fully in charge, and the alternative position will be foreclosed from presenting its opinions on the national proscenium. Under such an arrangement, the sachems of the ADA could sleep peacefully in their beds; whoever happened to win the elections, they could not lose.

While achievement of this objective would put the liberals in a position of future strength, the effort to get there suggests a present weakness. If liberalism is as overwhelmingly popular as we are led to believe, what is the objection to having a little conservative dissent? Why is it demanded that the liberal position control not one party but both? What is the urgent necessity of having the liberal view advanced by both protagonists in our political debate, conservatism by neither?

This fear of alternative opinion suggests that the liberal theoreticians are not so confident of their position as they would have us believe. In the evidence of a changing American mood, the growing anxiety of many of the liberal intellectuals, the restiveness of the young, we glimpse the sources of their anxiety. The professed object is to save the Republican party by injecting it with liberalism; the real object is to save liberalism by injecting it with the Republican party.

16:: DECLINE AND FALL

Sometime in late 1965 or early 1966—he does not specify which—political columnist David Broder of the Washington *Post* (then of The New York *Times*) experienced an illumination. It was apparently one of those moments when subjects previously confused fall into place, random phenomena organize themselves into patterns of order, and the sum of human knowledge is correspondingly expanded.

Broder had been puzzled, it seems, by the battle of conservative and liberal Republicans which was so prominent a feature of the 1964 election year and had continued sporadically in the intervening months. The *eclaircissement* was the realization that the conservatism-liberalism thing was not the real point at all: The real struggle was between Republicans who wanted to win, "to expand the party's base," and those who did *not* want to win, who were content to be a minority party forever.

Broder acknowledged that not all Republicans could be

fitted into these categories; but, by and large, he thought, this approach cleared things up pretty well. Republicans like John Lindsay, William Scranton, Nelson Rockefeller, and George Romney fit perfectly into the mold of "responsibles," men who are "trying to expand the party's base to the point where it can again compete effectively for the presidency . . . who want to see the Republican Party again exercise responsibility for the affairs of cities, states, and nation. . . ."

On the other hand, he stated, people like Everett Dirksen, Karl Mundt, Wallace Bennett, Frank Carlson, and James Utt, among others, are "influentials," satisfied to see their party lose perpetually so long as they can nuzzle up to interest groups willing to trade cash for trifling favors. People of this sort, Broder said, "have long since resigned themselves to a minority role—and do not really desire to have it change . . . [they are] quite content to market [the party's] influence to its financial clients."

So, at last we have the answer concerning the senators and congressmen who backed Taft and Goldwater. They not only are unable to win, they in fact *do not want* to win. Such was the nature of David Broder's illumination, as it is recorded for us in the April 1966 issue of *The Atlantic.*

All of which, in light of the matter previously reviewed, is roughly comparable to Galileo's having gazed at the heavens and suddenly concluded that, after all, the Ptolemaic astronomy was absolutely right, only more so. Broder's flash of insight is in fact a restatement, in more insulting terms than are usual in such matters, of the reigning theory: That liberal Republicans can win and conservatives cannot. And although he offers it as new and exciting doctrine, as though the idea of steering the GOP leftward is new and relatively untried, it is very ancient stuff indeed.

Far from being a bright untested inspiration, the course

suggested by Broder and his responsibles has been attempted repeatedly by the Republican party across a span of decades, with thoroughly lugubrious results. So far as Republican fortunes are concerned, it has been tried, and found wanton. It is the conservative approach, not the liberal one, which is relatively new.

Over a twenty-year span of American political history, the Eastern GOP has had numerous opportunities to prove its strategy could broaden the party's base of popular support, achieve majorities in Congress, and secure a majority in the Electoral College. The outcome was a long series of losses, decimation of the Republican ranks in Congress, and a drastic shrinkage of the popular base from near-parity with the Democrats to a quarter of the electorate.

If we consider the eight presidential elections between 1936 and 1964 in terms of candidates and strategies alike, the heavy preponderance of the liberal approach becomes apparent. In terms of personalities, the GOP has run six times with a "liberal" candidate (Landon, Willkie, Dewey twice, Eisenhower twice), once with a candidate of mixed tendencies acceptable to conservatives (Nixon), and once with an explicit conservative (Goldwater). In terms of strategy, the GOP has also run six times under the liberal banner—that is, in terms of the New York approach attempting to unite the Midwest and the liberal East (Willkie, Dewey twice, Eisenhower twice, Nixon), once with no discernible strategy at all (Landon), and once in explicit repudiation of the New York analysis (Goldwater).

Taken all in all, these eight elections show the GOP making seven attempts at the presidency in terms of liberal personalities and/or strategies, once in terms of a conservative personality *and* conservative strategy. (The 1960 Nixon race is obviously a borderline instance, but in strategic terms, as we shall note presently, it is classifiable with the Willkie, Dewey, and Eisenhower efforts.) Under the liberal banner, the party managed to lose four presidential elections in a row, picked up two wins in the Eisenhower races of 1952 and 1956, then reverted to the loss column with Nixon's defeat in 1960.

If we grant provisionally that Eisenhower's victories were attributable to the effectiveness of the New York strategy (a somewhat doubtful point), we are left with these conclusions: (1) The liberals, in presidential politics, have batted two for seven—not a very impressive performance for those who claim to hold the patent on presidential victories; (2) the liberals managed to lose four elections in a row before they came up with their first win—also not a very impressive record. Now the people who produced these results and dominated GOP presidential politics for twenty-four years say the conservatives, with their one try out of eight, have been excessively influential; the people who managed to lose four straight presidential elections before garnering their first win say the conservatives who have had a single chance should ever after be foreclosed from having another opportunity.

The presidency is not, of course, the only thing at stake in this debate. There is also the question of what liberal or conservative stewardship implies for party strength in general, in terms of public esteem, representatives in Congress, state offices. If we examine the results of liberal hegemony in this respect, we find that the record is very dismal indeed, hardly suggesting that liberalism can "expand the party's base." Consider the long-term findings of Dr. Gallup concerning the relative strength of the two parties in terms of public sentiment:

	Republican	*Democrat*	*Independent*
1940	38%	42%	20%
1950	33%	45%	22%
1960	30%	47%	23%
1964	25%	53%	22%

Thus the Republican party, which as an ideological force stood roughly even with the Democrats in 1940, had dwindled away to a feeble homunculus by the time the conservatives got their chance at the presidency. Equally striking is the fact that the decline continued at the same general rate when the liberal Republicans actually had control of the White House with its immense patronage and publicity resources—when they had secured the very goal to which everything else had been made subordinate.

In terms of congressional representation, the Republican record during this span was even worse. The Eisenhower years, when the moderate wing of the party should have been hard at work on base expansion, saw the congressional strength of the party sink increasingly lower at every by-election. In 1950, the Republican party gained 49 per cent of the vote for congressional seats. In 1954, this dropped to 47 per cent. In 1958, it plunged to a record off-year low of 43 per cent. The party which elected 47 senators and 199 representatives in 1950 found itself reduced, in the last Eisenhower Congress, to 35 senators and 154 representatives.

As Theodore White observes: "Divorced from the personal carrying power of his great name, in each measurable off-year congressional election under his administration the Republican Party lost ground. . . . With the Democratic triumph in the election of 1958, the fortunes of the Republican Party, as a party, had sunk to their lowest ebb since the zenith of the New Deal in 1936." To make the situation even more unpromising, the liberal Republicans had, and have, no program for righting this state of affairs, other than denouncing the notion of electing Republican congressmen in the South.

Congressional and other losses suffered by the GOP in the 1964 election are alleged as final proof that conservative Republicanism "can't win." It is therefore interesting to compare the outcome of the Goldwater race with the last election conducted explicitly under the sign of Eisenhower. In 1958, the Republican party sustained a net loss of 48 House seats compared to 38 in 1964. The party in 1958 lost a net total of 13 Senate seats—compared to two in 1964. In gubernatorial races, the 1958 GOP suffered a net loss of 5, winding up with control of 14 statehouses. In 1964, the party actually made a net gain of one governorship. In 1958, the party lost 686 state legislative seats; in 1964, it lost 541. In fine, the performance was uniformly worse in 1958 than it was in 1964.

The liberal GOP has managed to foment electoral disasters in presidential years as well. In 1948, when Dewey ran his New York strategy presidential campaign in a race he was supposed to win hands down, the GOP lost a staggering 75 seats in the House of Representatives, 9 seats in the Senate, and seven governorships—in each case, a far higher total of losses than those sustained in 1964.

It is true that in 1948 and 1958 alike the party began from a higher base than it did in 1964, both in terms of general public support and in terms of offices held. But it is also true that the lower base from which Goldwater had to operate in terms of public support and congressional representation was with marginal exceptions a legacy confected for him by his predecessors. The essential point is that, given the materials and the circumstances of the moment, the 1964 election was in fact a *lesser* calamity, not a greater one, than either 1948 or 1958.

It is obvious, of course, that there is neither comfort nor instruction for the GOP in any of these figures considered in isolation; the party is manifestly not going to achieve a great deal simply by trading recriminations about previous disasters. But when a misreading of history is made the premise for a long train of political analysis, the record must be corrected. The fact is that the charges hurled at the head of Goldwater, and the implication that modern Republicans alone know how to build the national party and win elections, simply aren't true. Far from being able to "win," the liberal Republicans hold championship marks for engineering GOP defeats.

There is one further point which, in this context, requires consideration: The question of what, if anything, the GOP will have "won" if it does manage to gain office through the modern Republican formula. As noted, modern Republicans in office tend to behave very much like Democrats. In many cases, the differences are invisible to the naked eye—*e.g.*, the record of Senator Javits in Congress, the performance of John Lindsay as Mayor of New York. The same was true, with some occasional distinctions, for the eight-year span during which the Dewey-Lodge-Brownell wing of the party had control of the White House.

The Eisenhower tenure in Washington served to make clear the central fallacy of the liberal Republican formula. Having accepted the Democrats' approach to public problems, the liberal GOP has no ideology; and having no ideology, it can have no major impact on the fundamental direction of the nation's politics. It is by definition a satellite of the Democratic party, a political *Doppelgänger* that moves only with the impulse of its original. Although Eisenhower has shown himself personally congenial to the conservative position since departing the White House, his tenure there saw Republican national policy on most domestic issues firmly in control of the Deweyites. The net result, with minor exceptions, was to ratify the major elements of the Democratic program. Lubell observes that "to solidify itself permanently in American life the New Deal needed at least one Republican victory" which would "endorse much of the New Deal through the simple device of leaving things untouched." That, for the most part, is what the Eisenhower administration did.

One result of this, as noted, was to alienate from the party the new majority which had temporarily surfaced in 1952: The taxpayers and homeowners who looked to the Republicans for relief, and who were rudely disappointed as augmented Federal spending and taxes shifted the costs of government more heavily on them than before. In consequence, the GOP emerged from the White House with little to show for its eight-year occupancy: A party base more shrunken than ever, repeated defeats in the battle for Congress, and no strategy for reversing things.

Liberal Republican vulnerabilities have emerged with notable clarity in three different presidential races which the GOP had every reasonable expectation of winning—1940, 1948, and 1960—but which, in pursuit of the New York strategy, it contrived to lose. Republican prospects in 1940 were aided by two powerful factors: Roosevelt's unprecedented bid for a third term, and growing public uneasiness over the possibility that the United States would become enmeshed in the European war. When Willkie was nominated at Philadelphia, all the indicia showed Republican chances to be excellent. A Gallup Poll taken in July gave Willkie 47 per cent of the vote to 53 per cent for FDR. On August 3, Gallup showed Willkie with enough strength to capture 304 electoral votes, sufficient to be elected.

In keeping with the New York strategy, however, Willkie immediately began stressing his own liberalism. In his kickoff speech in Elwood, Indiana, he declared that "party lines are down! . . . Nothing could make that clearer than the nomination by the Republicans of a liberal Democrat who changed his party affiliation because he found democracy in the Republican Party and not in the New Deal." He subsequently got off a good deal of other commentary in similar vein, agreed with Roosevelt on virtually all foreign-policy questions, and seconded the motion on most domestic policies as well. We are told that Roosevelt viewed Willkie's nomination as a godsend for the country "because it eliminated the isolationist issue from the campaign and reassured the world of the continuity of American foreign policy."

What the Willkie nomination mostly assured the world of, however, was the continuity of Roosevelt. By failing to develop any of the major issues against Roosevelt and by ignoring the party regulars at every possible turn, Willkie managed to lose an election Republicans had good reason to think they could win. The Gallup Poll electoral vote, which had stood at 304 in August, had dropped precipitously to 32 by October 1. In the actual election, Willkie got 82 electoral votes. He failed to carry New York, the prize toward which his strategy was angled, and simultaneously lost Ohio, Illinois, Wisconsin, and all of the Rocky Mountain states except Colorado.

In 1944, with the war in progress and Roosevelt campaigning as commander in chief, it was unreasonable to suppose Republican candidate Dewey could win the presidency, and win he did not. Even though the 1944 race was run on liberal Republican premises, it is unfair to suggest this as a significant test of what that strategy can or cannot achieve. A far better test, on every conceivable count, was the election of 1948.

Dewey went into the 1948 election with much in his favor. He faced, not the invincible Roosevelt, but the highly vincible (or so it seemed) Harry Truman. The Democrats had been in office for four long and troublesome terms. Truman was not a popular President, the Democratic party was split three ways, the country was ripe for a change. All the pre-election polls showed Dewey far out in front. But, accepting the liberal analysis in almost every particular, he contrived to blow it.

Dewey's 1948 run was a textbook study in liberal Republican strategy. Its ideological bias was heavily canted toward liberalism, a fact Dewey underlined by virtually disowning the Republican party in Congress and steering particularly clear of archrival Robert Taft. Dewey assumed that the Midwestern heartland of the party was secure, and that his job was to corral the liberal votes of the East. He also assumed the key to Republican success was in the cities—another theorem presently favored by the liberal GOP.

What happened? Dewey accomplished the major strategic objectives he thought were necessary to his election. He carried supposedly decisive New York State, as had Willkie before him, triumphed in Pennsylvania and New Jersey, ran strongly in the major metropolitan centers. Yet he lost the election because he failed to carry the Republican base he thought he could take for granted. It was the crowning irony of the New York big-city strategy that the 1948 election was lost through defection of the Midwestern farm vote. Dewey lost the key Midwestern states of Ohio, Illinois, Iowa, and Wisconsin by an aggregate of less than 100,000 votes, and thereby lost the election.

Why Dewey faltered in the Midwest was clearly indicated by an episode in the state of Iowa, which the liberal GOP strategists thought was safely in Dewey's corner. Malcolm Moos tells us that when Truman and Dewey were invited to address the National Plowing Contest in Dexter, Iowa, Truman accepted but Dewey declined, "largely on the advice of his managers, who pointed out that Iowa had gone Democratic only three times since 1872. . . . Moreover, it was argued, the polls showed Dewey leading with 55 per cent in Iowa against 39 per cent for Truman." So Truman had the National Plowing Contest all to himself, using the occasion to charge that the Republicans had "stuck a pitchfork" in the back of the farmer. Dewey lost the state by 28,000 votes.

The story was similar in traditionally Republican Ohio, which Dewey lost by 7,000 votes. Statistical analysis showed that the Republican vote in Ohio cities, according to the urban-appeal formula, was up, but that it was drastically down in the rural areas, with the result that this Republican bastion was overrun. Dewey also considered Ohio in the bag, and did not campaign there. Whether his strategy of avoiding Taft was wise may be gathered from the fact that Taft ran for re-election in Ohio two years after Dewey's defeat and won by more than 430,000 votes.

The principal effect of Dewey's strategy was to weaken the party in its Midwestern heartland. As one authority quoted by Moos puts it, "the agrarian wing of the GOP, particularly in the North Central states, was relatively weaker in 1948 than four years earlier," while "the industrial wing, particularly in the Northeast, was relatively stronger." In other words, the votes picked up in the East and the cities were not additional votes, but tradeouts. The Dewey strategy made the mistake of seeking new strength that was not conformable to the existing base. The net result was that in 1948 Dewey's vote was actually lower than it had been four years previously.

The Eisenhower elections of 1952 and 1956 tell us little about the merits of the New York strategy as opposed to an alternative approach. If winning the presidency *per se* is the party's only consideration, then the GOP is obviously well advised to find another Eisenhower, since in both his campaigns he won just about everything that wasn't nailed down. The irrelevance of conventional political strategy to the Eisenhower wins may be noted by scanning a map of the states he carried—everything from the Pacific Coast to the Great Lakes, conservative Texas and liberal New York, Indiana and New Jersey, Oregon and Florida. The people apparently voted for a likable father figure whom they felt they could trust, irrespective of ideological inclinations. By the sheer volume of success, Eisenhower's campaigns precluded firm lessons about one kind of political strategy as opposed to another; total victory makes either-or decisions about particular ingredients difficult.

The Nixon campaign of 1960 provided an opportunity for examining the New York strategy in the light of more recent developments, considered on its own merits and devoid of Eisenhower's charismatic benevolence. Like Willkie and Dewey before him, Nixon conducted an orthodox New York oriented campaign, and suffered similar disappointment. Those who fault Nixon with running a bad race do him an injustice. Given the assumptions under which he was operating, it is hard to see how he could have done much better. Beginning with the notion that he must carry the Republican heartland and super-add New York and other Eastern power centers, Nixon very nearly pulled it off. The TV debates, in which he appeared to agree with Kennedy, were obviously a necessary part of his strategy. That they hurt rather than helped him is testimony, not to Nixon's ineptitude, but to the fact that the strategy was mistaken.*

Unlike Willkie and Dewey, Nixon ran well in the Middle West, a result probably aided by Kennedy's own strong Eastern-liberal image. Nixon in addition squeaked out a victory in his native California and made a valiant bid for the big cities of the East. But the contrasts with Kennedy which allowed Nixon to carry the Midwest were precisely the factors which militated against his strategy in the East. For slightly different reasons, Nixon failed as Willkie and Dewey before him failed: He could not wedge the liberal East and the conservative Midwest into a single phalanx.

Nixon's efforts to make himself palatable to the liberal East were largely wasted: The meeting with Rockefeller to liberalize the Republican platform, selecting Lodge as his running mate, agreeing with Kennedy in the televised debates. All of this was mandated by the New York strategy, but none of it worked. Nixon could not out-liberal Kennedy, and in consequence lost New York, Pennsylvania, and New Jersey, and was of course easily repulsed in Kennedy's own Massachusetts.

The principal irony of Nixon's campaign was that he could very probably have won every state he did win without all the effort to project a "new Nixon," and that had

* According to a Gallup Poll survey following the first debate, 43 per cent of those questioned thought Kennedy had done the better job, as opposed to 29 per cent who thought Nixon's performance superior.

the liberalizing effort not occurred he might have picked up the votes he needed to become President. On the morning after the 1960 election, one major flaw in his performance should have been obvious even to his warmest supporters. He had grossly neglected a major section of the country which—without endangering the Midwestern base he carried with such success—could have supplied his margin of victory. The South, which had no central role in the Nixon campaign, stayed mostly with the Democrats. Texas, which had twice gone for Eisenhower, went by a narrow margin for Kennedy-Johnson (one instance in which the choice of a vice-presidential candidate was unquestionably helpful to the national ticket). Florida and Tennessee did go for Nixon, but the remainder of the South, with the exception of unpledged electors in Mississippi and Alabama, was Kennedy's. Had Nixon carried these states he would have been elected President. Yet the whole of his campaign strategy, angling for the New York votes he did not get, was of the sort to insure he did not carry them.

The net result of the evidence before us is that, in the absence of a transpartisan folk hero, ordinary Republican mortals are incapable of mixing the oil and water of Midwestern and Eastern politics. Neither Willkie nor Dewey nor Nixon, over a span of twenty years and four different elections, was able to mate the conservative Midwest with the liberal East. What goes over in Dubuque does not always go over, after all, in Spanish Harlem—and if one cants his philosophy far enough left to get the latter, he is likely to lose the former, and vice versa.

It was this history of frustration which the Goldwater strategists surveyed in 1964 as they set about the quadrennial search for electoral votes to unite with the Republican heartland. They believed that the logical course was not to unite like with unlike, but to match the conservative Midwest with the conservative South and West. As the story has it, they failed, and their strategy failed with them. But the end of that story has yet to be written.

17:: THE POWER OF NEGATIVE THINKING

On June 30, 1950, a smallish group of liberal Republicans foregathered in the city of Philadelphia to found "a new political era." Calling themselves "The Republican Advance," the fifty or so conferees put their names to a statement on various social and political issues, urging the GOP to embark on a bright new liberal course.

The principal ideological paragraph of this manifesto asserted that "the real issue against the Democrats does not lie with the goals. . . . The real issue . . . lies with the means of achieving these goals." Which meant, as a spokesman for the group explained it: "The Republicans have failed to sell themselves by attacking the product of the Democrats. They have not presented satisfactory alternatives to the Democratic projects they have attacked."

This was, it appears, a historic meeting. For the text it adopted has since become a kind of hornbook of alleged Republican sagacity—not only among GOP liberals but among some conservatives as well. It has become difficult in recent months to hear a Republican speaker of any stripe hold forth on party destiny without encountering something like: "We cannot afford to be negative. The Republican Party must project a positive image. Instead of opposing Democratic programs, we must come up with constructive alternatives of our own."

In essence, this argument is a reworking and recapitulation of inchoate liberal Republican ideas that have been bouncing around for years. But in this particular form, tricked out as constructiveness or problem-solving, the liberal GOP approach has made greater theoretical progress than in any of its other incarnations. Through the multiple confusions it is capable of generating, it has seduced many essentially conservative Republicans and has popped up from time to time in the pronouncements of Republican leaders in Congress.

This is, for Republicans, an unfortunate development. To date there is no evidence that the constructive approach has done the party any good, and a great deal of evidence that it has worked the party harm. If constructiveness is pushed much further and becomes established deeply enough in the thinking of enough Republicans, it could easily cancel the gains the GOP stands to inherit from the suburban revolution, the shift of American population, and the growth of popular resentments against the burgeoning costs of the welfare state.

The fallacy of the constructive view may be suggested by pushing it to its preordained conclusion. The logical extension of the argument is that when a bank robbery is under way, it is negative for the police to interfere and bring the proceedings to a halt. To protect their positive image, the police should have a constructive alternative ready—perhaps siphoning off the money through embezzlement, hitting three little banks instead of one big one, or maybe knocking over a series of gas stations.

Otherwise, the police are simply saying "no" without suggesting how the particular bank job in question ought to be done. The point, of course, is that the bank job shouldn't be done at all, because it is wrong, period. The alternative is the peaceful state of affairs that exists in the absence of it.

Precisely the same holds true for the myriad schemes proposed each year for ravishing the public treasury, wooing votes with the taxpayer's money, and transmuting America into a collectivist society. There is nothing constructive about offering a laundered version of this activity as an alternative to a more blatant version of it. The proper course for those who believe such things are wrong is to oppose them, not to invent some half-wrong to put in their place.

Almost as notable as the ethical confusions of the constructive argument are the verbal confusions. Determination of who is against or for something is, after all, a purely subjective matter. Every political program is both "for" some things and "against" others. The important question is: What is it for, and what is it against?

The particular danger of the constructive argument is that it passes over this very question; it demands that the Republican party omit substantive evaluation of issues and simply determine it is going to be "for" whatever the Democrats happen to be "for." It demands that the GOP abandon its own analytical framework and accept that of the opposition.

What the Republican party should in fact be for is clear enough on the record: It is for the American Constitution, limited government, maximum individual freedom, the right to own and dispose of property, to earn good wages in the free market and to enjoy the fruits of one's labor, to be secure in home and person against the depredations of criminals, to have the best possible defense against foreign enemies that ingenuity can devise and treasure can sustain, and so forth.

These are the hallmark principles of the Republican party. Anyone who is for them is, *per contra,* "against" big government, collectivism, rampageous inflation, high taxes, price and wage controls, wasted revenues, destruction of property rights, the sentimentalizing of hoodlums, retreat and conciliation before the onslaught of international communism.

It is by being for the first set of objectives and against the latter, moreover, that the Republican party can best realize its hopes of political success. According to the poll results, all of these issues are a source of increasing anxiety to the electorate and, if properly crystallized, could sunder the Democratic coalition. In attempting to surface such issues, however, the GOP confronts a major difficulty: defining the grounds of controversy. The Democrats, for obvious reasons, don't want to discuss rising taxes, governmental extravagance leading to inflation, the encroachments of bureaucracy. Above all, they do not want to discuss the broad question of *who pays.* They prefer to talk about *who gets.* The self-conceived beneficiaries of these myriad programs, after all, form the core of Democratic strength; the self-conceived victims form the core of Democratic opposition. So long as the debate can be confined to the question of *getting* rather than *paying,* the Democrats will be in excellent shape.

The fatal weakness of the constructive approach is that it tends to keep the debate on precisely these grounds—the grounds most favorable to the Democrats. It relinquishes the philosophical initiative. "Constructiveness" begins by letting the Democrats define what the "problems" in our society happen to be—poverty, or medical care, or urban congestion—effectively muting the Republican contention that the real problems are the various evils associated with leviathan government, *i.e.,* with the Democrats themselves. It thus confirms the belief, so hostile to Republican fortunes, that the essential difficulties in our society consist of deficiencies or lacunae in the performance of the market economy, rather than of taxes, inflation, and governmental compulsion.

Constructiveness thus manages to put the psychological emphasis in just the wrong places, encouraging thought patterns and emotional responses that play to Democratic strength and Republican weakness. By addressing the voters in their role as present or prospective beneficiaries of government rather than as victims of it, as subsidy-seekers rather than taxpayers, it helps focus attention on *who gets* rather than *who pays*.

In strategic terms, the constructive approach attempts to bid for the natural Democratic constituency while forsaking the natural Republican constituency. It in effect says welfare-minded citizens are entitled to two national political parties devoted to their aspirations, while the taxpayer, homeowner, pensioner, and suburbanite are entitled to none. Both Democrats and Republicans will go after the voters who make up the declining liberal coalition, and ignore the voters who make up the rising conservative coalition.

Constructiveness thus confounds, at a single stroke, the necessary elements of a successful GOP strategy, stressing all the things congenial to Democratic hopes, neglecting all the things congenial to its own. The virtues of this development from the Democratic point of view are obvious. What it can do for the Republican party is, however, more difficult to discern. The track record indicates that whenever the Republican party has acted on these premises it has maneuvered itself into heavy trouble.

In the 89th Congress, for example, Republicans were confronted by a renewed Democratic drive for the enactment of Medicare. Despite the demonstrated fact that such a program was not needed, that it would be highly expensive, and that it would intrude more government control into private sectors of American life, the GOP decided not to take a "negative" approach. Instead, the party came up with a constructive alternative in the form of its own Medicare program.

The result of this effort was that the Democrats freely borrowed those features of the Republican proposal which suited their taste, grafted them to their own design (thereby increasing the total cost of the program), and enacted the whole thing. Medicare was on the books, the tax burden was augmented, another government program came into being, the medical profession was marched several steps closer to regimentation, and the GOP was left high and dry without an issue.

Indeed, since the Medicare program contained several Republican-sponsored features (in addition to, rather than in place of, the Democratic ones), various Republicans were in fact partially responsible for it. And since no effective campaign of opposition had been mounted, there was not even an "I told you so" to present to the voters when the program began—as in the now-notorious "Medicaid" department—to malfunction. The Democrats reaped all the benefits of having enacted a welfare scheme, and were totally exempt from Republican criticism for its deficiencies.

Of similar tendency was the performance of the Senate Republican leadership in the 1967 controversy over the so-called consular treaty with the Soviet Union—an agreement which provided for an exchange of diplomatic offices between the U.S. and the USSR. The treaty presented the GOP with an unusual occasion for combining public good with Republican opportunity. FBI chief Hoover had, after all, described the treaty as "a cherished goal of Soviet intelligence," and although the Johnson administration subsequently tried to minimize Hoover's concern, he never retracted this statement. Nor did he back off from his many previous assertions that such outposts are focal points of Communist subversion and espionage.

In terms of the Republican effort to spell out the national-security implications of bridge-building with Moscow, this was a golden issue. It was direct and comprehensible as, say, disarmament, ABM defenses, and other technical subjects are not. Hoover's statement was clear, the fact that Communists use such installations for espionage was clear, the probability that such espionage would therefore be given increasing scope was clear. It was as perfect an incapsulation of major foreign policy issues as one could have wished.

So, what happened? The Republican leadership under Senator Everett Dirksen experienced a sudden siege of constructiveness, and for reasons not yet adequately explained switched from opposition to the treaty to support of it. The result was that Republican votes in the Senate provided the necessary margin for ratification, and a highly debatable move toward Cold War "accommodation" sailed through to victory without much debate. And, since the Republican leadership had opted for it, the Johnson administration was off the hook. Republican candidates who attempted to use the issue against pro-treaty Democrats could easily be rebutted by the comment that Dirksen and numerous other Republicans had voted for it. Thanks to "constructiveness," a bad treaty became law and a good issue went out the window.

Contrast with this the splendid job the Senate Republican leadership did on the question of Section 14(b) of the Taft-Hartley Act. In this episode, with the Democrats demanding that the clause be repealed, the GOP was theoretically in the same verbal bind as in most other cases: Since it was for freedom, it was necessarily against the Johnson regime's repealer effort. It was hopelessly negative.

Undaunted by that fact, Dirksen twice led filibuster efforts in the Senate which were supported by a majority of the voting members of that body, and knocked the repealer dead. The GOP, being "against" federally imposed compulsory unionism, conducted an intensive and highly educational "negative" campaign, drew many Democratic senators to its cause, and, by every available measure, elicited strong support from a majority of the American people.

In the case of 14(b) Dirksen won an important legislative battle, scored points on the opposition and handed the Republican party an issue—all because he had the audacity to utter a simple "no" and to stand by it when the pressures were turned on. By making clear the evil of the thing he was being negative about, he turned his negation into a political asset.

A related fallacy of the constructive approach is the idea that the Federal government is drawn into various zones of activity because somebody or some institution has failed to meet his (or its) responsibilities. If we are really concerned to prevent the growth of Federal power, it is argued, we can best do so by taking care of our problems ourselves. Effective problem-solving at the state or local level will forestall Federal entry into the field.

This argument misconstrues both the facts of history and the stated motives of the Federal interventionists. There is little to suggest that proposed "alternatives" or "responsible" action—hiking state welfare budgets, for example—can forestall Federal intrusion. State and local spending on public projects has been skyrocketing in recent years, but there has been no corresponding reduction in demands for Federal intervention. On the contrary, Federal efforts to intrude upon schools, medical care, welfare payments, unemployment compensation, and just about everything else have actually increased as state activity in these same areas has accelerated.

Indeed, the record shows that demands for Federal legislation to deal with various problems have actually been heightened by evidence that the problems were moving rapidly toward solution by local or private agencies. Medicare was passed, for example, despite the fact that, in 1962, some 75 per cent of the U.S. civilian population was covered by private health insurance and that then-current estimates projected 90 per cent coverage by 1970. A Federal college loan program was pushed through Congress despite the fact that a private group, United Student Aid Funds, was already in the field and doing the job; in essence, the Federal program was an effort to take over and manage USAF's pre-existent program. Federal aid to school construction was also passed despite the fact that states and local communities had for years been overfulfilling estimated needs for new classrooms and that the so-called classroom crisis of the 1950's had in consequence all but disappeared.

In such cases, the dominant motive cannot be that the problem isn't being solved. The more likely goad to action is the fact that it *is* being solved, and that in a few years' time there will be nothing left to intervene about. After all, we have it on the authority of various liberal spokesmen that their principal concern in questions of Federal "aid" is to get control.* And in that case evidence of successful activity by other than Federal sources will obviously cause them, not to relax their demands, but to press them the more urgently.

This does not mean, of course, that state, local, and private agencies should not take action on their own

*E.g., a pamphlet mailed out by the National Education Association says the problem with the schools today is that local community leaders control them, and that Federal aid to education provides a means of averting this local control. "Once public education has been made as much a Federal responsibility as national defense or national highways," the pamphlet says, "more money than was ever dreamed of will be spent on it." *The New Republic* has similarly remarked on "all the ways in which Federal money could be more wisely spent, if the myopic local school boards or the self-seeking state legislators were not in the saddle." U.S. Office of Education official Carroll Hansen put it, in 1961, that "the tradition of local control should no longer be permitted to inhibit Office of Education leadership."

recognizance when they feel that action is needed. But it does mean the argument for such action as a barrier to Federal intervention is a delusion, and that if this is the major reason advanced for Republican support of it, there is cause to question the proposal—particularly if it involves an increase in taxes. Efforts at Federal take-over will proceed irrespective of such action or lack of it, and such efforts will have to be combatted, on other grounds, irrespective of such action or lack of it.

The constructive argument about winning elections is less convincing still. Nothing is more provably erroneous than the idea that the GOP must have answers to Democratically-defined problems in order to get votes. There is no evidence at all that counterproposals, alternatives to the opposition's programs, or even being positive *per se* wins elections. It would be closer to some obvious truths of politics if this whole formula were simply turned inside-out. Perhaps the best-established fact of political life in America is that people vote "against" much more than they vote "for." And the most successful political candidates are not those who succeed in proposing things but those who do the best job of opposing other things.

In 1966, for example, what was the universal conclusion emerging from the GOP coast-to-coast sweep? That the Republicans had successfully projected counterproposals to what the Johnson administration was doing? Not at all. The GOP presentation from Edward Brooke to Ronald Reagan was so immensely varied that it would have been difficult to name any counterproposal on which the various Republicans could have agreed. The common element in all their victories was the fact that they capitalized on national feeling *against* the Johnson administration.

The same lesson emerges from 1964, when the Republicans lost so heavily and the Democrats swept into power. Did Johnson win that election because he was positive, spelling out concrete proposals for dealing with American problems? Quite the contrary. As we have seen, Johnson won because he succeeded in mounting a successful fear campaign *against* Goldwater.

In 1960—granted differences of personality and circumstance—the case was essentially the same. What positive proposals did John Kennedy bring forward in that campaign? What were his alternatives to the program of the Eisenhower-Nixon administration? Nobody knew. The Kennedy strategy was to attack; to declare he was "not satisfied" with the American performance of the 1950's; and to capitalize on a general feeling of unease which militated *against* the Republicans.

In none of these elections did constructive alternatives play a part. At best a general mood or impression of being positive served, in each of them, to forestall the opposition's own negative attack; but even in this tactical sense it is doubtful constructiveness packs much political muscle. The real job of stirring up the voters and winning elections depends chiefly upon the politician's effectiveness in mounting a negative attack against his opposition.

The Republican failure over the past thirty years or so has in fact been a failure to make its negativism prevail over that of the Democrats. The Democrats have conducted a successful negative campaign against Republicans as heartless ogres, tools of economic royalists, witch-hunters, Social Security destroyers and, of late, nuclear irresponsibles. In part, present talk of constructiveness is an effort by certain Republicans to dig themselves out of this hole. If only we are positive enough about enough things—so the thinking runs—we can demonstrate that we are not economic royalists, heartless enemies of the poor and tools of Wall Street.

But, unfortunately, it doesn't work that way. By assuming this defensive stance, the Republicans actually tend to confirm the Democratic indictment. The man who keeps protesting I am *not* heartless, I am *not* an enemy of the poor, I am *not* a nuclear maniac, is unconvincing. His very denials keep recalling the original charge, and his urgent effort to prove he isn't a monster raises doubts about his sincerity. He is in the position of the lady in *Hamlet,* who by protesting too much confirmed the suspicions she sought to deny.

It is of course necessary that one be able to parry as well as thrust. When the opposition mounts a determined attack, it is an obvious requirement of survival that the onslaught be blunted as effectively as possible. When the inhumanity or economic-royalist attack is pressed, it is desirable that the Republican party be able to defend its flank, and it is in this respect that it should advance and support self-help programs, private sector accomplishments, tax-credit programs for employment and educational opportunities. These things are good in their own right, and should be supported for that reason; and they also serve to dull the force of the Democratic onslaught. For both reasons they should be important items in the Republican-conservative rhetorical quiver.

Nevertheless, it must be understood that emphasis on such programs as a political tactic is essentially defensive and must therefore be an adjunct to, rather than a substitute for, the critique of the opposition. The substance of the GOP approach must be to convince the public that the social and economic costs of the Democratic program are *the* problem to be combatted. To give over this attack in favor of stressing private sector and self-help programs, to make even the most impeccably libertarian "problem-solving" devices *the essence* of the Republican program, is to commit a grievous political error. It is to assume an essentially defensive posture, making protestations of one's own innocence the burden of the discourse; and it is to reinforce the notion that the essential problems before the nation are the things the liberals say they are, rather than the liberals themselves.

The proper way of handling such matters—technically, if not morally—was exhibited by the Johnson campaign of 1964. Johnson was not viewed as a particularly trustworthy President; there were some doubts, subsequently much enlarged, about his handling of the Vietnamese war; there was the Bobby Baker mess; and, finally, there was Walter Jenkins. Any one of these elements, in some other election, might have been enough to cause him considerable trouble.

But Johnson emphatically did not set about to deny or disprove these negative factors. He simply ignored them. Rather than trying to prove he was *not* corrupt, that he was *not* botching the war in Vietnam, that he was *not* involved in the Baker mess, he passed over to the offensive. He and other Democratic campaigners succeeded in hitting Goldwater so hard on the nuclear and Social Security issues that public anxiety on these two points dwarfed everything else.

For Republicans, the indicated guidelines to success should be relatively clear: If they are going to win elections, they will have to make their negative presentation superior to that of the Democrats; they must make their version of the bad things that will happen to the country under Democratic rule prevail over the Democrats' version of the bad things that will happen to the country under Republican rule.

There are plenty of such negative materials around, handy to Republican use. The public is concerned about foreign policy, about inflation, about crime, and about the encroachments of big government on various aspects of American life. In 1966 the Republicans made considerable headway precisely because they took a negative stance on these issues while Johnson went positive, arguing that the people never had it so good. The negative position won going away at the tape. There is no reason the same result could not be repeated in future elections.

18:: A SHADE OF DIFFERENCE

In weighing Republican prospects for the future, we must never forget—to paraphrase Judge Cooley—that it is a political party we are construing. Few agencies are more crucial to the functioning of our system; few are more generally misunderstood.

There are many possible things to be said about political parties and their sometimes unpredictable ways, but none is more important than the fact that they invariably come into being because a group of people hold certain views or interests in common and want to have these represented in the governing process. The first principle of the political party, therefore, is that *it exists for the purpose of representing something distinctive*—some common nucleus of belief which draws its adherents together in the first place and will keep them together in the future.

This nucleus of belief may consist of virtually anything —adoption of the Constitution, rejection of the Constitution, strict construction, loose construction, low tariffs, high tariffs, free silver, prohibition, abolition, greenbacks, preservation of the union. The issues may be moral in nature, economic, mere pretexts for the pursuit of power; but they must be issues which, for the broad mass of the party constituency, make some kind of difference. In order to have a reason for being in the first place, a political party must provide a broad group of people some product they want but can't get somewhere else.

This rudiment of politics illustrates one of the principal hazards of the liberal Republican position. Since the liberal approach is precisely to assimilate the Republican party to the ideology of the Democrats, it removes from the Republican party the element most necessary to its continued prosperity: Its *distinctiveness*. Under the liberal Republican conception, there is really no reason to have anything called "the Republican Party" because the agency so named does not supply anything which cannot already be obtained from the Democrats. The technical difficulties entailed by ideological assimilation to the Democrats are, moreover, quite as great as the philosophical ones.

Since it represents only 25 per cent of the electorate, the Republican party's chief task is to persuade independents and dissident Democrats, situated in the correct strategic locations, to cross into the Republican column. It is precisely here, of course, that the liberal Republican outlook is supposed to be most useful. But is there any reason to believe the liberal Republican position, as such, actually draws either independents or unhappy Democrats into the Republican fold?

If there is one fact of life which is apparent from common-sense analysis and from the findings of the political scientists alike, it is that change from one political party to another must be motivated by the idea that there is a relevant *difference* between them: that Party A offers the voter something he is not getting from Party B. The difference, granted, doesn't necessarily have to be a real one; it must only be apparent enough to convince the voter he should make the change. To establish *an apparently relevant difference* between itself and the opposition must, then, be among the major goals of the Republican party.

There are essentially two different kinds of party changers: the long-term dissident and the perennial waverer. The long-term changers are people who have historically belonged to one of the parties and have come to feel uncomfortable about a growing disparity between their own beliefs and the stance taken by the party as a whole. At some point along the way they conclude that the party has drifted too far in an uncongenial direction, or that their own outlook has changed on certain essential matters, and therefore make a definitive break.

The waverers are less affected by long-term developments in the party than by aspects of the campaign itself. They make up their minds between the time the candidates are nominated and Election Day, often not deciding which party will get their votes until the last moment. These are the chronic "undecideds" of the poll statistics, and they are the group at whom campaign pyrotechnics are chiefly aimed.

There are of course a number of ways in which voters from either of these groups can be persuaded to vote Republican, irrespective of Republican performance. The voter may simply decide that, between two given individuals, he likes one better than the other. If the one he likes is a Republican, then the GOP gets his vote. Another possible motive develops when the voter has become so angry with the party of his original choice that he is ready to leave it no matter what the Republican party offers him, just to get a "change."

Both of these motives for party-switching are adventitious, and unrelated to the Republicans' ideological stance.

The personal characteristics of candidates and the voters' chemical reaction to them are matters difficult to judge until the votes are actually in and, on the record, have little to do with the *philosophical* position the candidates assume. Nor is the degree of disaffection from the parent party a matter under the control of the Republicans. A Democratic voter's perception that he and his party are drifting apart is chiefly dependent on his own patterns of thought and the Democratic performance.

Whether it be liberal or conservative, the Republican party will obviously try to get the most attractive candidates possible and will just as obviously hope that the Democratic opposition develops internal fissures. But if the GOP is interested in generating a cross-over vote on a programmatic basis, then the logical steps before it would seem to be comparatively plain. First, with respect to the long-term changers, it must seek to crystallize the political themes which are a source of deep concern to these voters, to hammer away at ideological points which are proven sources of dissension in the opposition ranks: second, it must provide the long-term changers with an alternative sufficiently different from the Democrats to make them feel it is worth the trouble to change parties; third, it must make an immediate impact upon the short-term waverers; and fourth, it must field a broad-scale political organization which will provide the all-important element of personal contact.

With respect to the long-term changers, the essential superiority of the conservative position is readily perceived. Although the Republican party may pick up an occasional liberal Democrat for romantic or individual-interest reasons (the Willkie syndrome), it is apparent that it is not going to pick up, on the *national* level, sizable numbers of disenchanted liberal Democrats. The Democratic party is, after all, *the* liberal party, and will for the foreseeable future continue to be more liberal than the Republicans. A liberal Republican party does not offer liberal-minded voters anything they can't otherwise obtain.

The more obvious source of new Republican votes is the large number of Democrats whose essential position is to the right of the over-all Democratic tendency—the Democrats whose presence is clearly reflected in the Gallup Poll surplus of conservatives over Republicans. These people, many millions of them if we can believe the pollsters, provide the GOP's natural target of opportunity. As self-conceived conservatives, they obviously cannot be happy with the tack the national Democratic party is taking, and therefore make likely converts to the Republican cause. This is in fact precisely what is happening in the South and West where many of these Democrats are located.

Such developments will obviously be encouraged by a conservative, but not a liberal, Republican party. Indeed, the liberal GOP approach is ill-equipped either to elicit internal Democratic differences or to bring the dissidents to the Republican standard once they emerge. Having defaulted the critique of the Democratic program through constructiveness, the liberal GOP provides such voters no occasion to believe there is anything essentially wrong with the Democratic approach to begin with, much less any reason to leave the Democratic party for the Republicans.

The liberal Republican strategy must depend entirely on adventitious pickups through personal appeal or an overwhelming discontent that is ready to try almost any change rather than stick with the existing arrangement. Its principal merit is that, when these conditions exist, its bland ideological diet does not interpose any particular *obstacles* to crossing over. When the question is "why not?" rather than "why?" the liberal approach is properly equipped to step back and let the crossovers enter the party. But it is totally unequipped to *attract* them. Which means, in essence, that winning national elections under the liberal GOP aegis becomes almost entirely a matter of fate, not of Republican policy: If the accidental factors of personal chemistry and Democratic discord combine to create the apparently relevant difference—as occurred in 1952—the Republicans will win. If the accidental factors do not so operate—as in 1940, 1944, 1948, and 1960—they will not.

This principle was clearly established in the Dewey campaign of 1948. Samuel Lubell observes that "Truman rather than Dewey seemed the conservative candidate to many voters in . . . Cleveland . . . a reaction I got in middle-class cities and in the farm belt." Lubell adds that "the harshest fact about the 1948 voting from the Republican viewpoint was how many ordinarily conservative persons feared a Republican victory," and concludes that "the net significance of the Dewey debacle was that it demonstrated the political liabilities of being neither fish nor fowl."

The accuracy of this comment is suggested by Dewey's diminished vote total in comparison with 1944; by the fact that some 682,382 voters in the election did not bother to mark a ballot for either presidential candidate; and by the fact that in sixteen states there was a larger vote for congressional candidates than for the presidential aspirants. Dewey himself observed, in the aftermath of the election, that it "looks as though two or three million Republicans stayed home." His explanation was "overconfidence," which may or may not have been the case. It is also possible the voters did not feel there was an apparently relevant difference which made it desirable to vote for the Republican candidate.

By way of contrast, the conservative Republican ideology, as has been clearly demonstrated in the South and West, is itself a major factor in inducing crossovers. In increasing numbers, Jeffersonian Democrats, working men in the suburbs, young people worried by increasing compulsions, elderly people concerned about galloping inflation, have become disenchanted with the Democratic program—to some extent because conservative Republican criticisms have focused on the crucial points of anxiety. Confronted by an essentially conservative GOP which takes its stand against high taxes, deficit finance and consequent inflation, rising crime and augmented compulsion, such people find a political alternative which provides the apparently relevant difference. When this occurs, the garnering of crossovers is no longer a matter of kismet; it is dependent on the content of the Republican program.

What about the short-term changers who don't make up their minds until the middle of the campaign? It is often assumed that these are people to whom the liberal Republican strategy will be especially appealing. They are conceived as voters who carefully match up the claims and personal characteristics of—*e.g.*, a Nixon and a Kennedy—then make a decision according to which of the two makes the more intelligent presentation of the issues, judge finely of the competing claims to administrative excellence ("I agree with Mr. Kennedy, but . . . ") and come to a hard-wrought, closely balanced decision between the two ideologically similar candidates.

An intensive study of party-waverers conducted by Paul Lazarsfeld, Bernard Berelson, and Hazel Gaudet suggests a different picture. This survey showed that the party-changers "were the people who were torn in both directions and did not have enough interest in the election to cut through the conflicting pressures upon them and come to a deliberate and definite decision. They drifted. These people, the only ones of the entire electorate to make a complete change during the campaign were: the least interested in the election; the least concerned about its outcome; the least attentive to the political material in the formal media of communication; the last to settle upon a vote decision; and the most likely to be persuaded, finally, by a personal contact, not an 'issue' of the election." The authors conclude that "the notion that the people who switch parties during the campaign are mainly the reasoned, thoughtful, conscientious people who were convinced by the issues is just plain wrong."

Philip E. Converse, commenting on this and other studies of party-switching and ticket-splitting, reaches similar conclusions. Although the data are difficult to assess (voters with low information and political involvement levels may also be presumed the least reliable in reporting their political behavior), all the available evidence points in the same direction: " 'Shifting' or 'floating' voters tend to be those whose information about politics is relatively impoverished." Converse notes that studies of voter shifts between the 1956 and 1960 presidential elections reveal a steady correlation between information levels and stability of party commitment.

The evidence of these surveys suggests people who are deeply interested in politics tend to make up their minds early in the game; that they tend to get in one party and stay there, changing only for overpowering reasons; and that the more intelligent and interested they are, the more difficult it is over the short term to swing them away from one party and into the other. *The very people who are most alert to the distinctions of the "I agree but" rhetoric are those who tend not to be swayed by a campaign conducted in terms of those distinctions; the very people at whom such rhetoric is aimed are the least likely to hear it in the first place, and the least likely to observe the subtlety of shading if they do hear it.* These facts suggest that the idea of being like the opposition but just-different-enough is not a very good tactic for winning uncommitted or floating voters.

To attract the favor of these voters the differences between the two parties must be more readily discernible than the "I-agree-with-Mr.-Kennedy-but" approach. The differences must be vivid, not subtle; broad, not narrow; clear, not hazy. They must be instantly perceptible, not dependent on complicated expositions of technique. They must be differences which evoke a favorable rather than an unfavorable reaction on the part of a sizable portion of the electorate. And, finally, they must be differences which do not erode the existing base of party strength. They should be issues which will garner new votes while insuring that existing votes are not chased into the opposing party's camp or induced to boycott the election.

The types of differences which fit these requirements are not unlimited in number. As it happens, however, the poll figures readily suggest two such issues: taxes and the constantly rising price spiral. These are subjects close to every voter, with immediate rather than theoretical impact. Given a proper Republican presentation, they can be, and have been, made vivid and politically seductive. Indeed, they are precisely the issues which are uppermost in the thoughts of the American electorate at large, and, as we have seen, most important in the estimation of such normally Democratic voters as the members of the labor unions. Republican concentration on these topics, as recommended in the conservative rather than the liberal approach, could galvanize the mood of national disenchantment, attracting long-term changers and party waverers as well.

More crucial than the direct impact of the issues in reaching undecideds, however, is the work of the party organization in supplying the personal contact Lazarsfeld *et al.* found to be a prerequisite of attaining their votes —a verdict confirmed by practicing ward-and-precinct politicians. In this respect, the importance of the Republican ideological stance is indirect, rather than direct. Its value consists, not in its appeal to the electorate at large, but in its ability to motivate party workers to do the necessary tasks of political organization.

It is in this category that the political disutility of the liberal Republican approach is most apparent. Just as it provides no metaphysical foundation upon which the party can rest and no reason to draw people to its cause, so does it fail to evoke the organizational energies necessary to political success. Because it provides nothing for people to believe in, no standard to which they can rally, it furnishes no incentive for them to do the many hard and unrewarding tasks of a political campaign.

Practicing politicians understand very well that elections are often won, not by high-sounding phrases, but by the prosaic work of ordinary citizens. The issues of moment to practical politicians are not especially profound, but they are important: Which party is doing the better job of taking the poll? Who is getting his voters registered? Who will turn out the vote on Election Day, provide baby-sitters and transportation? Who is out canvassing, politely urging people to vote for candidate X? Who is conducting the mass telephone campaigns? Who is manning the precincts, issuing challenges, insuring that the candidate isn't counted out?

For the Democrats, the answers to these questions have for a number of years been somewhat automatic: Work of this type is conducted in case after case by the AFL-CIO's Committee on Political Education, which goes at the matter as a daily and weekly job to be performed. The Democrats are able to draw on workers who are, in every real sense of the word, professionals; that is, people who are paid to do the work of political organization.

For the Republicans, the answers are not so automatic. The GOP has used "professionals," of course, but these are usually field men out of Washington, operating at a relatively high level. In the grass roots effort, the party must depend on the self-motivation of the voter and on volunteer workers who fill in the gaps by taking the poll, registering people, manning the precinct polling places, and so forth. For the most part, the Republican party has tried to counter the professional organization of the Democrats with a volunteer organization of its own. And, with few exceptions, that is essentially what it is trying to do today.

This dependence on volunteers is a Republican vulnerability in any event. But in the case of the liberal Republicans it becomes virtually annihilating, for the simple reason that the liberal GOP program does not motivate people to do this unglamorous kind of work. Again, the adventitious factors may in some cases overcome the deficiency—an attractive candidate motivating people to work for him as an individual, etc. But the difficulty inherent *in the program* persists. Volunteer work depends on motivation; and there is nothing less calculated to motivate people than the idea that the work they are called on to do does not, in the final analysis, make any difference.

This liberal Republican weakness was repeatedly in evidence in the 1964 campaign, as the moderates failed to mobilize their shock troops in opposition to Goldwater. Robert Novak notes that the Rockefeller and Scranton forces had suffered a number of unlucky reverses, but adds that "if they had had some nonpragmatic moral philosophy to oppose Goldwater and his conservatism, they might have survived the bad breaks." He further asserts that "Rockefeller and Scranton had nothing to offer the people but themselves. Goldwater had a moral philosophy that stirred enough people to the heights of enthusiasm so that the nomination was his."

How this difference worked out in practice was illustrated by the Goldwater-Rockefeller face-off in California. To get on the 1964 California primary ballot, it took 13,000 petition signatures—and the first to file the required number received the preferred top spot on the ballot. The Goldwater legions were in the field at the crack of dawn on the first day petition drives were permitted, and by noon had 36,000 signatures. Within two days' time, they had 85,000. The Rockefeller forces had no such volunteer army and were dependent on professional agents to seek the necessary signatures. It took them weeks to garner as many names as the Goldwater people had accumulated in a single morning.

The "personal contact" so vital in reaching the undecided voter was, precisely as the Lazarsfeld analysis suggests, the crucial factor in California. As one Republican leader quoted by White put it: "These guys who win by surprise—they've reached out and touched. . . . The question is: Which of the two will they remember when they go to vote? The Los Angeles *Times* editorial [endorsing Rockefeller]? or the [Goldwater] girl who came to the door? The Rockefeller group is class. The Goldwater group is the most messed-up, cluttered-up organization I've ever seen. But I think Mr. Goldwater is going to win on the doorstep."

This analysis is applicable to the entire 1964 nomination battle and, on a broader scale, to the whole gamut of American politics. It was personal commitment by people who believed their efforts made a difference which fueled the Goldwater effort from the primary battles, to the delegate contests in state conventions, to the floor of the Cow Palace. It accounted for one of the principal assets of the Goldwater movement, and of the conservative cause in general—the organizational work of F. Clifton White. His performance has been the subject of much awed commentary by liberal journalists, some of whom view him as a combination of Svengali, Mark Hanna, and Jim Farley rolled into one. And, because White is crisply professional, highly dedicated, and an intelligent student of the political process, the praise is well deserved.

What the commentators frequently miss, however, is the fact that White had a secret weapon: the conservative movement and the profound commitment of its partisans. White found in the legions of The Movement the people who would go out and make the personal contacts, ring the doorbells, sit through the precinct meetings. He found the people who were *motivated*—just as he himself was motivated—by the philosophy of conservatism. In the fall election of 1964, of course, this motivation was not sufficient to overcome the many handicaps under which the candidate labored. But without the commitment Goldwater would not have been in the race to begin with.

What is more important, this phenomenon persisted past San Francisco and past the deluge of November. In the campaign itself, the Republican party raised more money from more contributors—some 800,000 in all—than had ever been contributed to a presidential candidate. When the election results were supposed to have blown the conservative movement galley west, the conservatives picked up the pieces and started over. When party showdowns transpired in 1965, 1966, and 1967, the conservatives, time and again, had more horses than the opposition.

Congressional Quarterly, reviewing the 1966 primary results, concluded that the conservatives simply outorganized and outcampaigned the liberals. Ripon President Lee Huebner, discussing conservative victories in the Young Republicans, came to the same conclusion, and noted the GOP liberal deficiency in the matter of inspiring workers. The conservatives, he said, enjoyed "a highly disciplined organization and an effective and appealing ideology," while the "moderates, though toying now and then with the shadow of both, have yet to acquire the substance of either."

The same quality of spirit contributed to the most notable of conservative victories in 1966, that of Ronald Reagan. An interesting reflection of this fact emerged from the Los Angeles *Times* poll on the weekend before the election. The survey showed Reagan with a small lead over Brown among all voters polled—44 per cent to 42 per cent. But among "most likely voters," the ones who felt deeply enough about the issue to go to the polls, Reagan's lead zoomed upward. Here the margin was Reagan 49 per cent, Brown 43 per cent. The *Times* commented: "Reagan's narrow lead on the basis of the raw figures increases to 6 per cent largely because of the voters who feel strongly about the election, intend to vote, and have a consistent pattern of voting."

One of the chief jobs of the Republican party is to fire both its workers and its broad voting constituency with this brand of motivation. It is a sizable merit of conservatism that it can provide such motivation, just as it is a demerit of liberal pragmatism that it cannot.

19:: THE CONSERVATIVE TRANSFORMATION

Few presidential contenders have been better qualified for the office they sought than was the late Senator Robert A. Taft. As the leader of the Republican forces in the Senate, and indeed the nation, Taft commanded the profound respect of his party and his countrymen. His keen intelligence, skill in debate, and mastery of the legislative process were unsurpassed. And when he sought the Republican nomination in 1952 there was, quite literally, no other Republican in the United States who could have successfully challenged either his right or his ability to carry the party's standard.

Yet this superbly equipped and profoundly knowledgeable man was, at the Chicago nominating convention, abruptly swept aside, the prize he had sought over the span of a generation denied him forever. He was beaten on the first ballot by a rival who had no experience in politics, who, until the point had been nailed down a few months previously, was not even known to be a Republican, and who came into the convention on the short side of the delegate tabulation. It was a stunning, and, for conservatives, a bitter setback. The story of that reversal is, among other things, the story of a revolution in American politics.

It was, indeed, a kind of revolution among revolutions, since it concerned not substance but technique. It transformed not political ideas themselves, but the way in which political ideas are conveyed to the electorate. Taft was in fact the first notable casualty of the age of the image. Despite his manifold virtues, he was destined to lose to Eisenhower because he had two insuperable handicaps: He was not a glamorous figure, and—equally important—he did not understand the kind of politics in which glamorous figures are an important if not essential ingredient.

Taft vs. Eisenhower was a clash between the old politics and the new. Taft expected to win the nomination by employing the time-honored techniques of political advancement; he had labored long and hard for the party; his contact with Republican professionals could not be excelled; and his grasp of the issues was probably better than that of any other political figure of his time. A generation earlier, those qualifications were good enough for the Republicans. They were almost good enough in 1952. But in the age of television and the image-makers, they fell short.

The reasons for Taft's loss tell us something about the transformations of American conservatism. He began, of course, with the considerable hostility of the various segments of the media—a handicap which conservatives still have to bear, but which in Taft's case was particularly troublesome. When the columnists proclaimed him a non-winner, he had no way of going around them. His balding head, wire-framed glasses, and Midwestern twang were not the stuff of which popular dreams are made or political ground swells manufactured. In addition, his supporters did not understand the new style of political warfare that was being waged against them. Taft was run over by sloganeering and image-making techniques which he and his lieutenants could not counter because they failed to recognize them for what they were.

There was, to begin with, the insistently stated theme that "Taft can't win." In retrospect, it seems clear Taft indeed could have won in 1952, as he probably would have done in 1948. The issues and the times were not merely ripe for Republican victory but overripe. Even liberal commentators like Lubell acknowledge that Taft could have harvested the victory over Stevenson as well as Eisenhower, although no doubt by a smaller vote margin. There was, nevertheless, a grain of truth in the argument: Taft was simply not as merchandisable an item as the returning war hero, Ike. The "can't win" slogan was, in part, a reflection of the new age of image politics.

Even more to the point, however, the slogan was itself an *example* of image politics. It was an exercise in self-fulfilling prophecy, a variation on the theme which has been deployed by liberal Republicans against conservatives in every intraparty combat since 1940. It was part of the strategy of making a candidate unpopular by saying he is unpopular, and as such was not an argument to be met with elaborate refutation but a tactic impervious to rebuttal. Its purpose was not to convince the intellect but to stir the emotions.

Although the Taft managers in part recognized the "can't win" slogan for what it was, their major response was to view it as a serious charge which would have to be refuted. They went to the 1952 convention thinking this was to be the issue and were prepared to answer it. They failed to realize that, in the age of the image, such assertions are not meant to be debated; if and when conscious analysis is applied to them, the sloganeers merely shift their ground. While the literal-minded are busy refuting yesterday's incantation, the image-makers are equally busy manufacturing today's.

When the Taft partisans arrived in Chicago they were well equipped with arguments to prove he was a winner; had the battle been fought on those grounds, Taft might well have secured the nomination. But by the time the convention opened, such matters were largely forgotten. The forces backing Eisenhower had come up with a brand-new emotional cry which eclipsed the "can't win" issue and all other issues besides. Taft's backers found themselves confronted by the charge that their candidate, the most strait-laced and honest of men, was a thief. The convention rocked to the liberals' sententious declaration, "Thou Shalt Not Steal."

The merits of this controversy are, at this point, of antiquarian interest only. That the conservative forces were had seems obvious, but merely serves to underline the fact that they were not aware of the kind of world in which they were living. The liberal GOPers came up with the emotionally explosive "issue," and, with the help of the sympathetic media, made it stick. Against these skillful public-relations techniques, the Old Guardsmen were like babes in swaddling.

The "steal" charge against Taft revolved around three contested Southern delegations—those from Texas, Louisiana, and Georgia. Texas was the largest and most crucial. In that state's party conventions the preceding spring, Eisenhower supporters had beat the bushes for Democrats who would join the party for the purpose of voting for delegates to the state convention. Prospective voters were assured they could enroll as Republicans, vote for Ike, and then return to the Democratic fold. By this method a large number of Eisenhower delegates to the state convention were elected. The Texas Republican Central Committee viewed this device as a subterfuge, refused to seat the

Eisenhower delegates, and proceeded to elect a Taft delegation to go to Chicago. It was this certification which the Eisenhower supporters were challenging as a "steal."

The Taft supporters were caught flat-footed. They had not only let the Eisenhower backers seize the initiative by inventing an emotional issue to put before the convention, but were totally unprepared to counter the upheaval which resulted. When Ike supporters marched about the convention floor carrying "Thou Shalt Not Steal" signs and wearing masks symbolizing the theme of Taftian knavery, and when the press and the electronic media deposed on "the moral issue now before the convention," there was little the Taft supporters could do. On the defensive, they could get little help from the media on such points as the ersatz character of the Eisenhower Texas voters, or the fact that Dewey was bludgeoning Taft voters in New York into line with threatened loss of patronage. In the absence of effective counterattack in the press, of an offensive strategy of their own, and of sufficient preliminary work to secure the commitment of their delegates, they were swept under.

The episode clearly illustrated some of the difficulties under which conservative Republicans generically must operate, and the particular difficulties under which Old Guard Republicans specifically were operating. It was obvious that, if the conservative Republicans were going to have a chance at success in the national political arena, faithful articulation of grass roots sentiment, party loyalty, and legislative skills were not going to be enough. These would have to be augmented by something else. If Taft could not win on the straight Old Guard formula, nobody could. The conservatives would have to adjust to the age.

For a number of reasons we have already explored, the conservatives of the 1960s have made important progress in this direction. By 1964 they had come so far that they were able to accomplish what Taft, on three different occasions, had failed to do—win the nomination. To a large degree they were able to do so because of the economic and intellectual forces which were changing the balance of power in the nation and the party; but, to an equally large degree, they were able to do so because of changes in the conservative presentation itself. The nature of these changes was clearly suggested by the personal differences between Taft and Goldwater. Taft was in many ways a Republican in the good tradition stretching from Hayes to Hoover, an old-fashioned respectable. Goldwater was, in contrast, a most up-to-date article. He was a jet pilot and sports-car fancier, a ham radio operator and chronic gadgeteer. He was rather dashing in appearance and laced his public remarks with humor and colloquialism.

The personality difference, as well as the change in strategic environment, goes far to explain the fact that Goldwater succeeded where Taft had failed. Taft appealed almost exclusively to the intellect; Goldwater's style engaged the emotions. Goldwater won because he was able to capture the popular imagination in a way Taft could never do, and because his personality was more nearly fitted to the requirements of the age. It is significant, to take but one example, that Goldwater was projected into the national political picture by his dramatic appearance on television at the 1960 Republican national convention.

Goldwater also won because his backers appreciated—as Taft's backers did not—what image politics could do to them if their defenses were insufficient. The most notable difference between 1952 and 1964, if we except the altered substructure of the party, was the careful homework on this score done by the Goldwater forces. They understood that the charges and issues generated at political conventions are seldom matters of rational argument, but very frequently emotional counters employed for nonrational effect. Their defense against this was the best one possible: to secure as delegates men and women who were deeply committed to the cause, and who could not be budged by slogans or the most insistent pounding of the media.

Thus the 1964 convention in San Francisco saw repeated efforts by the liberal Republicans to seek "confrontation ground," as White puts it, and to stampede the convention. Thanks to the preparations of the Goldwater lieutenants, these efforts were totally ineffective. The effort to change the platform, minor squabbles over seating, the Scranton "letter," the daily blitzing in the press—all were to no avail. The world had turned over yet again since the Eisenhower nomination, and this time it was Lodge and Scott and the other "moderns" of 1952 who had been left behind. The liberals of San Francisco, trying to emulate the success of 1952, made Taft's mistake in reverse. They were trying to meet new conditions with an outmoded battle plan.

Conservative success in fending off these efforts did not mean, however, that the emotional element had been removed from politics or that the age of the image had somehow ended. On the contrary, the very fervor which held the Goldwater delegates in line was clearly the result of strong emotional appeal; and in the fall, as the media barrage and the accumulated lacerations took their toll, the potency of the image, for good or ill, was displayed more impressively than ever.

Goldwater and his followers had mastered the new situation sufficiently to win the nomination; but that, for the time being, was all. Beyond the confines of the Cow Palace, Goldwater's own image problems were in fact immense. The techniques which leveled Taft on the swings flattened Goldwater on the roundabouts. In the final reckoning, Goldwater was not able to cope with the problem any better than Taft had been. And, ironically, the very characteristics which made him a more appealing figure than Taft were turned strongly to his disadvantage.

Thus, Goldwater's role as a freewheeling conservative

missionary, discussing issues in an engaging style with quip or colloquial comment, built for him an immense following in the party. But it also put him on record in impromptu fashion on a thousand different issues in a thousand different places. The style which made him a popular personality was also to haunt him in the 1964 campaign.

Additionally, Goldwater shared with Taft a characteristic which was to be the undoing of both: Each believed that to speak the truth about the issues was in itself enough to win, that the people would respond to a forthright statement of the many troubles which afflicted the republic. Taft accepted this in typical Old Guard fashion, having his straightforward say without flair or discernible humor. Goldwater accepted it with the blunt hyperbole of the frontiersman, speaking with a certain *brío* that Taft lacked but also without sufficient forethought as to how his words would be received.

As a result, neither Taft nor Goldwater was a match for the arts of Madison Avenue. Taft was not of the new age himself and evidently could understand little of the way it operated; Goldwater was quite obviously of the age, but no more a student of its intangible techniques than Taft. He had the flair, but not the Kennedy-like expertise necessary to translate it into a national success.

Goldwater thus exceeded Taft's performance by almost exactly the same degree that he approximated the political requirements of the new era, and failed where that approximation ended. He was not of the Old Guard, and he won the convention; but he was not of the new guard either, and he lost the election. Having improved upon the Taft performance by approximately one half, he emerged with half a victory—triumph in the Republican party, defeat in the nation at large.

The conservatives of 1964 proved they were able to accomplish one part of their objective. The question remains whether they can accomplish the second part as well. As we have seen, they are considerably better equipped with respect to both issues and basic strategy than are their liberal opponents. Yet the disadvantages in terms of media hostility, general imagery, and the ideological boundaries imposed by the conservative position remain to be negotiated. The latent conservative majority in the presidential arena will be difficult to surface so long as these procedural barriers stand in the way.

In order to improve upon the Goldwater performance as Goldwater improved on Taft's, conservative Republicans must give augmented attention to such questions. Continued work within the party, appeal to the various emerging majorities by eliciting public concern on the tax-inflation issues, avoidance of the rhetorical failures of constructiveness, are necessary to Republican success, but not sufficient. The GOP must solve the image problem as well. It must give careful attention to the rhetoric in which its appeal is couched, to avoid committing verbal hostages to the opposition. And it must be able to neutralize the expectable hostility of a large segment of the media.

The Republican who has most clearly shown that these various objectives can be combined is Governor Ronald Reagan of California. In many ways, Reagan represents the same kind of qualitative adjustment to the character of the age vis-à-vis Goldwater that Goldwater represented vis-à-vis Taft. He projects the aura of excitement that has become so essential a part of the American political process; he is skilled in the use of the electronic media, perhaps more effective on television than any other extant politician; he has the free and easy style necessary to the age, but combines it with a careful attention to the quality of his rhetoric. And, as a result of all these things, he has been able to reach the electorate directly with his story, and with unprecedented results.

A study of Reagan's performance during his two 1966

campaigns and his tenure as governor offers a valuable blueprint for the successful articulation of traditional Republican principles in modern context. Reagan is a skillful verbalizer, who makes his points vividly with concrete figures, graphic images, humorous anecdotes. He neither overstates his case nor dissipates it through resort to safe but politically sterile abstractions. During his 1966 campaigns, the public always knew what he was talking about and why he was talking about it. He left the voters neither confused by verbal fog nor queasy over rhetorical violence.

Finally, Reagan overcame the barrier which, for most conservative Republicans, is the most formidable of all: the problem of the media. In some ways, he has been treated better by the national TV networks and the big national magazines than was Goldwater; yet the hostility to him has shown through in various different ways. In meeting and coping with this challenge, he has demonstrated one of the essential assets which must be a staple part of Republican strategy in our media-saturated era: his ability to speak over television.

Both during his campaign and during his tenure as governor, Reagan has used the medium of television more effectively than any political figure since the late President Kennedy. He understands fully that we live in the age of the image, and that the soundest ideas and the best performance in the world are of small avail politically if the voters don't know about them. As we have seen, the portrayal of conservative Republicans in an essentially liberal Democratic press is not always congenial. Reagan has in part coped with this by running a first-class political press operation, superintended by communications director Lyn Nofziger. But he has coped with it most effectively of all by conducting an end run—by conveying his story to the electorate, not through the distorting prism of somebody else's interpretation, but directly.

Indicative of Reagan's skill in this respect was his response to the critical onslaught when he curtailed government spending in California and was under strenuous attack from state employe groups and various newspapers. Reagan taped a one-and-a-half minute TV spot that was distributed to TV stations throughout the state, while the audio portion was made available to radio stations. The transcript, in turn, was distributed to the press. The net result was to put Reagan's version of the controversy directly before the electorate—with, according to the feedback supplied by opinion surveys, excellent results.

The National Observer notes of one such spot on which a poll follow-up was available: "The analysis of that spot indicates it was watched by an incredible 29 million Californians. That means, of course, that some individuals—hundreds of thousands of them surely—watched it five or six or even more times. Moreover, according to a public opinion poll, Mr. Reagan's argument was convincing to 70 per cent of his listeners and watchers."

The result was that, during his first year as governor, Reagan enjoyed the same kind of popularity that was so notable in the case of Kennedy and Eisenhower—popularity apparently unrooted in specific causes but attached to the political figure who has the appropriate sort of magic. This became so notable that the New York *Times* dubbed him "the Batman of politics," asserting that Reagan's popularity went up even when he ran into political trouble. The formulation suggests some *Times* hostility to Reagan, since in fact his accomplishments in office were rather impressive. But the point is well taken nonetheless. It is popularity of this sort which is most characteristic of successful political figures in the age of the image, and it is instructive to recall that President Kennedy's popularity, for a time at least, also tended to go up irrespective of performance.

Technical virtuosity cannot, of course, eliminate all the problems attached to the conservative political position, some of which are simply intrinsic to the position itself. Most notably, in the age of the pseudo-event and the people-machine, the conservative is ill equipped to play the game of competing promises. He is much less supple than the pragmatic liberal, who is willing to offer almost anything that will work—or, more exactly, anything that sounds as if it will work—as a method for getting elected. The conservative lacks the prime virtue of the modern politician—elasticity. He has a groove of principle that holds him fast, and makes it impossible for him to engage in artful maneuver designed to appeal to all the nation's interest groups.

How great the disadvantage is was clearly demonstrated by the 1964 campaign. In that contest, Goldwater all too obviously displayed the handicaps involved in the conservative position. He was not a manager, or a manipulator, or a poll-bred, computerized politician. There was little point in going to him with poll statistics proving one group wanted increased Federal expenditures and another wanted decreased Federal expenditures, and that he must make two different speeches in two different places. The conservative position precludes such reversals.

Nor was Goldwater's unavailability to the maestros of the pseudo-event the only handicap under which he labored. Because he was identified with the philosophy of conservatism, with its corpus of principle, he was subjected to a kind of scrutiny not accorded other candidates. He was expected to come up to the mark of consistency—and every deviation or nuance in his record became a matter of infinite discussion. While all this was taking place, the total reversals of Lyndon Johnson's career, as of Kennedy's before him, were passed over with the nonchalance reserved for the assessment of pragmatists.

Even in this regard, however, it may well turn out that conservatism has the advantages of its defects. The homogenization of thought which tends to result from the transmission of all the same impulses and ideas to all the people nightly at 7 P.M. is an unhappy development in many ways, yet it does have one virtue. It makes it increasingly difficult for a political candidate to follow the old routine of saying one thing one place and another someplace else; all utterances of important candidates now become automatically national, so that the whole electorate will hear a tidbit which previously could be directed only to one subdivision of it.

The liberal answer to this problem, as the Kennedy either-or approach suggests, has not been altogether satisfactory. The public doesn't like weakness in its public figures, and a candidate who talks out of both sides of his mouth on an issue is liable to get tripped up. The fate of George Romney as a result of trying to have it both ways on Vietnam is a perfect example. The very electronic revolution which ushered in the age of the image and the people machine has tended to discourage some ancient techniques of political trimming. This aspect of the matter works clearly in favor of the conservatives and against the liberals.

The conservative spokesman who knows what he is talking about and articulates his position carefully is much better suited to be a national candidate than is the liberal. His approach, practically considered, is to elicit the sentiments of the natural conservative majority which exists on the popular issues we have discussed and, in electoral terms, in the constellation of conservative states adding up to a majority in the Electoral College. He does not try to alter his pitch to match some subtle alteration in his audience. This fact makes it much easier for him than for the liberal to get on national television and say something clear and comprehensible. Thus his weakness in refusing to be all things to all people becomes his strength.

This ability to make a unified and coherent presentation has another advantage as well. This is the fact that the American people still like to know what a man stands for. They will respond favorably to a public figure who takes a stand for principle, even if they do not altogether agree with it. It was this feeling which first helped project Goldwater as a national figure, and his defeat on other grounds should not obscure the fact that his stand *for principle*—to the extent it was understood as such—was one of the things people liked most about him. Thus the Opinion Research poll of 1964 showed that, among the favorable qualities to which people responded in Goldwater, "speaks his own mind" was listed first (58 per cent of the respondents), closely followed by "has strong convictions" (45 per cent).

This is not to suggest that conservatives can say anything at all that is on their minds and win, or that they would be well advised to follow Goldwater's course and push controversial aspects of their program in the most disadvantageous places. Obviously, the conservative candidate should stress those aspects of the conservative presentation—low taxes, a halt to spiraling prices, curtailment of excessive spending, the battle against crime, support for the prayer amendment, et cetera—which touch the vital concerns of a majority of the electorate. The point is that a skillful presentation of the conservative view can be both popular and thoroughly consistent with principle. Further examination of the Reagan phenomenon will, I think, illustrate the point rather clearly.

20:: The Rise of Reagan

It is tempting to suggest that, if Ronald Reagan did not exist, conservative Republicans would have to invent him. Tempting, but mistaken.

The idea that the movement depends upon the man, rather than the other way around, was one of the principal factors working for confusion in the case of Barry Goldwater. Friends and enemies alike assumed Goldwater had somehow brought the conservative movement into being and that with his defeat it would wither and decline. The more accurate explanation was that, in a sense, the movement brought Goldwater into being—chose him, that is, as a repository for its considerable energies.

When Goldwater was defeated, conservatism did not cease to exist. It was, momentarily at least, without the necessary focus, the individual who could articulate its beliefs and champion its aspirations. But the inheritor of the conservative mantle, and a good deal more besides, had already made his appearance. By common consent, Ronald Reagan had made the most exciting and effective political speech of the 1964 campaign. In a late October television address, Reagan stated the case for the conservative position with force and eloquence, and drew more political contributions than any other single political address in history.

The speech caused Republican strategists in California to reflect that Reagan would make an ideal candidate for high political office—an intuition soon to be vindicated at the polls. Reagan went on to resounding triumphs in the 1966 Republican gubernatorial primary and in the fall election, and began almost immediately to attract national attention.

Had not Reagan appeared and enjoyed his phenomenal success, the conservative movement would have continued to exist and to grow, and would eventually have found another candidate who represented its opinions. There is little doubt that a force compounded of the strong ideological and demographic motives now changing the American landscape will attain, in one form or another, the political expression it has been seeking. The rise of Reagan or someone like him was therefore principally a matter of time. His television speech and his personal characteristics combined to make the time span shorter than it might otherwise have been.

It would be difficult to conjure up a political figure who more clearly summarizes the various themes of this book. Reagan's ascent to high political office in the largest of the states illustrates, almost point for point, the several items we have suggested as prerequisites for Republican success. Examination of the Reagan story can provide a number of clues to the Republican potential for the future, and suggest the fashion in which that potential can be converted into victory at the polls.

There is, to begin with, the fact that the Reagan saga has occurred in California, the state which most clearly adumbrates the various changes we have discussed: It is the most westward of the contiguous states in a nation moved insistently by the westering impulse; the most suburbanized area of our increasingly suburbanized society; the richest and largest subdivision of our expanding middle-class economy; and, simultaneously, the most hard-pressed of the states in terms of social unrest and welfarism, taxation and living costs, and consequent mounting concern about the trend toward liberalism in government. In all these respects, California represents the American tendency writ large; it is a prototype of what the nation, with all of its assets and liabilities, has increasingly become.

The futuristic aspects of present-day California society are conceded by most of our cultural soothsayers. The trend-spotters do not, however, usually go on to grant the same predictive value to the evolution of California state politics. They should. The evidence shows that the drift of California political opinion has been following, rather closely, the drift of California life in general —that the social and economic changes characteristic of the nation's largest state have produced a corresponding political style. California society features an increasing number of people whose self-conceptions have crossed the indeterminate line between beneficiary of government and prey of government; and the proliferation of welfare programs, the Berkeley riots, rising taxes and an even more rapidly rising cost of living, the inability of the authorities to quell social disorder and crime, have all served to jar the hostile nerve, elicit mistrust of welfare government, and crystallize a conservative majority.

Louis Harris' diagnostic sketch of the June 1966 California primary caught some of this development. Equally to the point is the analysis of California Superintendent of Public Instruction Max Rafferty, himself a conservative and a big winner in his two statewide races for public office. "There is a conservative trend running in this state and nation," Rafferty says. He notes that the trend began with the Republican gubernatorial primary of 1962, when the conservatives lost by a two-to-one margin: "The Goldwater-Rockefeller primary in 1964 was dead even. In 1966 the conservatives beat the moderates in the Republican primary by about the same ratio that they lost in 1962, and went on easily to win the general election. The trend is still building."

Thus it transpires that America's largest, most suburbanized, most affluent state has also become, in recent years, a principal bastion of conservative Republicanism. Once a forcing house for radical social ideas and spawning ground of liberal Republican hopefuls, California is now the premier example of conservative political success. The relationship is not accidental. It is, on the available evidence, a matter of cause and effect, and the lesson it provides for Republicans across the nation should be studied with care.

A good deal of attention has been paid to Reagan's effective speaking style, attractive appearance, and ability to use the medium of television. And all of these things are obviously important, necessities of a successful politics in the age of the image. But technique alone is all too clearly not the explanation of Reagan's victories. More important by far is the *substance* of the Reagan position —the essential points which his gift for articulation permits him to drive home to the electorate. The key to Reagan's success is precisely that he manages to reach the predominant concerns of the new conservative majority, addressing himself to those elements of the population that form the latent constituency of the Republican party.

In doing this, Reagan avoided the mistake which is the

perennial hazard of the liberal Republicans; he did not set out, either in the primary or the general election, to steal the opposition's clothes, to go after the votes that constitute the declining Democratic coalition, to be more royalist than the king. Instead he put together his own majority of taxpayers, homeowners, suburbanites—in sum, an antiwelfarist majority whose self-conceptions align them not with big government but against it. He surfaced all the anxieties which it should be the business of the Republican party, in the nation's interest and its own, to elicit and to assuage.

Fortune, in explanation of Reagan's success, offers this comment from one of his campaign managers: "We have become a state of homeowners. Working people in California have usually registered Democrat, but when they buy a house and get some roots down, they desire stability. They are against boat-rockers. They become conservative." To which the *Fortune* author adds the comment that "California's new middle class wants most of all to be left alone"—principally, left alone by the intrusive hand of government. To these Reagan's most salient appeal is said to be: "We stand between the taxpayer and the tax spender."

Reagan himself has emphasized the nature of the Republican constituency in explicit terms, approaching the subject as a matter of equity and practical politics alike. Addressing a GOP gathering in Eugene, Ore., he stated:

> There is a bloc out there that you and I should be talking to, and that bloc is made up of a great many unsung heroes. They're of every race and religion, they're in every economic bracket, and they certainly have every ethnic background. I'm talking about that great unsung body of Americans who've been carrying the load and paying the bills. They go to work, they send their kids to school, they contribute to their church or charity and they make the wheels go 'round with their contribu-

tions, civic and otherwise. I think that our banner, if we want them to follow us, must be that we say to them, "We offer equal opportunity at the starting line of life, but no compulsory tie for everyone at the finish line."

There could be no better rebuttal to the notion of the liberal consensus in America than the fact that by stressing such themes Reagan should have rolled to a two-to-one victory in the Republican primary and a 1-million vote majority in the fall. Assuming an ideological stance in every respect compatible with traditional Republicanism and hostile to the liberal presuppositions which are supposed to dominate American political thought, he not only won, but won overwhelmingly.

The importance of the welfare issue was noted in mid-campaign by columnists Rowland Evans and Robert Novak. "In a swing through the agricultural San Joaquin Valley," they noted, "Reagan's aides were startled to find that his references to welfare got a greater response than attacks on Brown's farm policy. Accordingly, in his next speech—before workers at the Hughes Aircraft Plant in the Los Angeles area—Reagan expanded on welfare. When Reagan asserted that 'able-bodied men should not be sitting on the front porch and doing nothing,' the blue-collar workers rewarded the Republican candidate with an animal roar of approval." Pat Brown encountered the same spirit in reverse, as Democratic defectors asserted, "Brown has let this welfare thing get out of hand"; "I'm paying taxes so other people can loaf"; "Brown is soft on the loafers." Evans and Novak wrapped it up by saying Brown's protestations "fall on deaf ears in this anti-welfare state."

Asked to explain his massive victory, Reagan himself pointed to the spending-welfare-big-government theme. "For me," he said, "the vote reflects the great concern of the people with the size and cost of government. They were disturbed, too, by our runaway crime rate and the excessive cost of welfare. There was a belief that, as far as welfare is concerned, we were not curing the problem—weren't helping people to help themselves. We were just building up a whole segment of society that was coming along for a free ride."

By taking this approach, Reagan was a long step toward surfacing his majority. The resulting political benefits can be tangibly demonstrated by comparing his performance among middle-income voters to Richard Nixon's showing four years earlier. In his winning race, Reagan received 57 per cent of the powerful suburban middle-income vote, compared to only 43 per cent for Nixon in 1962. The difference between Nixon's loss and Reagan's win was precisely the difference between an indecisive middle class and a middle class swinging strongly toward the Republican candidate. As noted in Chapter 4, this pattern prevailed in favor of the GOP in the 1966 balloting generally, but in Reagan's case the vote switch was considerably more dramatic than the norm.*

The latent concerns of these voters can, as we have noted, be screened out in a number of ways: By simple failure on the part of the Republican candidate to take up such issues and discuss them, by verbal misplays which

* David Broder and Stephen Hess, in their analysis of Reagan's victory, stress the importance of the middle-class surge to the Republicans. They state that "the California middle class, the youngish World War II veterans and their families who filled the developments in Orange, San Diego, and Los Angeles counties, and around Fresno, Sacramento, and the cities of the Bay area, came to conclude that government was costing them more than it was worth"; this despite the fact that many of these people, not too long ago, were in various ways beneficiaries of government programs and therefore presumptive members of the welfare coalition. What had occurred, Broder and Hess assert, was a "conservative counter-revolution in the suburbs." And "riding this revolution, speaking for it, was citizen-candidate Ronald Reagan. . . . In California—that most American of all states—'the alienated voters,' those who wanted nothing from government but to be left alone, found their voice in . . . Reagan."

serve to divert attention from the essential points at issue, or by the success of the opposition in generating tides of anxiety which override the questions conservatives seek to ask.

Reagan took all of these hurdles in stride. He did not commit the error of accepting the opposition's definition of what the issues should be. He did not dissipate his own majority backing by accepting the premise that poverty, or welfarism, or air pollution, or whatever were *the* issues, as they are said to be in the liberal conspectus. He understood that *the* issues were not the things liberals like to talk about, but the liberals themselves. The liberal disservice to the nation and to California through ever larger helpings of big government was the key to his campaign, and he never conceded that the real point at issue was or should be anything else.

Reading over a sheaf of Reagan speeches and press conferences, it is particularly interesting to note the manner in which he handled the constructive-alternative or positive image theme. His approach demonstrated admirably how Republicans can and should protect their flank from Democratic attack without relinquishing the initiative. As an adjunct to, rather than a substitute for, his critique of the Brown administration, Reagan stressed the powerful creative potencies of the private sector and the immense good it has achieved and can continue to achieve in the alleviation of want. He pressed home the self-help and local initiative themes which Richard Cornuelle, the late William H. Book, and others had advanced in years past, and in which Reagan himself had long since evinced a strong and continuing interest. (He is, for example, a leader of an excellent self-help organization called the Board for Fundamental Education.)

Reagan talked about such things because he obviously believes in them as an affirmative good in their own right, which they unquestionably are, and because they are just as obviously an effective counter to Democratic charges that Republicans are inhumane. Yet these themes did not form the essence of his campaign, were *not* the decisive element which ignited the interest of the public and fused that interest into a massive majority. In all his utterances, such things are ancillary to his critique of government, of the climbing tax rate, the expanding welfare bureaucracy, the crime explosion. The burden of his campaign was not to prove his own humanitarianism, but to demonstrate the nonhumanitarian consequences of the liberal program. In the metaphor of battle, his positive declarations were the shield, his critique of the Brown regime the sword.

That Reagan was an excellent campaigner and forceful proponent of traditional Republican principles came to be widely acknowledged. The question remained: What kind of governor would he make? He was a great candidate, the pundits conceded, but how was he going to do in office with his assertedly simplistic notions of government? By fall of 1967, the first major verdict was in: Reagan had proved to be as effective a governor as he had a campaigner. He dealt successfully with a Democratic-controlled legislature, guiding a handsome part of his legislative program through to enactment and winning the grudging admiration of Democratic legislative leader Jesse Unruh.

The new governor grappled with a budgetary crisis bequeathed him by the Brown administration, went into the legislative lion's den to seek his major objectives (budgetary slashes, student tuition at California state universities, a freeze on state employee hiring), and realistically brought out what he could. In almost every instance he succeeded in getting at least part of the objective accomplished (student fees, a new and more orderly regime at the University of California, record budget slashes, part of his crime package).

Among other things, Reagan made the largest single budget cut in California history, slashing proposed spending requests by $127 million. When the legislature tacked on still other spending items, he cut the final budget by $43.5 million. He inaugurated a pervasive economy drive, reducing full-time state employes by 2.5 per cent —reversing a long-term trend of annual increases under the Brown regime; reduced out-of-state travel by 74 per cent in the first six months of his administration; sold the state-owned airplane for $217,000; eliminated state printing of many maps, pamphlets, and brochures; cracked down on other projects, resulting in savings of millions of dollars; and eliminated $750,000 for a new governor's mansion.

In addition, Reagan pushed through a tax package putting California on a pay-as-you-go basis, pulling the state out of a chronic deficit position and paying off a $194-million debt left by Brown. Along the way, he launched a comprehensive self-help program, based on the work done by H. C. (Chad) McClellan in finding jobs for Negroes in the troubled Watts area; moved to restore order at the University of California; withstood pressures to override capital punishment sentences imposed by the state courts; and helped gain property-tax relief for hard-pressed California homeowners.

The single item in this program Reagan devoutly did not want—the tax hike—was, ironically, the one which won him plaudits from the liberal press. In point of fact, Reagan had little choice in the matter. As *Fortune* put it, the Brown administration had "utilized a number of fiscal gimmicks, culminating in 1966 in the switch from a cash system for accounting to an accrual system, in effect permitting the state to credit taxes collected in 15 months to a single year. This one-shot device not only permitted the state to spend substantially more than it took in during the single year; it also raised the standard of expenditures to a level that would produce an automatic deficit the following year even if the state's actual spending did not go up one nickel."

This was the deficit situation Reagan confronted when he assumed office. It was estimated by Reagan's finance director, Gordon Smith, that by continuing then-current outlays and maintaining the existing tax structure, a $500-million gap between needed appropriations and anticipated revenue could be expected. Given the fact that two-thirds of the budget consisted of mandated expenditures through constitutional or legislative provision, and that the legislature was reluctant to go along with proposed cutbacks in the mental health and education fields, Reagan had little option about the tax increase, although he did exert his administrative skills to get the kind of package he wanted and to avert the narcotic withholding-tax plan favored by some of the legislators.

Throughout the legislative session, Reagan explained these and other issues to the California electorate via weekly news conferences and special televised spots. The public clearly appreciated what he was trying to achieve, understood his reasoning, and strongly backed him. California surveys showed that, toward the end of the 1967 legislative session, his popularity was even higher than it had been on election day. According to the Field Poll, Reagan at midsummer 1967 secured a "good" or "fair" rating from an overwhelming 74 per cent of the electorate—a far higher score than Pat Brown had attained during his entire eight years as governor, and higher than any California chief executive since Earl Warren had been elected back in the 1940's with the endorsement of both political parties.

All of this made an impression on the national Republican Party and on the American electorate generally. During the 1966 campaign period and his first months in office, Reagan's national appearances were comparatively few. But those he did make were manifestly impressive.

In a joint 1966 appearance with George Romney in Washington, he wowed his audience while, in the estimation of both *Time* and *Newsweek*, Romney "bombed." In May, 1967, Reagan made another appearance with another major political figure, Senator Robert Kennedy of New York, and by common consent once more walked off with the honors.

The occasion for the Reagan-Kennedy confrontation was a transatlantic telecast called "Town Meeting of the World" in which the two American politicians fielded questions from foreign students, hostile to the United States. Kennedy gave an indecisive performance, in part agreeing with the students and appearing to apologize for American policies. Reagan challenged their misstatements, and articulated a calm, reasoned defense of the American position. Result: The response to Reagan was overwhelmingly in the affirmative, and Kennedy's partisans conceded their man had come in second.

In June of 1967, Reagan's star began moving rapidly into the national ascendant. Two events in particular served to put him into the headlines across the nation. He made a triumphant appearance at the Young Republican National Convention meeting in Omaha, Nebraska, where all the indices showed he was far and away the favorite of the party's junior echelon—a usually reliable index to the way sentiment is running in the national party. And he was the star attraction at two conclaves of Republican governors in the states of Wyoming and Montana. The Associated Press remarked that Reagan appeared to be "the major political beneficiary" of the Republican governors' conversations. And Governor Tom McCall of Oregon, himself a liberal Republican, stated that Reagan was the "hottest political property" in the country.

The Reagan speculation stirred by these two events was heightened still further as the summer wore on. Impressive evidence of continued GOP resurgence under Reagan's leadership in California was the election of Republican Milton Marks to a state senate seat formerly held by the Democrats, giving the Republicans a 20-to-20 tie in the upper chamber. This success was followed by Reagan speaking engagements in the Midwest and South, which gave Republicans in other parts of the country a chance to get a look at the new California governor—and apparently they liked what they saw.

Particularly significant was Reagan's foray into Illinois, his native state and a powerhouse in Republican conventions and national elections alike. Following his visit, *The Christian Science Monitor* quoted a top Republican official: "Reagan is getting good mention in Illinois. He appears to be a firm administrator. He managed to get his university situation under control. He's looking good here." To which the *Monitor* added: "Indeed, he is looking so good in Illinois that he attracted virtually every top Republican official to watch the library dedication [at Reagan's alma mater, Eureka College] and then meet him at the home of a local party leader."

Considered particularly important was the build-up given Reagan by Senator Dirksen, who introduced the Californian at the Eureka ceremonies. Dirksen was subsequently quoted as saying "we have a lot of old faces in the Republican party and what we need are new faces to win on the national level. Reagan has an attractive personality like the late President Kennedy. What did Jack Kennedy have that Reagan doesn't have? Reagan, as governor, is getting something Kennedy never had—administrative experience."

All of which gave additional weight to the pronouncements of Timothy P. Sheehan, chairman of the Cook County (Chicago) Republican party, who told a September press conference that "until recently I thought that Nixon was the strongest with Republican primary voters. In the last three or four weeks I have seen Reagan making a strong surge, and I am more and more of the opinion that before long he will be leading in Illinois."

If Reagan was doing well in the Midwest, he was even

stronger in the South. He drew plaudits from Republican leaders in Florida, Georgia, and South Carolina, and elsewhere in Dixie. Alabama GOP leader James Martin, who turned up at a Reagan gathering in Columbia, S.C., said, "I'm here to see the future. A ticket with Reagan on it would sweep the South." Reporters Robert S. Allen and Paul Scott gave this view of Reagan's impact in Columbia: "Reagan had to battle his way, inch by inch, through hundreds of admirers who turned a hotel reception into a mob scene as they reached out to shake his hand, demand his autograph, or just say to their friends, 'I touched him.' "

What these things meant in terms of general public support was clearly reflected by the polls, local and national. In his own state, surveys in September, 1967, showed Reagan had passed George Romney in the estimation of the voters as the Republican who "could win the general election for President of the United States" and was close on the heels of Richard Nixon. These results, published in the Los Angeles *Times*, September 17, 1967, were as follows:

Nixon	30 per cent
Reagan	26 per cent
Romney	19 per cent
Percy	9 per cent

This was a dramatic reversal from the preceding March, when Romney had led with 46 per cent, followed by Nixon with 16, Reagan with 11, and Percy with 8. The rearrangement was obviously precipitated by Romney's decline, but it was significant that Reagan made the greatest percentage gain of any of the candidates as the voters moved away from Romney. Reagan picked up 15 percentage points, compared to the 14 per cent for the long-established front runner, Nixon, and only one per cent for Percy.

Halfway across the nation, in this writer's home state of Indiana, similar signs of Reagan strength appeared. In a canvass of party officials in February, 1967, when the Romney boom was at its highest and Nixon was looked upon as the conservative stopgap against Romney, Reagan, who had barely surfaced as a national figure after a month in office, made a surprising showing. Nixon secured 44 per cent of the votes, Romney 27.5 per cent, and Reagan 19 per cent. Later Hoosier surveys of rank-and-file sentiment in the early fall of 1967 showed an even more pronounced trend towards the Californian.*

In December, 1967, an Associated Press survey of Indiana's delegates to the last GOP national convention showed Reagan closing rapidly in on Nixon—with 9 votes to the front-runner's 16. The following month, a new survey of county chairmen showed Nixon in front with 26 votes, compared to 10 for Rockefeller and 9 for Reagan. With Nixon out of the race, moreover, his supporters would flock to Reagan's banner. Asked to designate their second choice, the chairmen overwhelmingly picked Reagan. In this column he secured 26 votes, compared to only 4 for Rockefeller.

Similar results showed up in other areas as well. On April 30, 1967, the Tulsa *World* reported: "Richard Nixon is the overwhelming choice of Republican county chairmen in Oklahoma for their party's nomination for President next year. Their second choice is not Governor

* A September 1967 phone-in poll conducted by an Indianapolis TV station, WLW-I, showed a consistent pattern of conservative preference, with Reagan the clear winner. On successive nights, the poll showed Nixon beating Romney, 66 per cent to 34 per cent, Nixon beating Rockefeller, 64 per cent to 36 per cent, Reagan beating Nixon, 72.5 per cent to 27.5 per cent, and Reagan beating President Johnson 63.4 per cent to 36.6 per cent. Similarly, a post-card poll conducted by an Indianapolis Northside newspaper, *The Suburban Topics*, showed a strong surge toward Reagan. Asked to name their choices for the GOP presidential nomination, the readers responded as follows: Reagan 56.2 per cent; Nixon, 31.3 per cent; Rockefeller, 9.4 per cent; and Romney, 3.1 per cent.

George Romney, but Governor Ronald Reagan." In York County, Pennsylvania, to choose an example from the East, a survey of Republican committeemen and women showed Nixon the overwhelming favorite, with 92 votes, followed by Romney and Pennsylvania's own William Scranton, trailing him with 29 and 24 votes, respectively. Reagan, interestingly enough, had 19 votes, only five fewer than Scranton. And in politically crucial New Hampshire, an October survey taken by Republican Congressman Louis C. Wyman showed Reagan second only to Nixon. The results were: Nixon, 470; Reagan, 169; Rockefeller, 88; Romney, 61; and Percy 36. The Washington *Post* commented: "This is a surprising show of Reagan's strength."

The same indicia began filtering through on the national level. In August, 1967, when Reagan had been in office for only half a year, the Gallup Poll ran a trial-heat presidential race between the Californian and President Johnson. The result was Johnson 51 per cent, Reagan 39 per cent. A similar poll by Louis Harris yielded almost identical results, with Reagan doing slightly better: Johnson 50 per cent, Reagan 40 per cent. This was only slightly behind Nixon's showing, against whom Johnson ran a 51–43 race. Interestingly, Reagan polled as many votes in the Gallup survey from Independents as did Johnson. *U.S. News* commented: "For a man who has held public office a scant six months, Ronald Reagan has acquired political stature that impresses the professionals."

In November, 1967, Reagan improved on this already startling performance. An eye-opening Harris survey disclosed the California governor was one of four Republicans decisively favored over Johnson, whose popularity had hit a new low point. Reagan, in the eleventh month of his governorship, was favored by 46 per cent of the respondents to 41 per cent for Johnson. This compared with a 52–35 showing for Rockefeller, 46–37 for Romney, and 48–41 for Nixon. (The poll showed John Lindsay and Charles Percy neck and neck with Johnson, attaining 40–39 and 41–40 splits, respectively.) In other words, after holding public office for less than a year, Reagan was favored to defeat the incumbent President of the United States and ran popularity races comparable to the three long-established Republican presidential hopefuls.

Still another Harris survey, in October, 1967, suggested the electorate as a whole had a high opinion of Reagan. Harris concluded that Reagan "has made a major political impact on American public opinion in a remarkably short period of time. He is now known to 86 per cent of the electorate, and by 4 to 1 the public thinks he is doing a good job as governor." Harris found 82 per cent of the poll respondents believed Reagan was "right in wanting to put a firm hand to race riots," and 69 per cent thought he was "very attractive, charming and sincere."

Such findings obviously convinced Republicans across the nation that Reagan was a man who should be given consideration for the Republican presidential nomination. A Gallup Poll in September found Reagan had risen from fourth to third place as the rank and file choice for 1968 and was in a virtual deadlock for second. Nixon still led by a sizable margin, with 40 per cent of the respondents. Rockefeller was second, with 17 per cent, but Reagan was right on his heels with 16 per cent. Romney, who had been in second place the previous month with 24 per cent, had dropped to fourth place and 14 per cent. This positioning became the more important in view of previous findings which showed Nixon and Reagan support came from essentially the same sources, so that if for one reason or another Nixon were out of the race, much if not most of his support would go to Reagan. This was clearly reflected, for example, in the county chairman poll referred to in Chapter 6.

The same week that the Gallup results were tabulated, *U.S. News* relayed a cryptic but nonetheless interesting story which stated that "a prominent New York Republican who has the backing of the Liberal Party" was telling associates that Reagan "will wind up with the presidental nomination next year. His reasoning: The country is more conservative now than it was in 1964, and Mr. Reagan is in a position to capitalize on that mood."

In the months ahead, as he became increasingly subjected to the buffetings of political give and take, there would undoubtedly be some leveling off in Reagan's stratospheric popularity ratings in California, and some normal ups and downs in his national political ranking. No politician can go up all the time or stay universally beloved by everybody. Notwithstanding these considerations, Reagan's spurt from private citizen to major presidential contender in one year's time has to be accounted one of the most phenomenal stories in the history of American politics.

The strong trend toward Reagan in the fall of 1967 was suggestive of many things, but one fact in particular sticks out from all the rest: Given the enormous difference in circumstance, Reagan's brief tenure in office, the complicating matter of conservative regard for Nixon, and the enormous battering the conservative position had taken in the preceding interval—given all this, *the surge toward Reagan in the fall of '67 resembled, in its basic configurations, the surge toward Goldwater in the fall of '63.*

It is wise, of course, not to press the parallel too far, since so many things had been altered in the interim. But it is interesting to note that, in the fourth year of Lyndon Johnson's term, the image-world shattered by the Kennedy assassination had in large measure righted itself. Johnson the apparent middle-of-the-roader stood fully revealed, in all domestic matters at least, as a President fully as liberal as Kennedy. And the crystallization of sentiment against that explicit liberalism, vehemently expressed in objections to inflation and augmented taxes, was once more redounding to the benefit of the most conservative Republican around.

The rise of Reagan was thus indicative of many things, about the candidate himself, and about the broad constituency available to a Republican who handles issues adroitly. But it was perhaps indicative of nothing quite so much as the enduring strength of the conservative impulse in the Republican party and in the real American nation.

21:: Conclusion: THE SELF-FULFILLING PROPHECY

I have argued that, by developing the proper strategy and seizing the relevant occasions, the Republican party can work a major transformation of American politics: That it can halt the devolution of our system into a consolidated welfare state and foster a new era of decentralization, constitutional restraint of power, and reaffirmation of individual freedom.

It is standard doctrine, of course, that no such reversal of historical form is possible. Quite apart from the question of materials at hand or developing attitudes in American society, reversion from centralization to decentralization is supposed to be impossible. The long-term drift to collectivism, we are informed, is "inevitable." The twentieth century is the age of collectivisms, and it is foolish to think the United States can withstand the universal tides of history.

Among the many psychic barriers to conservative political progress, none is more formidable than this historical defeatism. Questions of political strength, population movement, the present or future state of public opinion, are to a certain extent measurable—although considerably less so than we might wish. It is possible to look at these things and decide whether realistic opportunities exist for conservative advance. But it is not similarly possible to examine the question of "historical tides."

The idea that there is anything inevitable about collectivist dominion is simply that, an idea. It stems from two sources: The fact that we do indeed have many kinds of collectivism in the world today, including our own diluted brand of it; and the fact that assertion of collectivism's "inevitable" triumph is itself a feature of leftist exhortation. In a society long dominated by collectivist thought, this idea will be abroad because it is what collectivists, from Karl Marx to C. Wright Mills, have believed.

Such notions have an obvious effect on conservatives and Republicans who do not want collectivism but feel there is little they can do about it. This is the self-fulfilling prophecy at work. If conservatives believe there is no hope of combatting the liberal welfare formula, they will fail to take the actions requisite to successful resistance. If they tell themselves they are beaten before they start, they in all probability won't start to begin with—or if they do, their efforts will be too halfhearted to be effective.

The particularly invidious effect of this conception is that it tends to neutralize the conservatives' principal asset: Their commitment to idea and principle. In an age of drift and indecision, the man who believes in something and is willing to work for it has, we have seen, an incalculable advantage; but that advantage can be canceled if the man of deep belief becomes convinced his point of view has no possibility of success. The self-fulfilling prophecy thus tends to demoralize precisely where morale could be the decisive factor.

The available data suggest there is no reason to assume

the permanence of liberal rule. On the contrary, all the pre-conditions of conservative revival are ready to hand: The suburbs, the middle class, the rise of the West and South, the conservative intellectual community, the new consensus liberals, the youthful conservatives on the campus, even certain aspects of the new left phenomenon—all indicate a heightening resistance to the extension of Federal power. Equally instructive is the rising level of public concern over the dangers of big government—concern which has tripled in seven years' time and which will in all probability continue to grow in the years ahead. Most important of all, perhaps, is the continuing popularity of the term "conservative."

A Republican party which stood forth clearly on the issue of limiting Federal power, relieving the tax burden, and resisting expansion of the Federal bureaucracy would have an excellent chance of uniting these elements into a common front. On the tax issue alone, it is already capable of mustering impressive majorities in statewide and congressional races, and has every reasonable prospect of doing so, at some future time, in the presidential arena. That prospect will fade only if the GOP, in pursuit of "moderate" doctrine, allows it to.

Even a confused Republican party will now and again get people into national office, of course, but the odds are that they will be the wrong people elected for the right reasons. The eight-year White House reign of the Deweyites provides an almost perfect example: A Republican regime—brought to power by an upsurge of anti-welfarist sentiment—which proceeded to extend the spread of welfarism. In consequence, the Eisenhower victory signaled, not the beginning of new Republican strength, but a continuation of the old decline.

The GOP can consolidate stable majorities only when it understands the reasons for its occasional victories and assembles a strategy for making them systematic. It can become a national majority party when it starts playing up to its own strength rather than that of the opposition. None of this will be likely to happen so long as the party hesitates between the substance of limited government and the rhetoric of welfarism. Until the GOP can make up its mind between the war on poverty and the need to reduce Federal tax levels, it will tend to fall between the stools of the old consensus and the new. Only by affirming the limited-government view can it surface its implicit majorities. Only by defaulting its opportunities can it make liberal victory "inevitable."

Also contributing its mite of inevitabilist confusion is the idea that there is something intrinsically hostile to the limited-government view in the rapid alteration of our technology. We are told that the complexities of the age demand augmented centralization and that local autonomies cannot survive in the era of the jet transport and instant communication. This facile assumption does not bear up under scrutiny.

It is unquestionably true that modern technology makes certain kinds of centralized power—the proposed "data bank," for example—more feasible than in the past. But this does not mean such power is either desirable or necessary. On the contrary, such developments suggest the dangers of centralization and have helped to spur resistance to it. The augmented feasibility of centralized power tends to make big government a less attractive rather than a more attractive proposition.

Nor are the anti-libertarian tendencies of consolidated power the only problems associated with it. There are also dangers of an economic and social character. The fact is that, as our economy becomes more and more complex, it is increasingly difficult for a government planner sitting in Washington to take all the appropriate variables into account and make a correct decision. He is better able to give a ruling and make it stick, but less able to make the right ruling in the first place. The complexity of the times, as modern industry has discovered, makes decentralization, not consolidation, desirable.

Like considerations obtain with respect to the technological factor which has concerned us most in the course of this discussion—the communications media. Again, it is assumed that the new communications technology is intrinsically favorable to the liberal position, unfriendly to conservatives. And since there are key aspects of modern communications which have served to disorient conservatives, this belief is understandable. It is mistaken nonetheless.

The notion that popular communications are *ipso facto* hostile to conservative opinion goes back to the invention of movable type and the spread of literacy. Such developments, it has been supposed, are contributory to the modern liberal temper; they have served to accelerate the spread of universal suffrage democracy, broken up existing culture patterns, and given birth to pamphleteering and popular journalism which have been useful to leftward revolutionaries. The continued expansion of mass political involvement through the electronic media is thought to have the same effect.

It would be foolish to deny that the spread of mass communications has had, in many instances, a liberalizing effect —or that it has this effect even now. Much of the preceding argument has been precisely to this point. But it is equally hazardous to suggest that these communications facilities *must* yield liberal benefits rather than conservative ones. It is always necessary to distinguish between the uses to which a given technology can be put, and the uses which are intrinsic to it. There is no more reason to suppose modern communications are *per se* hostile to conservatism than there is to suppose our nation is "inevitably" doomed to collectivism.

The disorienting impact of the media, their "certifying" power, and their ability to merchandise a point of view through extraneous appeals are all proper subjects for concern; but, unless one adopts the position that all objectionable things are somehow connected to the political opposition, it should be clear that these are not matters particularly associated with any single species of ideology. The harmful impact of these things on conservatives results from the fact that the media happen to be staffed with liberals—not from the nature of the media themselves.

In a certain sense, indeed, there is "conservatism of technology" which militates in the opposite direction. This has been true since the invention of type and it remains true today. The spread of printed books did serve, in some circumstances, to fragment traditional cultures; but it also made the preservation of the past, in somewhat tangible form, much more feasible than it had ever been before. Print can be an instrument of change; it can also be an agent of continuity. The recourse to historical documents, the citing of precedents, the vigorous defense of written tradition which are essential aspects of conservative advocacy became possible with the advent of printing.

Nothing could better illustrate this fact than the history of our own freedoms, built upon a mountain of documents and defended in a torrent of pamphlets. It was, precisely, the science of printing which allowed the British libertarian tradition to take root in America—where colonists like John Adams and James Madison read the works of Coke and Blackstone and Locke, then proceeded to put the printing presses of America to work in their own behalf. The technology of print, in sum, depends for its political effects upon the purpose to which it is put.

The same point emerges clearly from an examination of the contemporary press. The notion that newsprint journalism is necessarily liberal in its impact has long since been disproved; it can be argued, in fact, that the newspaper in

America is the most conservative of all the communications media. More regional variations emerge in the daily press than in national magazines or the TV networks, and more conservative expression also appears there. Conservative political columnists are published quite frequently, even in liberal papers, and there are of course a number of explicitly conservative papers as well. Few people would assert that *The Wall Street Journal* or the Chicago *Tribune*, two of the largest circulation papers in the country, have performed as instruments of liberalism.

All of this can be equally true of the electronic media. These outlets are highly serviceable to the liberal cause today, not because of an intrinsic technological liberalism, but because the people who are in charge of them are wedded to liberal doctrine. The same instruments can be and have been used by conservatives to sell their ideas to the electorate. Which means conservatives must not only look to their own morale vis à vis the existing bias of the media, but also perfect the media techniques necessary for getting around this hazard. This will involve full use of all the information furbelows, communications circuits, and public-relations expertise which modern technology affords. It will also involve finding attractive and articulate candidates who can go on television, make a good appearance, and speak convincingly. To be successful, conservatives are going to have to make use of all the most modern instruments of communication.

If there is no "inevitable" trend to the left, neither is there any "inevitable" drift to the right. The fact that many elements in contemporary America favor conservative renascence does not mean we shall necessarily see the triumph of conservatism; the impulses are there and will find some kind of expression, but whether that expression will issue in tangible political success depends on the activities of some highly individualistic and unpredictable citizens—the members of the conservative movement as such, and the members and leadership of the Republican party. If those activities are intelligent and timely, then success is probable. If they are hesitant and psychologically maladroit, then the opportunity can easily be defaulted.

The liberal ascendancy in American politics has come about because a number of people who believed strongly in the liberal view of things conducted a long educational campaign and seized a favorable psychological moment to merchandise their program. A conservative ascendancy can come about if other people who believe just as deeply in the conservative view spread their ideas and seize their moment in similar fashion.

Our example from American history is to the point. Men like Adams and Madison confronted, in many ways, a situation comparable to our own. Having enjoyed as a matter of prescriptive right the privileges of "free-born Englishmen," they found those privileges abridged by the growing power of the British government. Had they looked to the historical tide of the age, they would certainly have concluded that the triumph of highly-centralized monarchies was inevitable, and that a handful of American colonists could do little about it. And had they reached that conclusion, they would of course have been right—because they would have failed to do the things necessary to roll back the objectionable novelty of centralization.

But, of course, they didn't tell themselves anything of the sort. They believed that men make history, rather than the other way around. They resisted the encroachments of the British King and Parliament, and preserved their freedoms. They brought about the very reversion from centralization to decentralization which is supposed to be a historical impossibility.

There is no need to belabor the comparison: The circumstances are very different, the relationship of the American citizenry to their government is very different. In particular, full redress of grievances is open to all of us through the existing political process. But the essential point is the same: There is nothing "inevitable" about either free government or collectivism; the former is harder to maintain, and appears less often in the annals of Western history. It is nevertheless a function, not of historical drift, but of human effort. If the proper kind of effort is forthcoming, the future of conservatism can be very bright indeed.

Index